the cinema of AKI KAURISMÄKI

DIRECTORS' CUTS

Selected titles in the Directors' Cuts series:

the cinema of RICHARD LINKLATER: *walk, don't run*
ROB STONE

the cinema of STEVEN SODERBERGH: *indie sex, corporate lies, and digital videotape*
ANDREW DE WAARD & R. COLIN TATE

the cinema of TERRY GILLIAM: *it's a mad world*
edited by JEFF BIRKENSTEIN, ANNA FROULA & KAREN RANDELL

the cinema of TAKESHI KITANO: *flowering blood*
SEAN REDMOND

the cinema of THE DARDENNE BROTHERS: *responsible realism*
PHILIP MOSLEY

the cinema of MICHAEL HANEKE: *europe utopia*
edited by BEN McCANN & DAVID SORFA

the cinema of SALLY POTTER: *a politics of love*
SOPHIE MAYER

the cinema of JOHN SAYLES: *a lone star*
MARK BOULD

the cinema of DAVID CRONENBERG: *from baron of blood to cultural hero*
ERNEST MATHIJS

the cinema of JAN SVANKMAJER: *dark alchemy*
edited by PETER HAMES

the cinema of NEIL JORDAN: *dark carnival*
CAROLE ZUCKER

the cinema of LARS VON TRIER: *authenticity and artifice*
CAROLINE BAINBRIDGE

the cinema of WERNER HERZOG: *aesthetic ecstasy and truth*
BRAD PRAGER

the cinema of TERRENCE MALICK: *poetic visions of america (second edition)*
edited by HANNAH PATTERSON

the cinema of ANG LEE: *the other side of the screen*
WHITNEY CROTHERS DILLEY

the cinema of STEVEN SPIELBERG: *empire of light*
NIGEL MORRIS

the cinema of TODD HAYNES: *all that heaven allows*
edited by JAMES MORRISON

the cinema of ROMAN POLANSKI: *dark spaces of the world*
edited by JOHN ORR & ELZBIETA OSTROWSKA

the cinema of JOHN CARPENTER: *the technique of terror*
edited by IAN CONRICH & DAVID WOODS

the cinema of MIKE LEIGH: *a sense of the real*
GARRY WATSON

the cinema of NANNI MORETTI: *dreams and diaries*
EWA MAZIERSKA & LAURA RASCAROLI

the cinema of DAVID LYNCH: *american dreams, nightmare visions*
edited by ERICA SHEEN & ANNETTE DAVISON

the cinema of KRZYSZTOF KIESLOWSKI: *variations on destiny and chance*
MAREK HALTOF

the cinema of GEORGE A. ROMERO: *knight of the living dead*
TONY WILLIAMS

the cinema of KATHRYN BIGELOW: *hollywood transgressor*
edited by DEBORAH JERMYN & SEAN REDMOND

the cinema of WIM WENDERS *the celluloid highway*
ALEXANDER GRAF

the cinema of KEN LOACH: *art in the service of the people*
JACOB LEIGH

the cinema of
AKI KAURISMÄKI

contrarian stories

Andrew Nestingen

 **WALLFLOWER PRESS** LONDON & NEW YORK

A Wallflower Press Book
Published by
Columbia University Press
Publishers Since 1893
New York • Chichester, West Sussex
cup.columbia.edu

Copyright © Andrew Nestingen 2013
All rights reserved.
Wallflower Press® is a registered trademark of Columbia University Press

A complete CIP record is available from the Library of Congress

ISBN 978-0-231-16558-7 (cloth)
ISBN 978-0-231-16559-4 (pbk.)
ISBN 978-0-231-85041-4 (e-book)

Series design by Rob Bowden Design

Cover image of Aki Kaurismäki courtesy of the Kobal Collection

CONTENTS

Acknowledgements   vii

Introduction   1

1   The Auteur   18

2   The Bohemian   55

3   The Nostalgic   87

4   The Finn   113

Appendix: A Conversation with Aki Kaurismäki   141

Filmography   153
Bibliography   161
Index   172

For Ella and Willa

ACKNOWLEDGEMENTS

This book has benefited from the help of many colleagues and friends and the support of several institutions. Despite this help, if errors remain they are mine alone.

At the University of Washington, research assistants Rennesa Osterberg, Heather Short, and Maren Anderson Johnson helped me in various phases of the book's preparation. The University's Royal Research Fund provided the funding with which I began the project. I am thankful to students on the course *Scandinavian Auteurs* of spring 2010, with whom I shared many stimulating conversations about Aki Kaurismäki and Lars von Trier. Special thanks to Aija Elg and Ilmari Ivaska for helping me with some difficult deciphering. Thanks as well to colleagues in the Scandinavian Studies Department and in the Moving Image Research Group (MIRG), with whom I discussed the project: Eric Ames, Jennifer Bean, Yomi Braester, Sudhir Mahadevan, Marianne Stecher-Hansen, Jan Sjåvik, Cynthia Steele, and James Tweedie. I also want to thank Megan Kelso for sharing her thoughts with me about graphic design.

The book would have been impossible to write without numerous visits to the Finnish National Audiovisual Archive. I am especially thankful to Timo Matoniemi and Olavi Similä, who provided me with stacks of material and answered my questions. Thanks for the help, and for patience with my requests. Aki Kaurismäki let me interview him for the book, and Haije Tulokas of Sputnik Oy graciously and patiently helped to arrange this. Sputniky Oy also allowed me to use its images to illustrate the book, for which I am deeply thankful. Thanks as well to Anu Karjalainen for transcribing the interview, and to Aija Elg and Ilmari Ivaska for their help with it. I also wish to thank Taija Hämäläinen for her help with language questions.

I drafted much of the book during a year I had the privilege to spend at the Helsinki Collegium for Advanced Studies at the University of Helsinki. Colleagues there provided me with invaluable conversation and criticism. I am especially thankful to the director of the collegium during my time there, the late Juha Sihvola, who not only encouraged me to organise a symposium on Kaurismäki, but was happy to tell me about the arrival of punk rock in Finland over lunch. I also benefitted from the peerless research assistance of Jenni T. Laitinen, for which I am deeply thankful. Special thanks to Susanna Paasonen, Sara Heinämaa, and Pietari Kääpä, who read and criticised drafts. I also wish to thank Maxim Kupovykh, Arto Laitinen, Jason Lavery, Ilkka Pyysiäinen, Dmitri Panchenko, and Tuulikki Pietilä for their questions and interest. It was a pleasure to be a fellow at the collegium and I am thankful for the support I received. In Helsinki, I also wish to thank Paula Arvas, Henry Bacon, Anna Hollstén, Jukka Kuosmanen, Paavo Löppönen, Jyrki Nummi, Veli-Matti Pynttäri, Jussi Sipilä, and Matti and Kaisa Sinikara.

The book was strengthened by opportunities to present parts of it at the University of California-Berkeley, Department of Scandinavian Studies; the University of Tampere, Department of Media Studies; and the University of Jyväskylä, Department of History and Ethnology. Special thanks to Mark Sandberg at Berkeley for the invitation, and to colleagues who provided many questions. Thanks as well to Laura Horak for sharing her work on Greta Garbo and Mauritz Stiller with me. At Tampere, I wish to thank Jussi Ojajärvi, Kimmo Laine, and Pertti Alasuutari for their criticism, questions, and conversation. Laura Stark at the University of Jyväskylä also provided stimulating opportunity for discussion. Hanna Snellman, Marko Hakanen, and Heikki Hanka also shared their thoughts, and a special trip to Säynätsalo, which I will not forget too soon. I am also thankful to Yoram Allon and Jodie Taylor at Wallflower Press for their expert help with the book, as well as to Breffni Whelan for her work on the index.

Karen Baker always knew when I was off track, and helped me get back on. She also spent a year in Helsinki with me to make this book happen. I began this book before our daughters Ella and Willa were born; now they are big girls. This book is dedicated to them.

INTRODUCTION

'Who the Hell Are You?': Aki Kaurismäki's Cinema

> Am I not that dissonant chord in the divine symphony, thanks to the insatiable irony that mauls and savages me? That spitfire irony is in my voice and all my blood is her black poison. I am the sinister glass in which she looks on herself.
> I am the wound and the knife, I am the blow and the cheek, the limbs and the rack, the victim and the executioner.
>
> Charles Baudelaire[1]

Film critic Andrew Mann relates an anecdote about Aki Kaurismäki in his review of *Mies vailla menneisyyttä* (*The Man Without a Past*, 2002) for the *LA Weekly*. He tells of an incident that occurred at the Cannes International Film Festival in May 2002. It makes evident four stories that are ever present in Kaurismäki's filmmaking and films, as well as in the discourse that comprises the filmmaker as a public figure – Kaurismäki the auteur, Kaurismäki the bohemian, Kaurismäki the nostalgic, and Kaurismäki the Finn.

> When Kaurismäki took the stage at Cannes in May to receive his Grand Jury Prize, aka 'second place', he stopped first by jury president David Lynch and whispered something that put a look of alarm on the director's face. The most consistent story is that Kaurismäki muttered, 'As Hitchcock said, "Who the hell are you?"' Many, apparently Kaurismäki included, thought he would be taking the Palme d'Or. (Mann 2003)

Apocryphal or not, this anecdote helps us see the four stories. While Kaurismäki is often thought to be a retiring and quiet personality (a stereotypical Finn), in this story he plays the brash auteur performing for the media at the most important and heavily covered film festival in the world (see Valck 2007). Yet such a performance contrasts with the bookish, nostalgic remark about Alfred Hitchcock, a key figure

Kaurismäki twisting on the red carpet as he arrives at the Palais des festivals to attend the screening of *The Man Without a Past* during the 55th Cannes Film Festival, 22 May 2002 (photo: Anne-Christine Poujoulat/AFP/Getty Images)

in the history of Hollywood cinema and auteurism. Taken from another angle, we may see the incident as a case of Kaurismäki playing the bohemian, true to the art, disdainful of convention and the bourgeois aspiration to sophistication. Another incident at Cannes in 2002 provides further material for the bohemian story: Kaurismäki spontaneously twisted down the red carpet and into the theatre at the gala screening of *The Man Without a Past*, embarrassing Finnish Minister of Culture Suvi Lindén and her entourage, who were accompanying the director. The next day, Lindén was quoted as saying that public drunkenness was not appropriate for a representative of Finland on the international stage (see Tainola 2002).[2] Lindén rebuked Kaurismäki with an invocation of national culture. And yet Kaurismäki has long responded ambivalently to national culture, as he made evident in one interview:

> This nation is so insecure that it's just the greatest thing ever if some foreigner says something nice about Finland, or some Finn jumps or hops or bounces farther than anybody else. In that sense, when you have some success internationally, then that success is accepted here, too. Before that, my films were part of the freak show. (In Nestingen 2007)[3]

The small nation sees Kaurismäki's success as Finnish success, but Kaurismäki criticises such national enthusiasm. In the events at Cannes, paradoxes are clear when we analyse the anecdote in such terms as art and commerce, bohemianism and conservatism, nostalgia and scepticism, nation and cosmopolitanism. Tensions among these terms figure throughout Kaurismäki's cinema, and indeed in the art film as a worldwide phenomenon.

Anecdotes like these play an indispensable role in any critical analysis of auteur cinema. Critical writing, biographical narratives, interviews, and anecdotes – authorship discourse – shape our expectations, responses to, and understanding of a filmmaker and his body of work. By approaching Kaurismäki through analysis of the discourse around the films and filmmaker, along with analysis of the films, this volume seeks to offer a rich and variegated perspective on the director's films and career. No accessible English-language study of this noteworthy filmmaker's work is available.[4]

This study's methodology also seeks to extend revisionist authorship studies (see Koskinen 2002, 2009; Gerstner and Staiger 2003; Wexman 2003). Such studies have fruitfully built upon star studies' theories and methods (see Dyer 1979; Gledhill 1991), and also on earlier poststructuralist studies of authorship, which approached authorship as a textual effect (see Wollen 1998 [1969]; Wood (2008 [1977]). In this theoretical context, when we look at Kaurismäki's films at the same time as we turn his question to Lynch upon him – 'Who the hell are *you*?' – we are able to see the ways the films and authorship fit into a conjuncture defined by the rise of the film festival circuit, the globalisation of cinema and popular culture, the end of the Cold War, and the crisis of national welfare-state.

Before turning to the four stories, it is helpful to clarify what story means here. Story designates the organisation of events into a linked series. This correlates with narratologist Gerard Genette's notion of narrative as 'discourse which seeks to relate an event or a series of events' (1980: 25). Story or narrative are relative and vague terms, because their meaning depends on the institutional contexts in which they function, as Marie-Laure Ryan has argued (2007). Story and narrative here – as well as the term scenario, which refers to a rough amalgamation of story material – presume the argument that a scholarly study of an authorship discourse can intervene in the authorship discourse to make evident recurrent patterns of commentary and interpretation that organise relevant events into meaningful combinations. These overlap with the films, in many cases, attributing meaning to the films and the authorship. In examining the archive of material compiled on Kaurismäki and his films at the Finnish Audio Visual Archives, as well as the abundant popular and critical literature, it is plain that narratives have formed and are in circulation about his life and work. These inflect assumptions, expectations, and responses to his films. Closer analysis of these narratives allows us to see Kaurismäki's work in a more nuanced and plural way than we would if we were to bracket or ignore the authorship narratives, and focus only on the texts, understood as autonomous objects. In some contexts it certainly makes sense to adhere to a narrow, formalist definition of narrative as a cause-and-effect chain that is specific to cinematic or literary fiction, as some theorists of narrative do (see Bordwell, Staiger and Thompson 1985; Bordwell 1985; Bacon 2004). Yet the broader notion of narrative invoked here has provided enormous analytical value to cultural analysis. An example of such a narrative, highly relevant to Kaurismäki, is the national narrative, compellingly and critically theorised by Benedict Anderson (1991) and Homi Bhabha

(1990).⁵ Narrow and broad notions of narrative and story can coexist in cultural analysis, and do not threaten to erode concepts of narrative. Let us turn then to the predominant stories in Aki Kaurismäki's cinema, after which we will examine Kaurismäki's career in a brief overview.

The Auteur

The Cannes anecdote is at its most obvious the story of a professional clash, a contest of auteurs. A jilted Kaurismäki snubs Lynch by asserting a superior knowledge of film history. The insult's power comes from a cinephilic source, Kaurismäki's knowledge of Hitchcock's biography and films, but also his implicit familiarity with Lynch's cinema. Lynch's best known films – *Blue Velvet* (1986), *Lost Highway* (1997), *Mulholland Drive* (2001) – are arguably a postmodernist interpretation of Hitchcock's auteur legacy. Hitchcock and Lynch share a fascination with psychoanalytically derived character psychology, which they use to create narrative suspense. To the auteur Lynch, Hitchcock's aspirant heir, Kaurismäki growls, 'you don't know your Hitchcock'.

Such a remark stings because Kaurismäki claims a proprietary relationship to Hitchcock, a central figure in the *politique des auteurs* elaborated by Francois Truffaut, Jean-Luc Godard, André Bazin, and other *Cahiers du cinéma* figures who argued that Hitchcock and some other prolific directors in the Hollywood studio system of the 1930s–50s fashioned their industrial products into personal expressions, meriting their recognition as the authors of their work. They also found auteurs in the European cinema, arguing that personal expression was also salient in the work of Jean Renoir, Fritz Lang, Roberto Rossellini, Ingmar Bergman, and others. As a consequence, auteur film since the *politique des auteurs* has meant both a canon of Hollywood and European films and bodies of work, as well as films displaying a definitive personal element. Kaurismäki asserts his own status as an auteur by reclaiming the Hollywood side, in Hitchcock, and the European side, in his learned self-assertion.

There is another dimension of this contestation of authorship in Mann's account of Kaurismäki's insult, however, which is the story of a Hollywood outsider affirming his status as an outsider by thumbing his nose at the American pretender. This dimension correlates with the tried-and-true account of auteurism as an aesthetic discourse of modernist art, in contrast to the culture industry in southern California. In this view, the European auteur's cinephilia is understood in terms of modernism and the autonomous art object, which locate him in the high-cultural tradition of film art and distinguish him from the American auteur's financial concerns, which are relegated to the low end of the cultural continuum. This dimension of the auteur story tacitly places Kaurismäki in such a modernist account of European auteur cinema. Yet at the same time, the haunting presence of Theodor Adorno's culture industry argument and its many accompanying ghosts warn us of the paucity such binary accounts of auteurism can entail.

At the same time as Kaurismäki derides cinema as commerce, his films have embraced elements of the same commercial cinema, with their B-movie look, sentimental themes and expressions, and many allusions to popular music and culture

– which resonate with a notion of personal taste in authorship like that popularised by Andrew Sarris in 1962. The 'rock-n-roll' music and motif are in every film. *Ariel* (1988), *Leningrad Cowboys Go America* (1989), *Leningrad Cowboys Meet Moses* (1994) and Kaurismäki's music-video shorts are pastiches including plenty of Hollywood cliché. What is more, Kaurismäki has also proven himself a deft hand in the black arts of commerce, an owner not only of the rights to all his films, but also an operator of bars, restaurants, distribution companies and production companies, and also a sometime hotelier.

Kaurismäki's cinema prods us to rethink the fundamental categories and binary oppositions that often structure popular and scholarly discussions of film authorship. In this way, his work is highly relevant to revisionist approaches to European cinema (see Elsaesser 2005; Hjort 2005; Hjort and Petrie 2008), the art film and auteur cinema (see Galt and Schoonover 2010), world cinema (see Ďurovičová and Newman 2009), and authorship (see Gerstner and Staiger 2003; Wexman 2003). At the same time, an introduction to his cinema requires an approach that makes evident the problems raised by his films. Chapter one of this volume takes such an approach by understanding his cinema as an engagement with 'the archive'. It surveys Kaurismäki's feature production, suggesting that an important theme in his body of work is a tactics of disruption, in which the films inject alterity into familiar systems to suggest the relevance of a divergent socio-political ethos. This survey also works to provide an introduction to Kaurismäki's filmmaking, to place it in Finnish, European, and world-cinema contexts, as well as to sketch out some of the key interpretive frameworks within which it can be understood. In doing so the chapter also provides a background and set of references for the book.

The Bohemian

Another way to comprehend the remarks and twisting at Cannes is to understand them as part of a performance of bohemian identity. In this view, Kaurismäki's clash with Lynch and twist down the red carpet look like efforts to distinguish the artist symbolically from the commercial festival and state agendas, which would seek to stage-manage Kaurismäki's participation. The bohemian ridicules the commercial agendas that are part of the Cannes Festival and the state agendas that drive the attendance of Ministry of Culture officials. Kaurismäki has long presented himself as a bohemian filmmaker, and indeed his abiding interest in the theme is indicated as clearly as can be by his 1992 *La vie de Bohème (The Bohemian Life)*, an adaptation of Henri Murger's *Scènes de la vie de bohème (The Bohemians of the Latin Quarter*, 2004 [1852]), the basis for Puccini's *La Bohème*. From the beginning of his career, Kaurismäki's work has exhibited fascination with bohemian characters, whether the absurd author Ville Alfa in his screenplay for *Valehtelija (The Liar*, 1981), the unconventional artists of *Calamari Union* (1985), the criminals that surround Taisto in *Ariel*, Henri in *I Hired a Contract Killer* (1990), or the homeless characters in *The Man Without a Past*. What is more, Kaurismäki has often told the story of his entry into filmmaking and his subsequent career with bohemian tropes: kicked out of the army, homeless, scores of jobs, poor, devoted to his art, an underground filmmaker, micro-budgeted productions, and so on (see von Bagh 2006: 18).[6]

The term bohemianism has its roots in 1830's Paris, in which the modern bohemians defined themselves against an *arriviste* bourgeoisie who embraced conservative aesthetic tastes (see Seigel 1986; Gluck 2005). Naming themselves after the Roma people, or 'gypsies', whose home was reputedly in Bohemia, the bohemians adopted outlandish historical dress, theatrical modes of protest, and heightened rhetoric to make clear their distinction from the bourgeoisie, of whom they were in many ways also a part and upon whom the artists and writers among them depended for their market.

Bohemian in this book draws on historical scholarship concerning bohemianism that came down from Parisian bohemia of the 1830s and 1840s, rather than the myth of the rebellious, hungry, greasy-haired artist who lives only for his art and wholly rejects the middle classes and their values. Scholars have defined bohemianism as an ambivalent, self-reflexive relationship of the bourgeoisie to itself. Describing nineteenth-century Paris, intellectual historian Jerrold Seigel writes: 'Bohemia was not a realm outside bourgeois life but the expression of a conflict that arose at its very heart … It was the appropriation of marginal lifestyles among the young and not-so-young bourgeois, for the dramatisation of their ambivalence toward their social identities and destinies' (1986: 11–12). Building on Seigel's study, historian Mary Gluck has expanded a point about the cultural economics of bohemianism. Artists and intellectuals associated with bohemianism, emerged within post-revolutionary France, in which the patronage system had given way to an art market, making the constraints and excesses of both evident. Bohemian artists sought to link social, aesthetic, and economic contexts in dissent against the art market of what they saw as an insipid middle class, whose conservative aesthetic tastes and economic power they resented (see Gluck 2005). Yet these same bohemians' literature, theatre, and style also addressed the middle class, and depended upon it economically. The ambivalence Seigel and Gluck identify derives from the conflicted requirements and attitudes towards the economy of an art market, which opened up the arts to the historically new figure of the autonomous artist, at the same time as that artist was compelled to distinguish his art in an art market in which many others offered their work.

Kaurismäki's conflicted relationship to the middle class concerns both the art market and the political economy of the Finnish welfare state since the 1970s. Mainstream cinema is a commercial form, says Kaurismäki: 'I love the old Hollywood, but the modern one is just a dead rattlesnake … I am like a dog always barking about Hollywood because with its power, it could make some really good films. Instead, sixty-year-old men are creating boy-scout level – and boring – violence; crass commercialisation is killing the cinema' (in Cardullo 2006: 8). Today 'there's no sense in mixing up Hollywood and cinema. They're two different things. Hollywood is business, the entertainment business' (in Nestingen 2007). Consequently, Kaurismäki must distinguish his work in non-economic terms in a market dominated by 'Global Hollywood' (see Miller *et al.* 2001). The national audience offers no succour, for the Finnish welfare state since the 1980s has come to equate consumerism and citizenship;

this discourse is part of a longer post-war history, in which the Finnish welfare state sought to define itself around a middle-class consensus, in which labour is productive, capital grows, and the nation enriches itself (see Alasuutari 1996). Kaurismäki's symbolic distinction is in part evident in the absence of promulgators of this discourse: officials, the wealthy, and the middle classes in general figure little in the films. 'They're completely irrelevant; at most they're caricatures who play the fool for a maximum of thirty seconds ... they're just such dull characters, all of them' (in Nestingen 2007). And yet, just as Kaurismäki's cinema must distinguish itself in the context of Global Hollywood (see Miller *et al.* 2001) and a national context, so too his films belong to the period of the mature European welfare state, defined around the same middle-class perspective that is part of the Finnish welfare state, many differences between political systems notwithstanding. The ambivalence identified in nineteenth-century bohemians by Seigel and Gluck finds an equivalent in Kaurismäki's filmmaking and autobiography, as he has struggled to distinguish his films at the same time as he depends on the economy and perspectives he assails. It should be no surprise that bohemian ambivalence figures in the anecdotes at Cannes, and Kaurismäki's career.

Bohemianism ties into a broader problem in auteur cinema, for it too occupies a position of symbolic opposition to the mainstream, yet is also historically, institutionally, and economically entangled with it. The relevance of Seigel and Gluck's analysis of bohemianism is evident in the collection *Global Art Cinema*, which departs from the claim that art cinema as a discourse 'has provided an essential model for audiences, filmmakers, and critics to imagine cinema outside Hollywood' (Galt and Schoonover 2010: 3). Art cinema's identity also depends on non-economic distinctions on the cultural market. Yet as the editors point out, 'outside' does not entail a neat division, but many criss-crossing connections and dependencies, precisely the conflicting identifications that animated the bohemians.

Chapter two further develops a historical contextualisation of bohemianism in Kaurismäki's cinema, while at the same time critically tracing the use of the bohemianism trope in the Kaurismäki discourse. The analysis also serves to introduce the director's biographical narrative by tracing bohemianism as a trope within it.

The Nostalgic

There is another commonsensical, albeit equally ambivalent, narrative evident in the Cannes anecdote: a nostalgia story. Given the critique of capitalist modernity we identified in sketching Kaurismäki's bohemianism, it is easy to see why his films might also be understood as the construction of an idealised past. Kaurismäki's citation of Hitchcock could be seen as an expression of longing for a lost cinematic past and its great auteurs such as Hitchcock, George Cukor, Howard Hawks, Fritz Lang, Douglas Sirk, and others. This longing can easily be related to the disenchantment with post-classical Hollywood, which we have also observed. Furthermore, Kaurismäki's films offer much evidence of nostalgia in their aesthetics, *mise-en-scène*, and characters' attitudes. What we have in the insult, then, is also a putative declaration of nostalgia for a bygone film culture.

Commentators have told the nostalgia story about Kaurismäki's cinema innumerable times. Some have emphasised an emotional register, interpreting the films in terms of subjective melancholia (see Toiviainen 2002). Others have read the nostalgia as a moral critique that attacks winner-takes-all neoliberalism, affirming instead a disinterested solidarity of the past (see Timonen 2005; von Bagh 2006). Some have seen it as an aesthetic critique, Kaurismäki's films using old objects and visual styles to disrupt the digitally seamless design principles of capitalist modernity's visual culture (see Koski 2006). Another view understands the nostalgia as an archiving project, which seeks to conserve the past against a planned obsolescence engineered in contemporary objects and attitudes (see Kyösola 2004b). These arguments share the claim that the object of the director's nostalgia is the Finnish past.

In making Kaurismäki's nostalgia national, these arguments make him one more competitor for cultural and political power in a national context. In a sense, they argue that Kaurismäki's cinema is a 'musealizing' discourse (see Huyssen 2001), whose importance lies in its access to the reservoir of authority held in the national past.

To put it another way, the nostalgia story likens Kaurismäki and his films to the historical museum. The historical museum as an institution makes an objective claim to authority over the past as curators collect, organise, and display objects that embody the past. In their status as representative, these objects instruct us about the value of the past, as we view them in a cultural context of rapid, broad, and destructive change. The nostalgia story, in contrast, does not make an objective claim, but rather a subjective one. It is not a scholarly, curatorial agenda but Kaurismäki's sensibility and critics' interpretations that establish the relationship to the past. The nostalgia story ascribes to Kaurismäki a symbolic opposition to economic and political power, but it also involves an aspiration to cultural power.

Such arguments about Kaurismäki's nostalgia presume that the nostalgic expression in the films, and in the discourse, is emblematic of a larger cultural whole, for which it stands. The aged jukebox playing rockabilly, the crooner singing Finnish tango: these stand for a national past. But can we take such expressions as typical or paradigmatic? That is to say, should we understand these examples in terms of types, with a universal set of referents? Or are they particular, contingent images with a circumscribed representational scope? This question is raised by the photographer and theorist Allan Sekula in an essay on images of the criminal in mid-nineteenth-century photographic archives; the archive is both 'abstract paradigmatic entity and concrete institution', writes Sekula (2006: 73). On the one hand, the archive rests on an assumption of equivalence, in which its holdings can be organised to recognise types; on the other, it is contingency, the collection of a vast number of particulars. For Kaurismäki's nostalgia, then, we must ask, does the nostalgia that arguably figures in his films conform with the realist logic of type, or with the nominalist logic of contingency?

Chapter three examines the realist varieties of nostalgia adduced to Kaurismäki, while also arguing for the significance of contingency in the nostalgia in his films. This argument draws on the work of Michel de Certeau to suggest that contingency makes evident a tactic of disruptive resistance in Kaurismäki's cinema and authorship discourse, which introduces an alternative socio-political ethos into the market rationality of late capitalism, as it is a context for Kaurismäki's career.

The Finn

There is a final story we could tell about Cannes, as we witnessed in Minister Lindén's remarks: Kaurismäki was drunk. Kaurismäki's thirst often figures in the story of Kaurismäki the Finn. In this story, the man's national sensibility not only explains incidents like the one Andrew Mann recounts, but his entire work as a filmmaker. But as with the stories about authorship, bohemianism, and nostalgia, the story of Kaurismäki's Finnishness conceals ambivalence. For the Finnish story is often an essentialist account, which reduces complexity to the expression of a national stereotype. Chapter four shows that in contrast to such stereotypes, the narrative of nationality in fact involves competing accounts of nation at work within and beyond the borders of Finland. Kaurismäki's cinema helps us see the 'multi-local' and 'multinational' composition of a national cinema, that is the geographically and transnationally dispersed participants and audiences involved in the production, distribution, and consumption of Kaurismäki's cinema. Such parsing helps develop the term small-nation cinema.

Incommensurable constructions of Kaurismäki as a Finnish filmmaker make him many things to many people. This contested status is visible in a comment made by eminent filmmaker, producer, and jack-of-all-trades Jörn Donner, entitled 'Kännissä Cannesissa' ('Sauced at Cannes'):

> Aki Kaurismäki is a shy and reticent person, not unlike the characters in his films, quiet but also well spoken. However, liquor makes him wild, as it does some other Finns. Surprising and puzzling sentences start flying, which the lemmings of the international press then collect. (2003)

Donner's story of Cannes is not actually an explanation of the insult to Lynch, but of Kaurismäki's twist with Suvi Lindén, and the competing narratives of nation it involves. Donner's story helps us see the logic of the Kaurismäki the Finn story, and as such is a strand of Mann's anecdote. The logic here is one of revaluation, in which behaviour that is on the surface transgressive gets recoded as an expression of originality. For Donner, Kaurismäki's surprising behaviour is not boorish, but actually of a piece with a set of cherished national traits: honesty, terse eloquence, silence, and thirst. Kaurismäki only appears boorish if we align ourselves with the stance taken by the Minster of Culture, that is, the perspective of a governing elite – a group to which Donner also happens to belong, having served in parliament and in political appointments. Donner implies that Lindén and the institutions she represents wish to stage-manage Kaurismäki for the international audience, rather than support his originality. In Donner's account, Kaurismäki's drinking and dancing are an expression of rebellious originality, the source of his brilliance.

In the Kaurismäki the Finn story, we once again see competing claims to authority. A state representative asserts a normative definition of national culture, while another

Kaurismäki and his entourage at the Cannes Film Festival, including Finnish Minster of Culture Suvi Lindén (second from the right), 22 May 2002 (photo: Pool Benainous/Duclos/Gamma-Rapho/Getty Images)

commentator maintains that such a claim suppresses originality. Because figures like Lindén cannot recognise Kaurismäki's art, Donner implies they deserve precisely the kind of critique and correction that Kaurismäki provides.

The ambivalence arises from the transgressive performances that are required to make such claims to authority. Donner and Kaurismäki know very well that one of the obsessively repeated debates in the discourse of Finnish national identity has to do with alcohol. In making a case for Kaurismäki's originality, Donner revalues qualities often deemed shameful and in need of amelioration. As the folklorist Satu Apo has shown, alcohol is seminal in Finnish history within a discourse of self-stigmatisation, in which elites have used drinking practices to criticise the masses for their many alleged lacks, thereby justifying elite agendas, institutions, and action concerned with national improvement (see Apo 2001). But many, mostly on the left like Donner and Kaurismäki, have revalued what elites construct as a low-status position defined by lack, attributing to it romantic vitality, energy, humour, and life force. The literary scholar Pirjo Lyytikäinen has called this the 'transgression tradition', evident from such canonical writers as Rosa Liksom to Hannu Salama to Väinö Linna to Aleksis Kivi, the last commonly regarded as the father of Finnish literature (see Lyytikäinen 2004). The transgression tradition's claim to authority lies to some degree in contesting elites' construction of the nation, while at the same time asserting a moral claim by casting itself as the righteous victim of these same elites.

Another way to contextualise the national dimensions of Kaurismäki's cinema is to analyse it as an instance of small-nation cinema circulating in the realms of a transnational, world cinema. Small-nation cinema is a term elaborated by Mette Hjort (2005) and later in a collection of articles edited by Hjort and Duncan Petrie (2008). Hjort emphasises the way film production is enhanced and broadened by way of institutional innovation, creative leadership, 'gift culture', and other savvy collaboration. While such features figure in Kaurismäki's cinema, it is not so much production as distribution that is a key feature. Kaurismäki has used the film festival to advance Finnish cinema as a small-nation cinema, not only through the construction of his own reputation at the taste-making festivals such as Cannes, Berlin, Toronto, and Venice, but also through his work and development of the Midnight Sun Festival, which he founded with his brother, Mika, their collaborator Peter von Bagh, and the municipality of Sodankylä in the far north of Finland. Through invitations to many prominent figures in auteur cinema, Kaurismäki has created a consistent cultural input into his own cinema and Finnish cinema, developed a widespread professional network, and developed a reputation as a figure distinct for his exotic cultural background in the land of the midnight sun. Yet this reputation, as we saw in the conflicting dimensions of nationality in his cinema, is at once useful and an obscuring façade. Layers of small nation clash, but in their dissonance with each other help us see the way that Kaurismäki's cinema is an example that is interesting in its own right, but also helps develop further theories of national and small-nation cinema. Chapter four argues that the dimensions of national cinema in the Kaurismäki discourse are highly relevant to the films, but also misleading, inasmuch as Kaurismäki's cinema is a small-nation cinema that has grown through the transnational festival circuit and circulation as world cinema.

The criticism on Kaurismäki's films and career calls to mind commentary on the American humourist Garrison Keillor, a heuristic comparison that helps make clear this book's argument about Kaurismäki's cinema. Keillor is celebrated for his National Public Radio broadcast *A Prairie Home Companion,* which began in 1974. The two-hour variety show includes skits by a regular cast, performances by musical guests, and a twenty-minute monologue by Keillor about the fictional rural town of Lake Wobegon, Minnesota. The monologues relate stories about a stock set of characters, gently playing on ethnic stereotypes about their Scandinavian-American identities, Lutheranism, modesty, culinary habits, and other features of their everyday lives. Keillor tends to affirm stereotypes, often with a sentimental tone. Many commentators argue that Kaurismäki's characters express a similar affirmation, embracing and endorsing stereotypes of Finnish identity. From this view, the films' characters are modest, industrious, self-restrained, solidarity-minded, and silent, because Finns are. (As Bertolt Brecht famously quipped in reference to Finland's official bilingualism, Finns are the only people in the world who are silent in two languages.) Yet from another view, Kaurismäki's films are also ironic, the irony working to highlight the ambivalence of identities, representing as they do a period of rapid and tumultuous economic, political, and cultural change. The main critical paradigms for Kaurismäki's films – the auteur, bohemian, nostalgic, and Finn – entail clashing and contradictory elements, which seen together put the lie to readings that align Kaurismäki with the kind of stereotypes we find in Keillor.

Kaurismäki's cinema finds much more in common with writers like Sinclair Lewis, F. Scott Fitzgerald, and Jonathan Franzen, writers who, like Keillor, take up the legacy of immigrant identities and culture in the midwest of the United States. Such characters as Carol Millford in *Main Street* (1920), Nick Carraway in *The Great Gatsby* (1925), and Walter and Patty Berglund in *Freedom* (2010) struggle against the confining identities and social mores of the American Midwest – and in particular Scandinavian-American identities for Lewis and Franzen – seeking to distance themselves from their families and the region through professional, social, and personal transformation. Their efforts critique and divulge such identities' combination of emptiness and resilience, that is, their foundation in vacuous stereotypes, which the novels seek to analyse and criticise. They also analyse the grip of such stereotypes on their lives, influencing their characters' notions of themselves and others' perceptions of them. These novels stand in contrast to Keillor's sentimental affirmation of such stereotypes, which in his rendering disclose notions of authenticity, community, and intimacy. Novels such as *Main Street, The Great Gatsby*, and *Freedom* do not find authenticity, community, or intimacy, because their characters can identify with those in their social worlds in only conflicted and qualified ways. Kaurismäki's films share this quality, for his characters are invariably aliens in their social worlds, inhabiting the lower depths of society, cut off from family, unable to connect with romantic partners, and able to find redemption only in apparently ephemeral moments of solidarity, cooperation, and love. These experiences are those of subjects living in economic and political transition, destabilised by larger forces. In this world, static and essentialising stereotypes provide little footing. The novels of Lewis, Fitzgerald, and Franzen of course differ in any number of ways from Kaurismäki's films, yet they share some key themes, which help point us away from the conventional accounts of Kaurismäki's filmmaking and towards a richer account of it. Recontextualisation of Kaurismäki allows us to see a richer set of relationships to European cinema, world cinema, and the globalisation of cinema, but doing so first requires a brief introduction to the director.

Aki Kaurismäki

Aki Kaurismäki was born on 4 April 1957 in the town of Orimattila in south-central Finland, the third of four children. Kaurismäki's father worked for a variety of textile companies in sales and management. The family lived in seven different towns before Kaurismäki left home, after completing secondary school.[7] Kaurismäki left his compulsory military service in Finland's army incomplete, and applied to Finland's film school in 1977. The school denied him admission. Kaurismäki studied journalism for several years at the University of Tampere, but did not complete the degree. Between 1978 and 1981 his older brother Mika studied filmmaking at Munich's University of Film and Television. Mika's final project furnished Aki with an entry into filmmaking. Aki co-authored the screenplay for *The Liar*, in which he also played the protagonist. The film won the Risto Jarva Prize at Tampere's short film festival in 1981. Although the film sold only some five hundred tickets in its theatrical run, it made an impact on Finland's intelligentsia (see Hyvönen 1990). *The Liar* signalled the Kaurismäki brothers' distinct style. They parlayed the prize money and prestige of their prize into financing for three further projects during 1981 and 1982. Aki Kaurismäki made his directorial debut in 1983 with an adaptation of Dostoyevsky's *Crime and Punishment*. He followed up at a prolific pace, writing, directing, editing, and producing four more shorts and six more features by the end of the 1980s. His third feature, *Varjoja paratii-*

sissa (*Shadows in Paradise*, 1986), was selected for the Directors' Fortnight at Cannes in the spring of 1987 as well as for the Toronto International Film Festival later in the year. Subsequent films were selected for prestigious festivals, and since 1992 all of Kaurismäki's features have screened at the Toronto, Berlin, or Cannes film festivals. Nominations and awards received for *The Man Without a Past* secured the director's status as a leading figure in contemporary auteur cinema. At the time of writing, Kaurismäki has made seventeen feature films and eleven shorts.

The auteur categorisation fits Kaurismäki easily, as viewers, critics, and scholars have identified a consistency of style, theme, and vision across his body of work. He has exercised authorial control over all aspects of his film production from the beginning of his directorial career, and as the producer of his films, Kaurismäki has exercised total control over the films, including control of copyright. For example, he has used his control of his films' rights to refuse distribution of them in the People's Republic of China, protesting against China's record on human rights (see Latomaa 2010). His auteurship has also meant that Kaurismäki himself makes all aesthetic and budget decisions about production.

For many critics and scholars both in Finland and beyond her borders Kaurismäki is not only a European auteur, but also a Finnish one. Their interpretations find support in the films' silent, plain anti-heroes and old-fashioned aesthetics, which critics contrast to the determined achievers, acrobatic camera movements, and glossy look of mainstream cinema produced in Europe and the US. Kaurismäki's auteur identity is also the result of specific publications' enthusiasm for his work. Kaurismäki's films have received much attention on the pages of *Cahiers du cinéma*, *Positif*, *Sight and Sound*, *Filmihullu*, and other auteurist magazines. Critics at influential dailies, such as *Die Zeit*, *Parisien*, the *New York Times*, *Dagens Nyheter*, and *Helsingin Sanomat* have also favoured his films. Critics writing on these pages have often interpreted his films' idiosyncrasies as an expression of exotic Finnishness. High visibility on the international festival circuit, prestigious nominations and awards, and broad theatrical distribution have consolidated Kaurismäki's critical reputation as Finland's greatest filmmaker and one of the bearer's of the Scandinavian auteur legacy.

Yet if Kaurismäki has become known as Finland's greatest filmmaker, his greatness derives in part from the methods and critical agendas of his interpreters. Most critics and scholars have interpreted Kaurismäki's films by way of close reading and biographical criticism, methods that have come down from *Cahiers du cinéma*'s 'great man' theory of auteurism. Kaurismäki makes evident in his films and in comments that he is a devotee of the French New Wave, and critics have repeatedly emphasised the intertextual connections of his films to those of Jean-Luc Godard, among others. Kaurismäki has encouraged this, suggesting that his intense viewing of films during his twenties was modelled after 'Jean-Luc Godard during the early 1960s, only I didn't have a sports car' (in von Bagh 2006: 18). Close reading and biographical criticism have led to arguments that the director's brilliance finds expression in his films' moral themes, intertextual engagement with the 'high' tradition of auteur cinema, and humorous yet honest expression of national sentiments. Kaurismäki's influential interpreter, collaborator, and friend Peter von Bagh, for example, has devoted his career to championing auteur cinema in Finland, not least through his and others' commentaries on Kaurismäki's films in the magazine *Filmihullu*, of which von Bagh was long-time editor. Kaurismäki's 'working-class' films, argues von Bagh, combine a realist depiction of the everyday experiences of average Finns with cinephilic inspiration from the French New Wave as well as Robert Bresson, Mikko Niskanen, Yasujiro Ozu, Douglas Sirk, Teuvo Tulio, and other auteurs. Von Bagh argues that this combination of content and form articulates a moral challenge to a dehumanising Finnish state and the neoliberal economy it has embraced since the 1980s (see von Bagh 2006). The national interpretation of Kaurismäki has proved influential, as Finnish critics have disseminated it and the director himself has given it support through cryptic remarks about Finland in interviews. Commentators outside Finland have also noticed the lower-class characters and cinephilia, and while they give more emphasis to Kaurismäki's cinephilia and nostalgia for the cinematic past, they have also often construed the films' Finnish identity in an exoticising manner. Within this critical methodology, Kaurismäki is presented as a national auteur whose original engagement with the history of Western art cinema and culture transcends national identity, at the same time as the films powerfully express a specific 'Finnish-ness'.

Kaurismäki's status as a national auteur and example of Finnish national cinema is more complicated than Finnish and international critics usually consider, for his cinema's many contradictions raise the question, 'What is national cinema?' One of the points of reference in most answers to this question is film scholar and theorist of national cinema Andrew Higson's now-classic study of British cinema, *Waving the Flag* (1995). He argues that national cinema is not only a matter of traditions of national representation, but also involves economics of production, audience tastes, critical agendas and canons. In situating Kaurismäki within Higson's matrix, we find that the director draws on representations of the nation that come down from the auteurs within Finland's studio period: Teuvo Tulio, Valentin Vaala, and Nyrki Tapiovaara, developing their tradition of melodrama. Many critics have argued that Kaurismäki's characters' silence and long-suffering optimism represents national attitudes. On the other hand, one can see this silence as an aesthetic rejection of the Hollywood cinema's reliance upon method acting and dialogue-driven narrative, an affirmation of Robert Bresson's mute characters, and a distinct style of minimalist direction (see Nestingen 2007). Similar complexities touch production and audience taste. Since the 1980s Kaurismäki has assembled diverse funding arrangements for his films, with important production support coming from Germany, France, and Sweden, and production occurring in the Czech Republic, France, Germany, Mexico, Poland, the UK, and the US, in addition to Finland. And Kaurismäki's films have never been popular with Finnish audiences – as the freak-show remark cited above makes clear. While successful domestic releases reach audiences of one hundred thousand and blockbusters surpass two hundred thousand in Finland, Kaurismäki's biggest box-office success in Finland was *The Man Without a Past*, which sold 176,232 tickets, while total international ticket sales for the same film were 2,050,702.[7] Kaurismäki's critically praised *Juha* sold only 10,174 tickets in Finland.[9] Issues of aesthetics, economics, and audience taste suggest Kaurismäki's cinema cannot be categorised simply in national terms. Critics' zeal to identify a Sibelius of the cinema accounts to a significant extent for Kaurismäki's definition as a *Finnish* auteur. Von Bagh's influential stance on Kaurismäki's cinema is an especially prominent example of this position.

The Finnish state has also supported Kaurismäki's rise as a filmmaker through the Finnish Film Foundation (*Suomen elokuvasäätiö*). The Finnish Film Foundation was established in 1969, around the time that similar film institutes and funding programmes were established in other Nordic and European states to sustain the production of quality films. While the Finnish Film Foundation has since undergone many changes in its funding policies, it has annually provided approximately half the funding for film production in Finland – national television providing approximately another quarter. Kaurismäki's film career has received substantial support over the years. During the 1990s, for example, he was the single biggest recipient of support, receiving 13.4 million Finnish Marks (FIM) of the total 81.4 million FIM disbursed: 'Aki Kaurismäki is the only European-level director [in Finland] … and so he is treated as something of a special case in funding decisions', said Erkki Astala in 1999, while serving as director of production support at the Finnish Film Foundation (quoted in Arolainen 1999).[10] In addition to receiving funding, Kaurismäki has also played a seminal role as a model of international distribution for Finnish Films. His films have been widely distributed internationally since the late-1980s, when World Sales Christa Saredi began representing him. These distribution networks have made Kaurismäki a model for Finnish producers and filmmakers seeking to reach an international audience. He provides an example of how a small nation cinema can reach across and beyond borders. But such a cinema largely plays to a deterritorialised transnational audience in large cities.

What then is Kaurismäki's cinema? His films display a continuity of narrative, style, and mode. They are largely built on the same narrative structure: typically, the protagonist is displaced and isolated by a trip, a conflict, or other unexpected but not unusual events; the character struggles unsuccessfully in this new context to establish him- or herself; finally, the character experiences a weak, secular redemption. Stylistically, the films draw eclectically on the art-film tradition, but also borrow music and *mise-en-scène* from the history of cinema and post-war popular culture. Kaurismäki's *Tulitikkutehtaan tyttö* (*The Match Factory Girl*, 1990) is modelled on Bresson's *Mouchette* (1965), for example. Intertextual links to Charles Chaplin, Buster Keaton, Jean-Luc Godard, Rainer Werner Fassbinder, Yasujiru Ozu, and others are recurrent. Stylistic consistency is also evident in the films' static camera, anachronistic *mise-en-scène*, colour design, lighting, and darkly ironic humour. While the films are realist in a sense, depicting quotidian problems of working and family life, they also exaggerate their realist details into melodramatic revelations about the moral underpinnings of everyday struggles and problems. In this sense, the films share more than a little with the nineteenth-century literature that combines realism and melodrama, and which has fascinated Kaurismäki. Indeed, adaptations of Fyodor Dostoevsky, Henri Murger, Juhani Aho, and an earlier interrogator of moral conflicts, William Shakespeare, figure in Kaurismäki's oeuvre. Kaurismäki's characters are misfits, his style is an amalgam of postmodernist eclecticism, and he is a deeply, if oddly, political filmmaker.

This book studies Kaurismäki's cinema as a multiply constructed and contested auteur cinema. Kaurismäki's cinema includes not only the films but also their production history, circulation, reception, and the economic, political, and cultural dimensions these involve. In speaking of Kaurismäki's auteur cinema as multiply constructed and contested, I mean to stress that diverse elements comprise Kaurismäki's, which cinema are best studied as parts of ongoing dialogues whose character and significance vary by institutional context and location. This book finds its methodological sources in star studies and revisionist studies of film authorship (see Dyer 1979; Gledhill 1991). Star studies has convincingly shown the extent to which stars are comprised of multiple semantic strata, which cohere and contrast to produce continuities and divergences of meaning. A star can embody excessive heterosexual masculinity on one level, yet a counter discourse can qualify that excess by making the star's sexuality a riddle. To see these continuities and contrasts, we need to study a broad discursive field rather than a circumscribed set of texts. Revisionist studies of film authorship have suggested that star and authorship discourses share much in common, even if there are significant dissimilarities in their cultural and economic function. Multiple semantic strata connect a broad set of meanings and expectations to a subject and his or her creative work (see Koskinen 2002, 2009; Gerstner and Staiger 2003; Wexman 2003). Further, the subject and the creative activities consist of multiple narratives, affects, and images, which cohere and clash. This has long been evident in biographical film criticism, which in linking two levels of meaning, film narrative and biographical narrative, has often altered our notions of a body of film. By discovering Carl Theodor Dreyer's adoption by Danish parents and his Swedish mother's accidental suicide, for example, Martin Drouzy (1982) forever altered the narratives in circulation about Dreyer's filmmaking. This study is not concerned with creating a biographical narrative of Kaurismäki, however, but rather with interconnecting the many narratives that have circulated about his cinema.

Because Kaurismäki's cinema presents us with a set of contradictions which involve some of the key issues in film studies scholarship and criticism since the 1970s, including not only authorship but melodrama, national cinema, nostalgia, and the cultural politics of cinema, an account of the multiply constructed and contested characters of Kaurismäki's cinema gives us not only a richer and more nuanced account of the director as a cultural figure but also a richer account of these categories and their potential for meaning and revision in debates around them.

Notes

1   Ne suis-je pas un faux accord/dans la divine symphonie/Grâce à la vorace Ironie/ Qui me secoue et qui me mord?/Elle est dans ma voi, la criarde!/C'est tout mon sang, ce poison noir!/Je suis le sinister miroir/Où la mégère se regarde./Je suis la plaie et le couteau!/Je suis le soufflet et la joue!/ Je suis les membres et la roue,/Et la victime et le bourreau!' (Baudelaire 2006 [1861]: 163–4).
2   Lindén resigned her post as Minister of Culture a few days later, when she was caught up in a scandal of a conflict of interest. The Ministry of Culture's budget

includes amateur sport; the ministry had allocated an unusual amount of funds to Lindén's golf club.

3   My previously unpublished interview with Aki Kaurismäki is included in the present volume as an appendix. It is listed in the bibliography as Nestingen 2007.

4   Roger Connah's study *K/K: A Couple of Finns and Some Donald Ducks* (1991) is the only book-length study of Kaurismäki in English. It only covers the first ten years of Kaurismäki's thirty-year career and it is not easily available, published by a small Finnish publisher and held by few libraries outside Finland. Its style is also inaccessible.

5   It is difficult to conceptualise the postmodern moment or condition without the concept of 'grand narrative' as elaborated and criticised by Jean-François Lyotard in his argument that recurrent foundational stories, such as the 'narrative of progress', no longer sustain belief (1979).

6   In his interview with von Bagh (2006: 18), Kaurismäki says: 'In the fall of 1976 I was removed from the army...'. Kaurismäki's choice of words implies he was discharged without completing the required compulsory service. The most common way of describing successful completion of compulsory service would be to say 'kävin armeijan' ('I served in the army') so-and-so years. Kaurismäki is effectively saying, 'I was kicked out of the army'. Such an outcome was not unusual for musicians, artists and other dissident youth during the 1970s, before civilian service was offered as an option to complete compulsory service.

7   'Hyvinkää, Orimattila, Lahti, Toijala, Kuusankoski, Kouvola, Kankaanpää' (von Bagh 1984: 8).

8   Interestingly, *The Man Without a Past* arguably reached these sales figures in Finland because of the film's success at Cannes and a nomination for Best Foreign Film at the 2003 Academy Awards. On 30 June 2002, *The Man Without a Past* had sold only 72,066 tickets (see Näveri 2002b). Also see an earlier comment on Kaurismäki's audience by the daily *Helsingin Sanomat*'s longtime film critic Helena Ylänen (1991).

9   Numbers taken from the Lumiere Database on admissions of films released in Europe, http://lumiere.obs.coe.int/. See Korhonen (1999) for an explicit statement of this argument.

10 Astala had previously worked as a publicity agent and production supervisor for Kaurismäki and his brother Mika at Villealfa Filmproductions. He left the Finnish Film Foundation to work for the Finnish National Television Service's (YLE) features department. YLE funds about twenty-five percent of Finnish film production.

CHAPTER ONE

The Auteur

> Now I just drop everything into the same-size cardboard boxes with a colour patch on the side for the month of the year. I really hate nostalgia, though, so deep down I hope they all get lost and I never have to look at them again. That's another conflict. I want to throw things away as they're handed to me, but instead I say thank you and drop them into the box-of-the-month. But my other outlook is that I really do want to save things so they can be used again.
>
> Andy Warhol[1]

The posters for Aki Kaurismäki's films tell us a surprising amount about those films. The posters' large, silhouetted figures and their grim expressions evoke the films' anti-heroes. The slanted titles, hand-drawn lettering, and bold colour schemes echo film noir posters, and in so doing bring to mind the noir register of Kaurismäki's films: the low-key lighting, the characters' doomed fates and unwavering yet troublesome moral convictions, the films' shadowy streets, inhospitable cities, and false-hearted authorities. The correlation between posters and films points to an overarching consistency in Kaurismäki's film authorship. What is the character of that consistency?

One of the most conspicuous features of Kaurismäki's films is their contradictory, quality, nowhere more evident than in the contrast between quotidian realism and stylised pastiche also visible in the posters. While realism follows certain conventions and *topoi* of representation to create a plausible view of lived experience, pastiche combines aesthetic conventions incongruously, breaking down and rendering implausible realist dramatisation, while also sometimes folding realist conventions into the pastiche. We see Kaurismäki's realism in his inclusion of typical realist *topoi:* the workplace, eating and drinking, and domestic spaces, among others. He also employs formal elements associated with realism that call to mind André Bazin's theory of realism

Matti Pellonpää in *Shadows in Paradise* marketing material (courtesy of Finnish National Audiovisual Archive, used with permission of Sputnik Ltd.)

(1967): the long take, static camera, long shot-scale and depth of field, for example. Yet Kaurismäki also has, in the words of one commentator, a 'penchant for pastiche [for] thrusting classics (Dante, Dostoevsky, Shakespeare) into modern-day Helsinki; for singing rockabilly songs with a Finnish accent and casting Hollywood film techniques into a post-Godardian reflexivity' (Bloch 1989: 1, 4). There are many realist elements in Kaurismäki's cinema, yet they paradoxically find their place in a pastiche style in which realism is but one element. Critics have emphasised the salience of this combination, coining the term 'Kaurismäkiland' to describe the distinct cinematic world the director has created (von Bagh 1997: 5). Others have suggested we see the syncretism in Kaurismäki's films as magical realism (see, for example, Mazierska and Rascaroli 2006: 13–32).

The relationship of realism and pastiche is evident in *Shadows in Paradise* (1986) and in an image used to market the film. The poster image bears many marks of film noir. It features protagonist Uolevi Nikander (Matti Pellonpää) staring out of a window through venetian blinds, employing noir imagery and lighting, which recur throughout the film. Yet Nikander's plate of food in the poster lends a realist domesticity, qualifying the stylised image of alienation. The full plate calls to mind the habits of a lonely bachelor. Nikander's unfashionable polo shirt further diminishes the noir style. Noir is also present in the film. The portrayal of Nikander's love interest Ilona (Kati Outinen) bears a whiff of the femme fatale, if you abstract her actions in the film: she commences a relationship with Nikander, makes him an associate to a crime she commits, betrays him, and is finally united with him in escape. Yet at the same time, Nikander and Ilona are characters rendered in realist terms. They are workers in dreary Helsinki, a garbage collector and a trainee cashier. The film underscores their identity as labourers from the beginning, the opening sequence an ellipsis of a day on the job for Nikander. Indeed, the realist opening sequence in the workplace becomes an unmistakable Kaurismäkian trope. Images of workers also open *Crime and Punishment*, *Ariel*, *The Match Factory Girl*, *I Hired a Contract Killer*, *Pidä huivista kiinni, Tatjana* (*Take Care of Your Scarf, Tatiana*, 1994), *Kauas pilvet karkaavat* (*Drifting Clouds*, 1996), *The*

Man Without a Past, Laitakaupungin valot (*Lights in the Dusk*, 2006) and *Le Havre* (2011). (On the other hand, *Shadows in Paradise* opens musically on non-diegetic jazz by the Klaus Trauheit group, but jazz largely disappears from Kaurismäki's repertoire after the 1980s.)[2] The realism of the opening sequence combines in pastiche with the noir that also figures in the film. While the noir invokes a placeless fantasy about the history of cinema, the realist images locate the film in a specific place, with specific power structures operating.

A larger question arises, then: How can we make sense of the contradictory pastiche that we see in *Shadows in Paradise,* and which is characteristic of Kaurismäki's films in general? We might see Kaurismäki's cinema as an instance of postmodernist aesthetics. Postmodernism as an aesthetic trend that flourished in the 1970s and 1980s clearly influenced Kaurismäki's cinema. Evidence for such a view is offered in many places, not least the posters. The posters place multiple, contrasting traditions in a floating, timeless image, featuring 'mixing of diverse type sizes and weights, overprinting, cluttered pages, deliberate "mistakes", unpredictable historicist references, blurred photographs, and in some cases an embrace of general messiness' (Eskilson 2007: 336). The posters for *Hamlet liikemaailmassa* (*Hamlet Goes Business*, 1987), *The Bohemian Life*, *I Hired a Contract Killer*, and *Juha* (1999) are all built around paintings by Paula Oinonen, Kaurismäki's spouse. The posters include three distinct elements. Often the film's title is rendered in a strong diagonal, which is done with hand-lettering or in a

The Bohemian Life (1992) poster, Paula Oinonen (courtesy of Finnish National Audiovisual Archive, used with permission of Sputnik Ltd.)

Juha (1999) poster, Paula Oinonen (courtesy of Finnish National Audiovisual Archive, used with permission of Sputnik Ltd.)

font that evokes hand lettering, making a direct reference to the pulp and noir tradition. The hand lettering matches the *serif* fonts. The combination cites the craft tradition of advertising in the 1930s and 1940s, in which experienced draftsmen created film posters and other large advertising copy by hand. Yet the posters also commonly feature *sans serif* fonts associated with the modernism of the international style. Such streamlined, clean design elements sit oddly with the hand lettering and *serif* fonts. Each poster also features the main characters of the film in profile, with their eyes directed beyond the plane of the image to create a cinematic sense of spatial continuity and, hence, drama. Bold planes of colour divide the characters. They call to mind pulp covers, although they omit their sexual and violent elements. In combination these contrasting elements yield more pastiche. The design elements and varying styles, sizes, and weights of type create floating, timeless documents that do not belong to the present, but yet cannot be dated to any particular historical juncture.

Placing emphasis on pastiche in the posters and the films makes Kaurismäki's cinema appear to be an instance of postmodernism, yet such an account overlooks the weight of the realism, and the films' melodramatic seriousness of moral purpose. In this sense, the films might be more richly situated in a modernist framework, hewing to intellectual convictions, as they do, for which they seek a new and challenging formal expression. In this dimension Kaurismäki differs from such postmodernist filmmakers as Quentin Tarantino, Richard Linklater, Wes Anderson, the Coen Brothers, and Christopher Nolan, for in Kaurismäki's films we find moralism alongside pastiche and humour, and so he can be more suggestively likened to such filmmakers as Lars

The Man Without a Past poster (used with permission of Sputnik Ltd.)

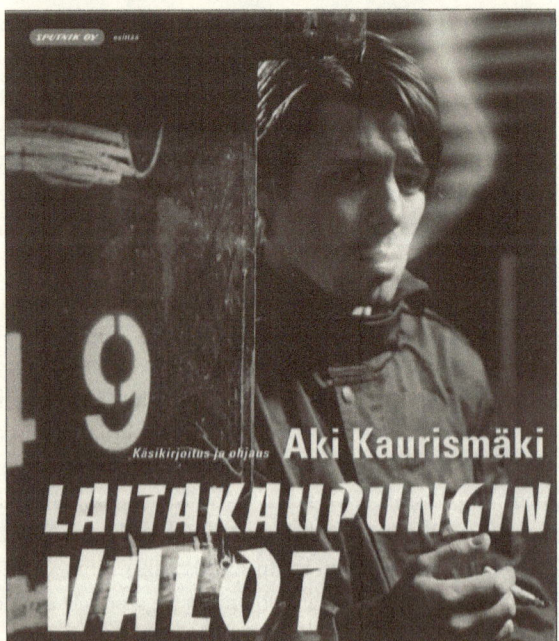

Lights in the Dusk poster (used with permission of Sputnik Ltd.)

von Trier, Michael Haneke, and Steven Soderbergh, some obvious differences with these filmmakers notwithstanding.

The posters from *Hamlet*, *The Bohemian Life*, and *Juha* are instances of pastiche and postmodernist graphic design, at once puckish and morally serious engagements with the cultural archive. It is evident that the style of these posters carries through to more recent films, such as *The Man Without a Past* and *Lights in the Dusk*. A rich way to approach and situate Kaurismäki's films is to analyse the way the films use the archive. What materials does Kaurismäki use? What does he eschew? Towards what ends? Kaurismäki's inclusion of diverse aesthetic traditions in his films indicates his access to and use of a vast cultural archive, but also his self-reflexive alignment with specific genealogies within that archive. This self-aware use of the cultural and cinematic archive is definitive of Kaurismäki's authorship.

The archive here is an aggregate of interwar and post-war popular culture texts, but also Kaurismäki's use of some of that material in his cinema, a sort of personal archive. The film scholar Satu Kyösola (2004b) has argued that Kaurismäki's cinema can be understood as an archiving project, which seeks to conserve certain elements of the past as an aesthetic and moral resistance against capitalist late modernity. Yet as we saw in the discussion of Allan Sekula's argument about the logic of the archive in the Introduction, different notions of the archive involve quite different cultural consequences. For example, is the archive a box like the one Andy Warhol kept, into which he dropped everything for a month before having the box taken away and put in storage? Is it an archive of survivors' testimony? In contrast to these instances, the relevant notion more closely resembles that described by Hal Foster in 'The Archival Impulse' (2006), which he associates with such artists as Thomas Hirschhorn, Sam Durant, and Tacita Dean. The practice identified by Foster is an archival sampling that takes place in a context in which the museum has failed as coherent cultural system, and the artist instead seeks to elaborate new, informal forms of cultural memory. This is not a melancholic project, according to Foster, but an 'institutive' one, which seeks alternative modes of archival practice. Kaurismäki's use of the past is fruitfully likened to the archival impulse theorised by Foster. We are able to see the pattern of sampling from an earlier era of mass culture, which is seminal in Kaurismäki's cinema. And yet Foster argues this is not a repetition of the museum project or a quest for lost objects and sentiments, but a means of engaging a fragmented and transitional symbolic order, about which many questions need to be asked. The archive as a trope in Kaurismäki's cinema can help us see his questions, as well as to raise some questions of our own.

Kaurismäki and commentators writing about him have often implied that access is at the root of his film education. He learned about cinema by watching hundreds if not thousands of films in the Finnish National Film Archive's Orion Theatre, the cinema clubs operating in Helsinki and Tampere during the 1970s and 1980s, and on Finnish State Television's TV2 film programming (see von Bagh 2006). Furthermore, he placed himself among such directors as François Truffaut, Jean-Luc Godard, Jim Jarmusch, Quentin Tarantino and others whose voracious consumption of films during their teens and twenties shaped their own filmmaking. Each of these filmmakers have situated themselves in various relationships to cinema by creating different accounts and lists of their relationship to film through textual allusions, writings, and criticism on film history, interviews, and performances. Kaurismäki's access to and command of film history is evident in his remark in the *Sight and Sound* Top Ten Poll: 'Everybody knows how hard it is. Top hundred might be a human task, but even that is tough (I have tried)' (BFI 2000). Kaurismäki has defined his cinema through his access to the cinematic and cultural archive.

The vastness of the cinematic and cultural archive now available to filmmakers causes accessing and using that material to involve a cultural politics. How does one use and align oneself in a context of near-universal access to the history of film? Film has been an artefact of the age of mechanical reproduction, to use Walter Benjamin's term. Such analogue reproduction enables a distribution and exhibition system in which a Finn like Kaurismäki can learn the cinema by viewing the films of D.W. Griffith, Luis Buñuel, and Yasujiro Ozu in film archives, clubs, and on Finnish television. Yet since Kaurismäki began as a filmmaker in 1981, access to the archive of moving images and popular culture has undergone a sea change. Digitalisation, new media, and globalisation have increased, broadened, and intensified access to the point where bits of a large amount of everything recorded, written, and shot has become available on YouTube, iTunes, Google Books, and other online repositories. Yet in contrast to the maximalist, futuristic ambitions of Apple and Google, Kaurismäki chooses celluloid over code, jukebox over iPod, analogue over digital. Kaurismäki chooses carefully how he accesses and uses the cinematic archive and the media that make it available. In the copy of the Finnish manuscript of the synopsis for *I Hired a Contract*, this care is evident in Kaurismäki's revision. 'I made the film "I Hired a Contract Killer" because as a ten-year-old I saw Henry Kass's film "The Last Holiday" on television, and I have not since been able to dispel the impression it made...' (Kaurismäki 1990a).[3] To the cinema Kaurismäki is true, cultivating a myth of his fidelity to it through repetition and erasure of qualifying historical details. It is no mistake that a clip of Godard's *Bande à part* (*Band of Outsiders*, 1964) appears in *The Liar*, a clip of Sergei Eisenstein's *Ivan Grozniy* (*Ivan the Terrible, Part I*, 1944) appears in *Calamari Union*, and posters for such films as Bresson's *L'Argent* (1983) appear in his films' *mise-en-scène*. Classic prints in the analogue cinematic archive interest Kaurismäki. In a context of ubiquitously available cultural texts, in multiple formats, one defines oneself as much by what one eschews as by what one chooses. This ethos uses the archive to fabricate a cultural politics from postmodern eclecticism. We can see this stance in the choices that define Kaurismäki's body of films.

On one hand, this chapter studies Kaurismäki's ecclecticism in terms of a conventional, *politique des auteurs* approach to cinematic authorship, accepting the premise that we can study a filmmaker's body of work as a director's creation. This premise applies to Kaurismäki, who is screenwriter, director, producer, and sometimes editor of his films. On the other hand, the chapter refuses the expressionist premise of the *politique des auteurs* claim, namely that films exteriorise the personality or soul of the filmmaker, as Andrew Sarris would have it in his interpretation and popularisation of the *politique des auteurs* notion of authorship. As part of the book's larger argument about authorship, the chapter seeks to recognise what we might call Kaurismäki's 'auteur scenario', that is the rough series and pattern of events comprising Kaurismäki's cinema as a meaningful body of work. Such a scenario is one dimension of his authorship, and created as much by commentators and audiences as by the director himself. Furthermore, as a scenario, the argument acknowledges the many ways in which Kaurismäki's authorship can be constructed; there is no one or true construction. My analysis thus seeks to identify a scenario, but also to note its contradictions and harmonies, explore its connections to other accounts of Kaurismäki's cinema, and to connect these. The advantage of this approach is that it acknowledges the point Tytti Soila (2003) has made in an article on Kaurismäki, that audience and critical interest in auteur filmmaking necessarily involves interest in the figure of the auteur, while recognising the multi-layered, discursive construction of the authorship, which revisionist theories of cinematic authorship have contributed. My discussion in this chapter seeks a tension between a conventional *politique des auteurs* approach to authorship and a poststructuralist one, which understands authorship as a changing intersection of multiple, unstable images and statements.

The auteur scenario developed here concerns the role of the cinematic and cultural archive in Kaurismäki's body of work. In arguments about 'Kaurismäkiland' or the magical realist quality of Kaurismäki's films, critics have acknowledged the consequence of pastiche in Kaurismäki's cinema. At the same time, in arguments about the ostensibly nostalgic character of Kaurismäki's films, other commentators have emphasised the importance of the past in Kaurismäki's films, whether it is made manifest through old objects, songs, or citation of earlier films or cinematic style. There is a link between the two, which has not been explored, but the exploration of which advances our understanding of his cinema. Kaurismäki uses the archive to articulate moral opposition to contemporary discourses of culture, economics, and politics. His films juxtapose symbolically archival objects, images, and music with symbolically contemporary material, creating contrasts which interrogate the ethical and moral systems on which the contemporary social order rests. These contrasts give voice to an oppositional position, which can often be read as an affirmation of innocence, a point that will come up for analysis in the discussion of the films that follows. In looking at his body of work in this way, it becomes clear that Kaurismäki uses the archive less for nostalgic reasons, to record what would otherwise be lost, but rather to gain access to material that the filmmaker can reuse and revise to intervene in contemporary cinema, culture, and politics.[4] We can understand this in terms of what Michel de Certeau (1984) calls 'the wig', the diversion of production materials from economic practices into other tasks, which introduce into economic tasks alternative socio-political ethics. Archival material provides a means of challenging the capitalist, market function of cinema, and of appealing to other values. This argument is developed below, but most explicitly in the discussion of nostalgia in chapter three.

This chapter works as something like a primer coat for the discussions in the chapters that follow, identifying key thematic and formal elements in Kaurismäki's cinema, providing an introduction to the filmmaker and his career, but also providing a basis and point of reference for further layers of analysis and elaboration. Other scholars have furnished us with useful introductory essays on Kaurismäki's cinema, such as Peter von

Bagh's insightful, humorous analytical overview (1997), Sakari Toiviainen's auteurist essay (2002; 2004), or Roger Connah's analysis of Kaurismäki's postmodernist eclecticism (1991). Film scholar Pietari Kääpä has written a deeply researched and thoughtful overview of the representation of nation in the Kaurismäki brothers' films (2008). In Finnish, film critic and filmmaker Lauri Timonen provides a highly readable introduction, *Aki Kaurismäen elokuvat* (*The Films of Aki Kaurismäki*, 2006). Kaurismäki's many interviews in English also provide rich introductory material (see Romney 1997; Cardullo 2006), and Jonathan Romney has provided us with a rich short essay on Kaurismäki's cinema (2003). This chapter seeks to build on these sources, but since many of them are not easily available, to develop an overview of Kaurismäki's films and to develop some provisional analysis of them.

Kaurismäki's project becomes most clearly discernible by categorising the films according to the kind of cultural material he draws upon, that is, through categories provided by an archival logic. Yet as von Bagh observes, the films are 'categorised awkwardly', for they 'defy categorisation… and are indivisible as a whole' (1997: 5). This observation notwithstanding, the categories here are roughly literature, cinema, theatre and cinema, and music. Seen from the angle of narrative mode and genre, these categories might be rendered as literary adaptations, road films, melodramas, and concert films. Labelling them in this way also adds a second layer, indicating not only the 'archival' medium in question (literature, cinema, theatre and cinema, and music), but the narrative structures around which Kaurismäki constructs his engagement with the archive. The relationship between archival material and narrative structure in Kaurismäki's films will be our first concern, after which we will look at the four categories comprising Kaurismäki's body of work.

Exile, Community, Music

At the heart of every one of Aki Kaurismäki's feature films, including the early films he made with his brother Mika, is a live musical performance. The performances and music give a good impression of what I have in mind in my argument about Kaurismäki and the archive. The diegetic performances included in the films are not trivial; they often span several minutes in films that are ninety minutes or less. They feature overlooked, forgotten, and underappreciated performers, archival because of their pop-cultural relevance yet lack of commercial status. The performances valorise vital, do-it-yourself, communally experienced, subversive musical experiences. The vitality present in the musical performances lies in an ethos that contrasts with the commercial, popular, and aesthetic notions on which much popular and cinematic music often rests. Performance and musical expression articulate characters' emotions and moral reasoning, glossing central conflicts in the films, rather than serving as showcases for musical stars, commercial hits, or the display of attitudes. At the same time, music functions to create strange juxtapositions with other material in the film, producing contrasts that destabilise typical associations and expectations about contemporary places, character types, and institutions. So, for example, the cinematography depicting Joe Strummer's cameo appearance playing a gig in *I Hired a Contract Killer* affirms the

Mika Tuokkola of Melrose performing in *Lights in the Dusk* (photo: Marja Leena Hukkanen, used with permission of Sputnik Ltd.)

materiality of his guitar and the performer, while erasing any markers of celebrity. It captures a vigorous and exceptional midday experience in a pub; at the same time, Strummer's song about alienation and travel towards a new home – 'Burning Lights' – thematises the narrative conflict of the film, Henri's (Jean-Pierre Léaud) isolation and aspiration towards transformation through love. The Strummer performance is alien in a world of over-produced, digitalised, marketed, commodified music, just as Henri is also a misfit in a world that differs from him. Depicting contrasts and using archival or quasi-archival material to enliven the typically stigmatised pole of the contrast, Kaurismäki challenges us to think about contemporary social order, whether that is the way we fetishise music or the social place of the misfit (or maverick).

While music is one formal means by which Kaurismäki stages contrasts, we might say that most of the contrasts that do concern him share a fundamental structure, a conflict between the alien and the social order he inhabits. Indeed the films could also be categorised in terms of the narrative and aesthetic means by which they produce their alienated protagonists. The literary texts Kaurismäki has adapted all involve protagonists who stand alone in their social world, isolated by a fateful choice or act or their commitment to a certain worldview, Raskolnikov and Hamlet epitomising this tendency. The journey film separates characters from their homes. There are also the loser melodramas, in which traumatic misfortune unmoors the protagonist, isolating him in his own world. Kaurismäki has called a triology of his films –*Shadows in Paradise*, *Ariel*, and *The Match Factory Girl* – the Loser Trilogy. My discussion of what I call the loser melodramas argues for a different and broader critical categorization,

Reijo Tapale performing the Satumaa Tango in *The Match Factory Girl* (used with permission of Sputnik Ltd)

as elaborated in chapter one. There are finally the concert films *Total Balalaika Show* (1993) and *Saimaa-ilmiö* (*The Saimaa Gesture*, 1981). The artist, and in particular the musician, typifies the conflict that concerns Kaurismäki, for as a cultural figure the musician is the loner, a figure made exceptional and isolated by his absorption in his art, its performance, and himself. The performance moreover culturally isolates him, placing him alone before the audience and staging his separation from the world he inhabits. Closer analysis of the performance of music in Kaurismäki's cinema shows that the music summarizes the central conflict in his films, the antagonism between the exile and his social world. Since this conflict underpins our categorisation of the films, it is useful to sketch further some of its features to prepare the way for discussion of the films.

A fruitful point of departure for this analysis is to note ubiquitous music and musical performance in Kaurismäki's cinema. In *The Liar*, made in 1981, co-written by Aki and directed by Mika, Aki, playing the male lead Ville Alfa, ventures into a club gig being performed by the Juice Leskinen Slam. Ville Alfa sways, mesmerised by the performance, shot with extensive close ups that also capture the performer Leskinen's sweaty pate. After that film, the brothers made a documentary about Leskinen and the rise of 'Suomirokki' (Finnish Rock) *The Saimaa Gesture*. In addition to Leskinen and his band, the film featured the punk-inspired bands that helped create the indigenous rock scene in Finland during the early 1980s, Eppu Normaali, and Hassisen Kone featuring Ismo Alanko. *The Saimaa Gesture* concludes with a performance of Finland's national anthem, 'Maamme laulu' ('Our Land') by the entire cast of musicians, calling to mind Jimi Hendrix's performance of the 'Star Spangled Banner' at Woodstock. A number of the musicians in *The Saimaa Gesture* appear in *Calamari Union*, which includes a giddy live performance by the entire cast of the satiric song 'Bad Boys'. The 1987 *Hamlet Goes Business* features a performance by the Finnish band Melrose of their song 'Rich Little Bitch'; Melrose return in 2006, performing in *Lights in the Dusk*. *I Hired a Contract Killer* features the cameo performance by Joe Strummer.

Juice Leskinen performing in the *The Liar* (copyright Villealfa Filmproductions Ltd.)

Leningrad Cowboys Go America and *Leningrad Cowboys Meet Moses* (1994) feature extensive performances, as the eponymous band performs on their first journey from New York to Mexico, and later during their journey from Mexico to the Urals. Punk-rock legend Nicky Tesco even joins the Cowboys to perform the Steppenwolf hit 'Born to be Wild' in *Leningrad Cowboys Go America*. The *Leningrad Cowboys* films culminate in the concert picture *Total Balalaika Show*, recorded as a live performance to an audience of some seventy thousand in Helsinki's Senate Square. And then there are the performances of tango and post-war-era rock-n-roll, which figure prominently in *The Match Factory Girl*, *Take Care of Your Scarf, Tatiana*, *Drifting Clouds*, *Juha*, and *The Man Without a Past*. These include performances and recordings by such key figures in Finnish Tango as Reijo Taipale, Markus Allen, and Olavi Virta, but also by remarkable acts like The Renegades, British pre-Beatles rockers (reminiscent of The Shadows) who enjoyed brief but incandescent stardom in two markets, Finland and Italy.

Ville Alfa (Aki Kaurismäki) attending Leskinen's performance in *The Liar* (copyright Villealfa Filmproductions Ltd.)

These performances, and the diegetical use of musical recordings as well, affirm the disjunctive, the unconventional, and even the odd – consider the Cowboys. We can see this dimension by pondering what Kaurismäki has not included. The music is not chosen because of its popularity, glamour, or the celebrity of the artists who perform – even Joe Strummer is presented as though he were an unknown local musician playing a midday gig. The performances in the films do not take place in large venues, arenas, or concert halls nor by groups that play them – with the exception of *Total Balalaika Show*. There are no current mainstream performers. *The Saimaa Gesture* and *Calamari Union* qualify this claim, since the bands featured in *The Saimaa Gesture* enjoyed popularity at the moment of production and their national celebrity and charisma was relevant to their casting in *Calamari Union*. Even in such cases, however, the depiction of the musicians goes against the grain, rather than presenting them in ways that seeks to confirm stereotypes about them. For example, the ensemble performance of the tune 'Bad Boys' in *Calamari Union* is a burlesque performance, inasmuch as it purposely seeks to lower the musicians' cultural role. The films' music repudiates the gaze of the fan or the tourist, instead cultivating fascination in the performance and music itself. Even the live tango performances, which might be mistaken for a conventional form of popular culture, can be understood as expressions of a dissident post-war popular culture, defined by its defiance of the high-cultural, edifying aspirations of the Finnish welfare state, which has long sought to use various means of governance to invigorate and disseminate high culture. Kaurismäki figuratively digs into the archives to present the audience with odd musical performances, which at once highlight the distance of the performer from the viewer, yet in their vitality and downright weirdness in some cases simultaneously beckon the viewer to embrace the music. A similar, ambivalent dynamic is at the heart of the films as well: the isolated protagonists inhabit their odd roles and alienated lives, while also seeking reconciliation with their community; yet they refuse compromise with their community's institutions and structures of power.

The opening sequence of *Crime and Punishment* offers a good example of the ambivalence related to music in Kaurismäki's cinema. The film adapts Dostoevsky's novel, an object of interest for Kaurismäki not only because Hitchcock had told Truffaut in an interview that the novel could not be adapted to the screen, but also because Bresson, a source of inspiration for Kaurismäki, had adapted it as *Pickpocket* (1959). Kaurismäki's adaptation narrows the focus to his Raskolnikov figure, called Rahikainen (Markku Toikka) in the film. He heightens Rahikainen's isolation, eliminating Raskolnikov's family and engagement, as well as the Marmeladov subplot. Further, whereas Raskolnikov murders the loan shark Alyona Ivanovna and her sister Lizaveta for philosophical reasons as well as to deal with the debt he has accumulated, Rahikainen murders the businessman Honkanen (Pentti Auer) to avenge the death of his fiancée, whom Honkanen killed in a drunken driving accident, of which he was acquitted. This shift gives the protagonist's isolation a different motive. Raskolnikov's internal struggle, both mental and philosophical, explain his erratic behaviour and growing isolation. Rahikainen's murder is of course also illegal, but morally justified, inasmuch as it sets right an injustice he has suffered. As a consequence, his isolation has a comprehensible moral justification. The conflict between an isolated individual's moral justification and the legal but immoral function of institutions recurs throughout Kaurismäki's career. Rahikainen is no innocent, but he does have a justifiable reason for what he does. Kaurismäki's protagonists will roughly follow Rahikainen's pattern, and music helps figure the complex relationship between such figures and the society they inhabit.

The opening music of Kaurismäki's career is Harri Marstio singing Schubert's 'Ständchen' ('Serenade') in English, in a Tom Waits style – albeit as a recording rather than as a diegetic performance.[5] Marstio also appears later in the film, performing a gig in a bar visited by Rahikainen. In his rendition of 'Ständchen', Marstio growls the plaintive words of melancholic longing for a distant lover, and the arrangement's atonal chords heighten his rough performance. The performance contrasts on several levels with the lyrical and pastoral expression of desire in Schubert's *lied*, but convincingly represents Rahikainen's tortured, solitary emotional world. In this register, 'Ständchen' also tells us Rahikainen does not belong in the abattoir, as a morbidly intellectual student who works dismembering animals with band saws, cleavers, and his hands, prying and pulling them apart. What we have, then, is a dissonant performance of the *lied*, which makes the music ugly to reflect the ugly setting, while preserving its beautiful expression of desire to comment on Rahikainen's desire. In this sense, Rahikainen is a more sentimental character than Raskolnikov. In such a contrast we see the moral alienation of Rahikainen. He is aligned with the narrating persona of Schubert's *lied* – indeed, later in the film we see him attending a performance of *The Marriage of Figaro*, another text concerning longing, desire, and romantic union – and he is out of place in the abattoir (even if he has been forced to acquire its skills). By contrast, Rahikainen's victim, the businessman Honkanen, is associated with the slaughterhouse. The opening sequence ends on a close up of blood washed down the drain, with a cut taking us to Honkanen pictured in close up in a taxi arriving at his apartment. The abattoir epitomises capitalism, and Honkanen belongs to this world. He is a patriarch whose good standing in the halls of power – he is head of the Finnish Wholesalers' Association, we later learn – insulates him from the bloody exploitation from which he renders his profits. These contrasts and associations articulate the film's central moral question: should Rahikainen maintain fidelity to Schubert and Mozart, with their aspirations to redeeming, romantic union, or should he reconcile himself to the rules of the slaughterhouse, as represented by Honkanen. Ultimately, Rahikainen chooses to remain unreconciled and unredeemed but affirms his moral stance; he murders Honkanen, accepts prison for his crime, and rejects the romantic union offered by his Sonja, Eeva (Aino Seppä). The film closes on 'Ständchen' as Rahikainen returns to his prison cell after a visit from Eeva, alone again.

The use of 'Ständchen' concisely marks the gap between subjective desire, and its moral aspirations, the order of the slaughterhouse and its institutional and legal foundations. The persona who narrates the *lied* seeks to transform his beloved with his expression of longing, for the beloved cannot be or will not do what the persona wishes. Similarly, there is a gap between the social order Rahikainen longs for, and what he experiences. Like the persona in Schubert's *lied* he seeks to enact a transformation, only by murder not song. As he says at the end of the film, 'I killed a louse, but became one myself. The number of lice did not change.' The struggle to reconcile alienated social experience and an aspirational order of wholeness is ongoing. The archive provides the source material for acting out this ambivalent struggle. Often, music is key to such performances in Kaurismäki's films. Let us examine how the other literary adaptation films deal with the ambivalent relationship between Kaurismäki's protagonists and their social world, before turning to the other films.

Literary Adaptations

Kaurismäki's literary adaptations all concern the relationship between the protagonists' moral convictions and the order of community and society with which they come into conflict. In *The Bohemian Life,* Murger's artists constitute a subculture, which seeks to negotiate a relationship to the social order that surrounds them, represented by bourgeois aspiration, sensibility, and profitable business practice. These bohemian artists have been popularised and interpreted by Puccini, by the New York theatrical production *Rent* (1996) and its film adaptation (2005), and by Sally Potter in her short *Thriller* (1979), among others; in each case the bohemian artists have given voice to a critique of bourgeois order and its values. Another of Kaurismäki's literary adaptations is of the Finnish author Juhani Aho's novel *Juha* (1911). In the novel, the eponymous protagonist is a cuckold, as well as a moral hero, who pursues his notion of justice to its logical end. Kaurismki has, as noted above, adapted Dostoevsky's *Crime and Punishment* and also Shakespeare's *Hamlet,* titled *Hamlet Goes Business.* Both adaptations focus on the protagonist's efforts to tally his moral reasoning with the tasks it calls for, which lead him to differentiate himself from his society. In *Hamlet*, the prince's avenging of his father ultimately claims the life of his murderer Claudius, but also uncovers his mother's involvement in the crime and brings about the death of Gertrude, Polonius, and Ophelia. Kaurismäki's adaptation also includes these deaths, but heightens Hamlet's moral isolation by making him the scheming, insolent, dumb and repulsive heir to a Finnish industrial family's wealth and business interests, which he insouciantly seeks to run according to his view of things. Kaurismäki's twist is to make the soldier Barnardo the working-class hero Simo (Hannu Valtonen), who ultimately outmanoeuvres Hamlet and murders him. It is not so much Hamlet's isolation that is at the heart of the film, but rather the class-based alienation of Simo, who patiently puts up with it all and bides his time. As a consequence, Hamlet's famous existential angst is played as silly parody. For example, Kaurismäki borrows from Orson Welles' *Citizen Kane* (1941) in a number of places, not least in his choice to seat Hamlet at the head of an extremely long dining table for dinners with his mother or by himself. Kaurismäki's table is longer, and his wide-angle lens exaggerates the gulf created by the long shots of the diners, creating a parodic isolation. By heightening the trope into absurdity, Kaurismäki signals his awareness of what he is doing, but also makes sport of Hamlet's existential isolation, lending his backing to Simo. Simo's isolation is what matters, which correlates with the sympathies of Kaurismäki's other films. Simo is an alien within the family concern, and he ultimately affirms his alienation by poisoning Hamlet, fulfilling a fantasy of class vengeance.

In *The Bohemian Life,* alienation and exile are embodied by the artist and immigrant subject, rather than by the class subject, and once again the alien is the moral agent standing in opposition to the representatives of capital. In the film, the latter include a nationalistic landlord, the publisher Gassot (Samuel Fuller), and the sugar-manufacturer patron (Jean-Pierre Léaud). In adapting Murger's stories, Kaurismäki alters both *dramatis personae* and historical setting. He eliminates the philosopher Colline, leaving Marcel, Rodolphe (Rodolfo for Kaurismäki), and Schaunard. He also diminishes the role of Musette and expands the character Mimi, making her romance with Rodolfo the central dramatic conflict in the film – her romance is with Marcel in Murger. These changes also work to put Rodolfo in the foreground, making Marcel and Schaunard sidekicks. Further, in Murger it is Mimi and Musette who are true outsiders, for they are *grisettes,* excluded by gender and class.[6] In Kaurismäki's adaptation, Rodolfo becomes the representative outsider as an Albanian *émigré*; the change underscores his status as an alien, positioning him on the wrong side of such lines as East and West, centre and periphery, rich and poor. *The Bohemian Life* is an episodic film, roughly following the organisation of Murger's short stories. Schaunard (Kari Väänänen), Marcel (André Wilms) and Rodolfo (Matti Pellonpää) meet on the day that Marcel is evicted from his apartment. They eat and drink together, support each other in their artistic work, meet and form relationships with women, help out Rodolfo when he is deported, develop their relationships, undergo break ups and reunifications, then witness the death of Mimi (Evelyne Didi), on which the film ends. The film moves from insouciant irony to sentimental moralism, as the outsider Rodolfo is separated from Mimi then reunited with her only to face her death. The film's meandering opening and middle are tied together in an affirmation of Rodolfo's dignity and moral conviction amidst his poverty and middling success as an *émigré* artist.

The same gap between alienated moral conviction and communal and social institutions and practices is present in Kaurismäki's other literary adaptations – *Likaiset kädet* (*Dirty Hands,* 1989) and *Juha. Dirty Hands* was made for Finnish TV2 (YLE) with Matti Kurkikangas as cinematographer and Lasse Liitovaara as sound engineer, an exception to Kaurismäki's usual arrangement of Timo Salminen and Jouko Lumme respectively. Kaurismäki had less control of the film than in his own productions, and distanced himself from it after its release (see von Bagh 2006: 70–5). The film is based on Jean-Paul Sartre's *Les mains sales* (*Dirty Hands,* 1948), which concerns the existentialist registers of political action, and is set in the closing phase of World War II in a fictional Eastern European country. Hugo Barine (Matti Pellonpää) is a committed communist. He is persuaded by a party leader, Louis (Pertti Sveholm), to take on the mission of assassinating the leader of a rival faction in the party, Hoederer (Sulevi Peltola). Hugo and his wife Jessica (Kati Outinen) go to work for Hoederer, but Hugo does not carry out the assassination. When Hoederer makes advances towards Jessica, Hugo shoots him. Hugo subsequently comes to understand the cynical strategy involved in Louis' assassination plan; but he also realises he is now vulnerable as a knowledgeable agent of theirs. Hugo ultimately makes the Sartrean decision, deciding to go with Louis' men at the end of the film, although he faces the certainty he will be murdered. In other words, he recognises and affirms the nothingness of his subjectivity, rather than fleeing death in a self-deception about his own identity. Like *Hamlet,* however, *Dirty Hands'* themes of isolation and alienation are ironised. The actors' understated levity is one of the key sources of the irony, and it prevents the film from generating the emotional tension that is present in Sartre's play. As a consequence, the gap between moral conviction and social convention, also at the heart of existential philosophy, is diminished.

Kaurismäki's *Juha* adapts Juhani Aho's 1911 novel, which is a canonical text within Finnish literature as well as another example of an alienated but not victimised protagonist who stands by his principles. *Juha* has been adapted as an opera, for the theatre, and for the big screen, with Mauritz Stiller making the first film version in 1921, Nyrki Tapiovaara making another in 1937, and Toivo Särkkä yet another in 1956. Kaurismäki's distinction is to have made *Juha* as a silent film, complete with a sweeping score by Anssi Tikanmäki, a Kaurismäki collaborator from the early 1980s. Remarking on his reasons for making a silent adaptation of *Juha,* and on his perception of the film's failure, Kaurismäki says:

> We can never again make films like *Broken Blossoms, Sunrise,* or *Queen Kelly* because since film started to gamble with mumbling and all that 'hoochie-coochie' and fancy words, stories have lost their purity, cinema its essence: innocence. (Kaurismäki 1999)

The film develops a rich and varied notion of innocence. Juha (Sakari Kuosmanen) and Marja (Kati Outinen) own a farm, which is visited by an out-of-towner, Shemeikka (André Wilms), who impresses Marja with his flash ways. She disappears with him, and Juha goes after her. As soon as Shemeikka gets Marja to the city, he pimps her out in his nightclub. When Juha finds her, she has had a child by Shemeikka and has been forced to work in his nightclub. Juha discovers Shemeikka did not abduct her; Marja wanted to leave with him. Juha liberates Marja, but invites his death by confronting Shemeikka and his men alone, armed only with an axe. Kaurismäki does not adapt the novel as psychological realism, to which the novel would lend itself. Rather, he makes it moral allegory, with symbolic characters, histrionic acting, exaggerated costuming and make-up, and an operatic score. Juha is an agent of moral conviction, defending his home and wife against the intruder Shemeikka. Shemeikka is the promulgator of an alienating capitalist modernity, driving a 1967 Corvette, operating a night club, and trading in flesh. Marja is a tragically determined ingénue. The narrative conflict is given an allegorical register by way of temporalisation in the *mise-en-scène*: Juha and Marja represent the countryside as a site of past innocence and moral conviction, and Shemeikka represents the city, and contemporary capitalist pragmatism. One of two moments of diegetic sound occurs when Juha sharpens his axe and shaves his face with an ancient electric shaver, before heading to the city. Such excess also includes a Sirkian irony signalled by the Sierck hood ornament on the corvette driven by Shemeikka, as Kaurismäki remarks in an interview (see Nestingen 2007). Douglas Sirk (Dietlef Sierk) made a number of melodramas in Hollywood during the 1950s which became known for their ironic critique of US society. Invoking these films with Sirk's German surname, Kaurismäki signals that his film shares Sirk's spirit of ironic critique. A literalist reading of the film would see the opposition of country and city, Finland and the continent, as an opposition between moral tradition and amoral, capitalist modernity. Taking the irony into consideration, the film also involves a critique of national self-image. This irony is clear in the way the innocence in question is inflected in an aesthetic and film-historical way, as indicated by Elina Salo's musical performance of the French standard 'Les temps des cerises' ('The Time of the Cherries').

Irony complicates matters and here as well it is a musical performance that matters. Tellingly, the most powerful moment in the film is the sound performance by longtime Kaurismäki favourite Salo of 'Les temps des cerises', which disrupts the silence of this silent film (the scene precedes Juha's axe sharpening). Salo plays Shemeikka's sister, a chanteuse in his club. Her performance shares some of the dissonance of Marstio's performance of 'Ständchen', which in this case is further heightened by a disjunctively edited match between sound and visual tracks. The song, moreover, is a classic of the French left, indeed a song of the Communards in 1871. It was also the musical foundation of a film Kaurismäki has frequently praised, Jacques Becker's *Casque d'or* (*Golden Marie*, 1952), itself an elegy to French poetic realism's favourite theme, doomed love (Andrew 1995: 338). Kaurismäki's films frequently draw on the French poetic realist films of the 1930s. In *Golden Marie*, 'Les temps de cerises' 'expresses the delicious fatality of poetic realism ... but it evokes simultaneously the warmth of the Popular Front that ... mature friendship ... where workers implicitly count on each other', which it summons as a force relevant to contemporary politics, as film scholar Dudley Andrew argues (1995: 342, 344). Performing in the nightclub, Shemeikka's sister sings not only of Juha and Marja's doomed love, in the poetic realist sense, but also reminds us that the forces of oppression Shemeikka represents are dialectically entangled with forces of emancipation, in a Marxist sense. Salo's sound performance can be seen to mark a moral gap. It is a singular moment of sound, an instance of beauty, conviction, dissent, and critique of Juha and Marja's dehumanisation, which differs from the camp and allegorical adaptation of the novel that surrounds it. Yet, in forging a single moment of terse beauty, hidden within Shemeikka's nightclub, the film suggests that it conceives of beauty not in terms of purity, but rather as entangled in contrasts that make beauty and dissent possible, sound and silence, the nightclub and the cinema, which take shape through the forces of Western capitalist modernity, yet in so doing also produce opportunities for resistance. This is a counterpuntal moment recalling 'Ständchen' in the dissonance of the performance, in its crisscrossing semantics, and in the ambivalent relationship between alienation, separation, and exile

Such beauty contrasts with the naively innocent Juha, who is a surrogate for the innocence of the cinema that Kaurismäki remarks upon above, and which he has frequently discussed. Characters like Juha are common in Kaurismäki's films. The Leningrad Cowboys, Valto (Mato Valtonen) in *Tatiana*, M (Markku Peltola) in *The Man Without a Past*, and Koistinen (Janne Hyytiäinen) in *Lights in the Dusk* are all innocent men. But it is not really innocence that concerns Kaurismäki. To be sure, he has long spoken of the lost innocence of the cinema: '*Crime and Punishment* is a homage to those golden years when one murder was sufficient for one crime film', was a tagline for his first film. The idea also encompasses cultural innocence. About *Tatiana,* he said, 'This film is my personal farewell to the Finland in which I grew up, but which to my dismay has been lost forever'. Yet judging in a literal-minded way, we can see Kaurismäki violates his own notion of innocence: *Hamlet, Ariel,* and even *Juha* each includes multiple murders. What is more, innocence remains a fundamental narrative and cultural category of the mainstream cinema Kaurismäki consistently opposes, especially in Hollywood. Innocent children, innocent couples, innocent natives, and innocent animals remain stock characters.

It is not the absolute category of innocence that concerns Kaurismäki, but the exceptional stance of the dissident who holds convictions that appear innocent in their contrast to the expedient and cynical compromises of political-economic life. His is not a cinema of innocence, then, but rather of moral objection, which produces the appearance of innocence. It is in this relative stance that we find the rationale for his literary adaptations, and for the key feature we have traced in them, the ambivalence around which they are constructed. The texts that appeal to him are ones whose key theme is moral objection to the compromises and concessions of the world. This inclination helps explain Kaurismäki's preference for noir aesthetics. Noir is not a world of innocence, but a world of compromise. It involves characters who know how to play by the rules of that compromised world; yet at least one of them remains true to his moral code. Such moral characters are also familiar from French poetic realism, on display in Jean Gabin's Pépé in *Pépé le moko* (Julien Duvivier, 1937) or his Jean in *Le quai des brumes* (*Port of Shadows,* Marcel Carné, 1938*).* We would miss such moral objection if we took the ironic Kaurismäki at his word on the topic of innocence. The literary adaptations are concerned with the relative categories of moral dissent, which is the driving notion behind their narratives and their aesthetics. They also articulate an aesthetic and political objection to the cinematic context in which they circulate by recalling noir, poetic realism, and various music from the archives. These same concerns figure prominently in the Kaurismäki journey films.

The Journey Films

Aki Kaurismäki's five journey films narrate the moral dissent of outsiders, a theme to which the journey narrative lends itself. The journey films also shed further light on the cinematic and cultural positioning of Kaurismäki's cinema, not least on the notion of innocence. The journey films include *Calamari Union, Ariel, Leningrad Cowboys Go America, Leningrad Cowboys Meet Moses,* and *Take Care of Your Scarf, Tatiana.* These are all road movies, with the exception of *Calamari Union.* While *Calamari Union* may not technically deal with the semantics of the road movie (a narrative built around a trip by motor vehicle with recurrent shots of landscape seen from the vehicle), it does employ the syntax of the road movie (conflict among the travellers and with the strangers and institutions they encounter in the effort to reach some final destination). 'Kaurismäki has taken the road movie genre to heart more than any European director save Wenders', writes Jonathan Romney (2003: 43). The road movie meshes with the concerns of Kaurismäki's authorship, for its generic elements allow Kaurismäki to create plausible and compelling outsiders, whose journeys permit a critical exploration of the eclectic cultural, temporal, and moral dimensions of the late-modern West. The journey narrative also rests on the gap between outsiders and the communities through which they pass, offering concrete contexts to stage conflicts between outsiders and agents of social order.

The correlation between travel, exile, and divergent historical moments is evident in Romney's arguments about Kaurismäki's road movies. He compares Kaurismäki's use of this genre to country and western music, writing that

> my favourite English subtitle comes in Aki Kaurismäki's *Take Care of Your Scarf, Tatiana*. As its two middle-aged slackers awkwardly sit down together, one tells the other, 'Move your ass, said Johnny Cash' ... The Johnny Cash reference is inspired, not just for its note of barroom swagger, but also because it pinpoints the flavour of Kaurismäki's films. There's almost no country music to be found amidst his eclectic soundtracks, which in their way provide as thorough a self-portrait as Scorsese's jukebox choices: blues, lachrymose Finnish tango, snatches of Shostakovich and Tchaikovsky, and copious fifties and sixties rock and R&B ... [Kaurismäki's] films are themselves country and western songs of the old school: stories of taciturn loners with hidden sentimental streaks, trying to walk tall in a world where there's not enough work and too much vodka. (Ibid.)

Romney's comparison to country music gets at a central register in Kaurismäki's journey films: the conflict between the traveller's convictions and the values of the world through which he travels – a conflict that can also be seen as a longing for the world the traveller left behind. The reason for the resonance between Kaurismäki and country and western is that country music is a genre of displacement and diaspora. It often tells tales of people who are out of joint with the world, and who long for lost homes and loves. The reason for this tendency lies in the history of country music. It is the music of poor, white southerners who migrated to the north and west of the US between 1900 and 1920, where they became known as 'hillbillies' and 'Okies'. They were displaced geographically and by class. Hank Williams Jr., Johnny Cash, Merle Haggard and many others came from and have written for this displaced population. Such singers and their audience are taciturn because they cannot go home, for economic reasons, yet feel a longing to return, hoping for an alternative to their new homes in California, Pennsylvania, Ohio, Minnesota, and the like (see Gregory 2005). Yet Romney is also wrong in his comparison, for there was another side to this music of American diaspora, which actually does figure prominently in Kaurismäki's films. It is the music of poor, African American southern migrants of the same period. African Americans spread blues, R&B, soul, jazz, and gospel to the North and West of the US, in some ways a historical mirror image of country music, yet also the music of cultural struggle, self-definition, and the civil rights movement. In *I Hired a Contract Killer*, for example, recordings of Billie Holiday singing 'Body and Soul' and 'Time on My Hands' are included, and *Drifting Clouds* opens with African American jazzman Shelly

Fisher singing 'Lonesome Traveller'. While not a journey film itself, the opening of *Drifting Clouds* helps explain why Romney associates the spirit of country music, and by extension blues, R&B, and jazz, with Kaurismäki's road films. They are films about lonesome travellers unable to find new homes and unable to return to old ones. The journey films stage exile and alienation within a circumscribed and malleable narrative form, providing the filmmaker a means of exploring a key theme within an accessible and comprehensible cinematic language.

Calamari Union, *Leningrad Cowboys Go America*, and *Leningrad Cowboys Meet Moses* link the journey narrative to music, and as we saw in the literary adaptations, music often conveys pivotal semantic content in Kaurismäki's films. With musicians making up the lion's share of the cast in all three films, Kaurismäki creates a tone of bohemian insouciance punctuated by occasional musical performances, which display emotional energy. All three films also share ridiculous premises. In *Calamari Union*, a group of fifteen men all named Frank, and one named Pekka, collectively decide to leave their working-class Helsinki neighbourhood, Kallio, and depart for the bourgeois neighbourhood Eira. The film unfolds in stylised action and loosely connected episodes. The Franks steal cars, fight, get picked up by women, make misogynistic remarks, take drugs, perform a concert, get gunned down, run cafés, drink iced water, sit in parks, and steal hearses from funny-looking drivers. Two finally escape Helsinki by dinghy, headed for Estonia. Likewise, *Leningrad Cowboys Go America* features a large cast, in this case the eight living members of the Leningrad Cowboys, their deceased ninth, their manager Vladimir (Matti Pellonpää), and the village idiot Igor (Kari Väänänen) who follows them. The group shares the same torpedo-style haircut – except Igor. Vladimir is a tyrant, whom the band resignedly tolerates. Vladimir has scheduled a gig in the US, and has aspirations for them, but their polka repertoire earns insults. A promoter sarcastically offers them a gig in Mexico, and they cheerfully set off from New York in a giant black Cadillac sold to them by Jim Jarmusch, who appears in a cameo performance. Their journey takes them through Memphis, Natchez, Mississippi, New Orleans, Houston, Galveston, San Antonio, and finally into Mexico. *Leningrad Cowboys meet Moses* tells the story of the group's return journey to a collective farm in Siberia. The collective farm is a promised land, to which they are delivered by Vladimir, whose time in the Mexican wilderness has transformed him into a Moses-figure. This journey goes from Mexico, through New York, to Brest, Frankfurt, Leipzig, Dresden, the Czech forest, Poland, Ukraine, and finally into a fantastical Soviet countryside, the promised land to which Moses has led them, but which he himself never reaches. The cowboys are pursued by CIA agent Johnson (André Wilms) along the way, who is after the nose of the Statue of Liberty, which Vladimir has stolen and is seeking to return to the collective farm, for it is the true home of Liberty. Once again, the cowboys make their way from gig to gig, playing country, gospel and blues in addition to their polka and rock repertoire.

The three films are built on improvisation, and indeed *Calamari Union* never had a script. Kaurismäki would write dialogue for the characters on the set, as he followed a map of Helsinki he had drawn up as a plan for the film. This was possible in part because the film was made with a low budget, and received no funding from the Finnish

Film Foundation. Improvisation and a self-reflexive embrace of low production values are not only the mark of underground cinema, but also associated with the French New Wave, to which tradition the film belongs (see Romney 2003). Yet the narrative structure of these journey films locates them squarely within Kaurismäki's storytelling method, which can be summed up as: isolate and alienate the protagonist/s; watch him or her try to get somewhere better. The journey creates protagonists, outsiders, and a destination, and also stages a series of juxtapositions and conflicts through which the films engage in cultural-political debate.

Ariel and *Take Care of Your Scarf, Tatiana* are less improvisational than *Calamari Union* and the *Leningrad Cowboys* films. They do not develop the bohemian register of these films either. *Ariel* and *Take Care of Your Scarf, Tatiana* narrate the journeys of lower-class men who find themselves displaced in their worlds. The protagonists are naïve and pitiful, yet resilient and hopeful. *Ariel* follows Taisto Kasurinen (Turo Pajala) from a closed mine near Salla in northeastern Finland to Helsinki, from Finnish Lapland to the southern capital city. The laid-off miner seeks work, which he never finds, but instead finds love with Irmeli (Susanna Haavisto). His bad luck accrues over the course of the journey, leading to a conviction and a prison sentence for aggravated assault. The film becomes something of a buddy picture through the prison episode. After spending some time in prison, Taisto breaks out with his cellmate Mikkonen (Matti Pellonpää), who is murdered before he and Taisto can follow through on their plan to escape from Finland. Taisto, Irmeli, and her son Riku do escape Finland on the ship *Ariel*, bound for Mexico – the pulp conclusion directly recalling Godard's *Bande à part*, which ends shipboard *en route* to South America; it also recalls doomed plans for escape by ship in some of the poetic realist films, such as *Pépé le moko* and *Port of Shadows*.

Like *Ariel*, *Take Care of Your Scarf, Tatiana* has elements of road film and buddy picture. It is set some time in the 1960s. The film begins with Valto (Mato Valtonen) rebelling against his oppressive mother, when she refuses to replenish his coffee supply. Valto and Reino (Matti Pellonpää) set off to pick up some coffee, but become involved in a longer trip when they pick up Tatiana (Kati Outinen) and Klavdia (Kirsi Tykkyläinen), stranded Soviet tourists trying to make it to Tallinn. The film follows the four from a barn dance, to a hotel, to a café, and on to the harbour, where the two men decide to continue with the women across the Gulf of Finland to the Soviet city of Tallinn. Even though Reino and Valto fail to speak to Tatiana and Klavdia beyond a couple of words, Reino falls in love with Tatiana, and she is willing to give him a chance. He stays on in Tallinn, while Valto travels back to his mother.

Kaurismäki's journey films involve two of the main features of his cinema: they stage experiences of alienation and isolation, as the travellers are by definition outsiders in the areas through which they travel; and the journey narrative lends itself to the pastiche of cinematic and archival elements that we have identified in Kaurismäki's posters and films. In *Leningrad Cowboys Go America*, for example, the Cowboys stage their version of a jazz funeral, angering the local police and landing them in jail. The travellers do not understand New Orleans, or have a permit to transport their dead bandmate. Kaurismäki plays the scene for its absurdity. Yet it illustrates the premise of his journey narratives. The Cowboys are outsiders in the world they traverse, yet wish to identify with it – whether by staging a jazz funeral for one of their own, or by adapting a mariachi style in Mexico. Their moral stance and ethical inclinations mark them as outsiders unable to enter the world around them.

The journey film's many locations simultaneously lend the form to pastiche and archival exploration. As the travellers follow their route, the stops on their itinerary can be just about anywhere. Kaurismäki uses this openness by making the Cowboys' journey temporal, inasmuch as the travellers pass through institutions of the past, which persist in the present. In *Leningrad Cowboys Meet Moses*, for example, the Cowboys' journey concludes in a utopia given form by a Soviet collective farm, despite the film's release in 1994, several years after the dissolution of the Soviet Union. The eclectic musical repertoire of the Cowboys' performances is another instance of the jumbled temporality of their journey. As they play blues, rock, gospel, and polka in different venues, they seem to enter different times. For instance, when Igor (Kari Väänänen) solicits a country and western performance from a barber in Memphis, the setting and action seem to date to the 1950s or 1960s. Later, the country bar Zhivago in Houston evokes the film's moment of production, the late 1980s. A biker bar the Cowboys subsequently visit evokes the 1970s, and the rise of the Hells Angels and other motorcycle gangs, but also the emergence of punk. The Cowboys' lost cousin, eminent punk-rock figure Nicky Tesco, gives a wild performance of 'Born to Be Wild'. Finally, the Cowboys themselves are an anachronism, arriving in New York ignorant of rock-n-roll, the most ubiquitous form of music in the West since the 1950s. They never fully make the transition to the present, inhabiting a liminal space between past and present, as their costumes, musical styles, and haircuts make clear.

The temporal dimensions of the journey films are equally prominent in *Tatiana* and *Ariel*. Kaurismäki situates *Tatiana* specifically in the past, setting the film in the 1960s and dedicating it to the memory of his childhood Finland, gone forever. The title underscores the archival dimension. *Take Care of Your Scarf, Tatiana*, refers to the fashionable style of riding double on motorcycles during the 1960s. The female passenger sat on the back with her legs to one side, 'Amazon', because fashionable mini-skirts prevented her from straddling the seat; the female passenger typically wore a scarf (but no helmet) to keep her hair from becoming windblown. Images of such motorcycling comprise the film's opening sequence. The first image includes motorcycles and riders whizzing by, but also store windows and a car-filled street, which date the film's diegetic world. Further images of men and women nonchalantly riding 'Amazon' at high speeds complete the credit sequence. These women need scarves to keep up their coiffed style. In contrast, Tatiana and Klavdia are not on the back of motorcycles, are not going fast, and encounter little danger of mussed hair. They hardly need to mind their scarves. The temporal allusion in the title divulges a warmly ironic remark about the hapless Reino and Valto. The allusion to 1960s' youth culture and motorcycles underscores the irony.

In *Ariel*, the journey from a closed mine in the north to the capital city of Helsinki, invokes several temporal strata. On the one hand, Taisto Kasurinen makes the mythical modern journey from the country to the city in search of work. The film is also

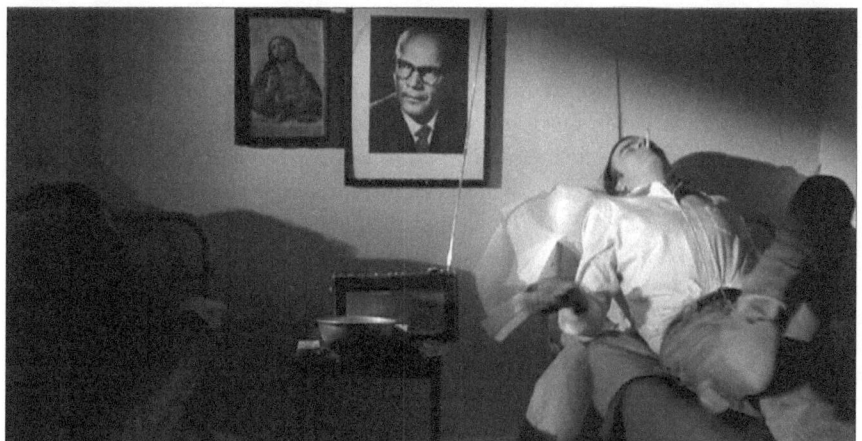

Taisto (Turo Pajala) with his portrait of Kekkonen (used with permission of Sputnik Ltd.)

a specific story of Finnish modernisation and urbanisation, linking Taisto to the automatisation and modernisation of extractive industries and agricultural production during the 1960s and 1970s. More efficient systems made Finland's rural population redundant. People left home looking for work. Some half a million Finns moved to Sweden during the 1960s and 1970s. Many more moved to southern Finland – as Taisto's father remarks in the film's opening sequence. This historical journey stands in contrast to the specific narrative of the film set, as it is, in the 1980s. The 1980s saw the rise of the so-called Casino Economy, the shift to a post-industrial economy, created by economic deregulation and the opening up of markets. When Taisto arrives in 1980s' Helsinki he finds people like his soon-to-be-companion Irmeli consuming hungrily with the help of easy credit. Their spending requires multiple jobs to keep up with payments on their debt. Industrial work is no longer available, as Taisto discovers. His journey makes him a man pulled between different historical strata. He takes a temporary job as a stevedore in the Sompasaari Harbour, at a time in which that harbour had already been automated, containerised, and emptied of stevedores. Stacks of containers are even visible in the harbour scenes. Such anachronistic juxtapositions receive further emphasis through the portrait of Finnish President Urho Kekkonen, which Kasurinen apparently steals from the Helsinki city hall to hang above his bed at a men's shelter. Kekkonen resigned the presidency for health reasons in 1981 after twenty-five years as head of state. The Casino Economy depicted in the film was made possible by economic deregulation that contrasted sharply with Kekkonen's paternalistic and protectionist policies. The presidential portrait also involves historical contradictions. Such presidential portraits were routinely displayed in schools and government offices through the 1970s, so Taisto's regard for the portrait implies that he is a man brought up in the old primary schooling system before its reformation, beginning in 1972.[7]

The journey films' combination of alienated protagonists and exploration of the cultural archive generate a cultural politics. The juxtapositions are value-coded, with representations of the present often placed in antagonism with representations of the past. In *Leningrad Cowboys Go America*, the Cowboys' most demeaning performance occurs at Zhivago, where they perform a country set to a night club whose few patrons agree that the Cowboys are 'absolute shit'. In contrast, the most intimate and richest performances occur in run-down but vital community institutions, such as Earl's Bar in New Orleans, or at the final wedding performance in Mexico. While a case can be made that the juxtaposition of past and present expresses nostalgia, the irony evident in the title of *Tatiana*, or in Taisto's theft of the Kekkonen portrait, disrupts any simple nostalgic reading of the film. Archival material provides a means of staging contrasts, which raise questions, rather than presenting the past as valuable in itself. The cultural politics are more complicated than a nostalgia for the past, for such a reading cannot account for the eclecticism and irony of the journey films.

The Losers

The loser melodramas are also built around narratives of alienation, but in these films Kaurismäki does not stage exile by adapting well-known literary examples of it, or by adapting genre conventions of the journey, but by alienating characters through traumatic experiences that change their lives. The loser films are built around quotidian traumas: the death of a friend in *Shadows in Paradise*, unemployment in *Ariel* and *Drifting Clouds*, parental abuse and unplanned pregnancy in *The Match Factory Girl*, assault in *The Man Without a Past*, and workplace bullying in *Lights in the Dusk*. Trauma here comes from Cathy Caruth's influential discussion. Trauma is conventionally understood as a wound to the psyche. Caruth points out that it is a double wound, for the wound

> is experienced too soon, too unexpectedly, to be fully known and is therefore not available to consciousness until it imposes itself again, repeatedly, in the nightmares and repetitive actions of the survivors ... Trauma is not locatable in the simple violent or original event in an individual's past, but rather in the way that its very unassimilated nature ... returns to haunt the survivor. (1996: 4)

As Caruth observes, the wound comes as a surprise to its recipient, causing incredulity, which leads to repetitious behaviour that seeks unsuccessfully to understand the origin of the wound. The surprised recipient doubts the wound, unable to tally his emotional and intellectual experience before and after the wound. He repeats the wounding in seeking to come to terms with what has happened to him. This can lead a subject to begin to fall socially, as the wound and its reverberations disrupt jobs, relationships, families, and so forth. Still, the films conclude with inconclusive forms of redemption.

The loser melodramas include *Shadows in Paradise, I Hired a Contract Killer, The Match Factory Girl, Drifting Clouds, The Man Without a Past,* and *Lights in the Dusk*. Some critics have called the films the Proletarian films, and indeed the trilogy of *Shadows in Paradise, Ariel,* and *The Match-Factory Girl* is commonly called the Proletarian or Workers' trilogy in Finnish, English, and otherwise. Kaurismäki (1990b) points out in an interview that the term worker or proletarian is a mistake, for it constructs the films' protagonists as class subjects, which they are not in his view. Their alienation tends to make them either unaware of their class status or indifferent to the politics of class.

These films are the most clearly melodramatic of Kaurismäki's body of work – although all of his work belongs to the melodramatic mode. Kaurismäki's definition of melodrama explains the connection.

> Melodrama depicts all the events and feelings of everyday life to the second power. Quotidian events are taken to the extreme, and the music too. When it storms, it's a real storm. When dark clouds appear, the clouds are black and there's a lot of them. Melodrama doesn't differ from naturalism except that everything in melodrama is slightly exaggerated. (In Nestingen 2007)

Melodrama takes the events of everyday life and multiplies their intensity, according to Kaurismäki. One's workmate does not die of a heart attack in his sleep, but on the job in the middle of the day, behind the garbage truck. One does not only get pregnant through a one-night stand, but awakens to a couple of large-denomination bills on the adjacent pillow and a scornful partner. One does not just lose one's wallet to a pickpocket, but gets beat with a baseball bat by the Finnish equivalent of Alex de Large of Kubrick's *A Clockwork Orange* (1971). One does not get laid off, but gets dumped and humiliated in front of one's colleagues. One does not just get played by a femme fatale, but also gets set up as a fall guy by a criminal gang using the femme fatale. One becomes a loser. Kaurismäki's films operate according to the 'melodramatic imagination' theorised by Peter Brooks (1976), in which emphasis on character traits works to convey the moral dimensions of character and narrative. Yet these traumas do not produce victims, for the protagonists endure and struggle in dignity, for which they are rewarded (see Elsaesser 2011). The balance between being a loser and maintaining one's dignity is drawn through Kaurismäki's repetition of the cinematic and cultural archive. While the traumatic events that initiate these films might play as horrific, they are often staged by way of ironic repetition of image and music from the archive, which underscore the narrative meaning of the episode while disrupting its affective intensity with the fizzy irony of the viewer's recognition of the citation. This balance gives the films a deftness, evacuating their realism and replacing it with black humour, intertexual references, and a combination of exaggeration and understatement.

One example of the balance in question occurs in *The Match Factory Girl*, which is widely regarded as Kaurismäki's gloss on Bresson's *Mouchette* (1967). In Kaurismäki's film, the ingénue Iiris (Kati Outinen) is alienated from her alcoholic parents, her indifferent employer, and her bleak city. She fantasises about love as an escape, reading romance novels, buying a dress, and going dancing by herself. She meets a man at a discotheque, who impregnates her in a one-night stand. He rejects her and humiliates her. She attempts suicide, but survives. In vengeance, she poisons her parents, her lover, and an anonymous man in a bar. The film ends with her apparent arrest. Kaurismäki wrote in a comment on the film that he conceived the film after a manic episode, when he lay despondently in bed, full of self-loathing. 'In vengeance, I decided to make a film that would make Robert Bresson look like a director of epic action movies' (Kaurismäki 1990c). In the connections to *Mouchette,* we see several of the main features that distinguish Kaurismäki's loser films. He adapts Bresson's narrative, with many of the changes discharging the seriousness of Bresson's film. He shortens Bresson's seventy-eight minutes to sixty-eight. Kaurismäki also tells the story of a guiltless young woman's ostracisation, exploitation, and ultimate fall. Where Bresson's film ends in suicide, with Mouchette's deliverance implicit, Kaurismäki's character redeems herself through humorously excessive vengeance. By substituting death with the satisfaction of desire, Kaurismäki turns Bresson's tragedy into tragicomedy. The changes also secularise Bresson's narrative. Second, Kaurismäki mimics Bresson's film intertextually. Mouchette's father is a drunk, Iiris's stepfather is a drunk. Mouchette does all the work at home, Iiris does all the housework. Mouchette receives a dress, Iiris buys a dress. Kaurismäki composites some of *Mouchette*'s events, having Iiris's father call her a 'whore' for having bought a dress, instead of a neighbour as in *Mouchette*. Mouchette's moment of flirtation on the bumper cars transforms into visits to a dance and to a disco in *The Match Factory Girl*. In these specific instances of intertext, Kaurismäki repeats Bresson with a difference, lending his film a self-reflexive, ironic humour. Such transformation of referents is typical in the loser melodramas.

Third, exaggeration of the intertexts creates irony, for we are prompted to ask why Kaurismäki made the changes. Mouchette's symbolically white dress becomes pink. Mouchette's selfish father becomes lazy yet officious in Esko Nikkari's performance in *The Match Factory Girl*. Bresson foreswore music in *Mouchette* (although did not follow through), Kaurismäki includes live musical performances and jukeboxes, which create a level of metadiegetic commentary on the film. For example, the film ends on the Finnish crooner's Olavi Virta's 'Kuinka saatoitkaan', otherwise known as 'Oo! What You Do To Me', and best known for Jackie Gleason and Buddie Hackett's performance of the song. The song's tone is sufficiently excessive to discharge the pathos Iiris has generated over the course of the film, the humour absorbing the pity the viewer may feel towards her. She deserves her vengeance, savours it, and perhaps carries it out in Mouchette's name. Kaurismäki ironically adapts narrative and intertext in an eclectic way to revitalise Bresson's legacy, yet make it his own legacy at the same time.

The Match Factory Girl affirms its status as a transgressive film, which seeks to align itself with a film history in exile – Bresson in a world of globalised American popular culture. The filmmaking practice aligns itself with the social and philosophical position of Kaurismäki's characters in the films. Over and again, Kaurismäki's films embrace overlooked elements of the cinematic and cultural archive, and insert them into configurations that revitalise them. Bresson's moralism, Ozu's restraint, Dreyer's classicism, and Keaton's physicality, among others, are redeployed. The repetition with a difference works as a plain and elegant filmmaking style, even if one overlooks the references. When the references are read for their semantic contribution, the films take on further layers of criticism and humour. On all levels, though, the films work by situating their protagonists at odds with the community around them, and depicting their conflict as a losing and humorous struggle, but one which affirms the virtues and moral stance of the outsiders. The sources also fit oddly within mainstream cinema, classics which no longer enjoy cultural let alone economic importance.

The loser melodramas emphasise the events that 'traumatise' their protagonists, while this trauma is easy to overlook because of the minimalist way in which it is represented. In *I Hired a Contract Killer* and *Drifting Clouds*, for example, the protagonists' exceptional status is established through unemployment. The protagonists lose their jobs due to vague neoliberal changes. The scenes depicting termination of the characters' employment are tied together formally. Henri (Jean-Pierre Léaud) and Lauri (Kari Väänänen) are both depicted at the moment they realise their fate with a zoom from medium shot to extreme close-up of their eyes. This is exceptional camera movement and shot scale for Kaurismäki, which gives the moment a special emphasis. Further, this is camera work typical of cinematic executions, as the condemned is depicted in a close up that captures his recognition that it is he who faces death. The close ups of Lauri and Henri Boulanger convey such disbelief. Lauri denies the event, insisting 'Minä olen minä' ('I am me!'). Henri seeks to repeat the wounding, only carried to its end, by engineering his murder. The traumatic experience distinguishes these characters from the world around them, as their unconscious struggles with their wounds single them out and transform their sense of themselves.

The traumatic narrative is never placed in the foreground in the films, which would construct the characters as victims. One of the main ways in which trauma is de-emphasised is the films' acting styles. Kaurismäki has embraced a minimalist, affectless approach which recalls such different acting styles as those used by Buster Keaton and solicited from actors by Robert Bresson. It also recalls the restrained stylised acting methods employed by such filmmakers as Jim Jarmusch, Wes Anderson, Dagur Kàri or Jared Hess. Yet Kaurismäki generates his style by a means that stands in contrast to Bresson, for example.

> I'm much nicer than Bresson. He was just mean. Remember the old woman who performed in the final sequence of *L'Argent*, washing clothes before she and the rest of the family were murdered. Bresson made her wash clothes for hours, until he was satisfied that she was washing the clothes the way he wanted. I don't believe in aerobics. Get the lead out. Ten minutes to practise the dialogue, then we take a look at it. I shoot the first runthrough. If something goes wrong, then I shoot it again. In general I do one take. (In Nestingen 2007)

The affectless style comes from a conscious effort to eliminate both the overtly aestheticised performance Kaurismäki sees in Bresson, but also the method acting, which constructs the narrative by linking plausible emotion, goal-oriented motivation, and action. Kaurismäki places the characters in situations and spaces, and invites the viewer to construct his or her own notion of their significance. This style is evident in the many medium and long shots Kaurismäki uses, his static camera, and his preference for two-shots over shot-reverse-shot to handle dialogue sequences. This style is relevant to trauma, for it de-emphasises the depiction of emotion usually used to represent trauma. Instead of using close-ups to depict emotional responses to the traumatic event, Kaurismäki tends to depict them by way of actions and situations that transpire from the event – hence the exceptional status of the termination scenes in *I Hired a Contract Killer* and *Drifting Clouds*. In the latter film, for example, we see Lauri and Ilona (Kati Outinen) on a date one month after Lauri had received his pink slip. In the two-shots of the couple, Lauri delivers the bad news, puffing on a cigar. The scene indicates the nature of the trauma by emphasising the extent to which Lauri has suppressed his unemployment. Smoking the cigar to celebrate his 'last day of work' makes the trauma evident, but at the same time does not construe the character as an object of pity. If Lauri's actions foregrounded pathos by way of acting and cinematography, Lauri would become a victim, soliciting spectator sympathy. By minimising the trauma, through use of acting style and cinematography, the depiction differentiates Kaurismäki's characters as misfits, and even losers, at the same time as they maintain their dignity and humour. They are proud and walking wounded.

Such a depiction of trauma is central to the narrative in all of the loser films. The death of a colleague disrupts Uolevi Nikander's life and plans in *Shadows in Paradise*, although this film is perhaps the least 'traumatic' of the loser films. Matti Pellonpää's performance conveys a combination of sensitivity and studied indifference in Nikander, who wishes to be relieved of his loneliness, but suffers traumatic misfortune and setbacks. Kaurismäki tells Nikander's story again in *Lights in the Dusk*, only in this case the symbolic occupation of the protagonist has shifted from garbage man to security guard. Both are the 'janitors' of their economic system, the one disposing of the consumption that defined the 1980s, the other enforcing the boundaries and zones regulating consumer access in the neoliberal state (see Lea 2002). In the connection, we see that Kaurismäki treats his own filmmaking as part of his archival material. The lonely Nikander becomes the lonely Koistinen (Janne Hyytiäinen). The pivotal event for Koistinen occurs when he meets the femme fatale Mirja (Maria Järvenhelmi). Mirja is involved in another relationship with a more prestigious man, just as happens with Ilona in *Shadows in Paradise*. Yet in *Lights in the Dusk*, the man is a businessman and organised-crime boss, who engineers Koistinen's deception as part of an ambitious robbery. Ilona's love interest was only a petty bourgeois clothing-store owner. And where Nikander wins back Ilona and escapes Finland, Koistinen is humiliated, defeated, imprisoned, humiliated further, and beaten. Still, the parallels between the films are signalled by Kati Outinen's cameo as a grocery store clerk in *Lights in the Dusk*, Ilona's occupation in *Shadows in Paradise*. The traumatic narrative of the earlier film repeats itself again, with more cynicism and more force. The little redemption offered to Koistinen is so subtle as to make one wonder if it only exists in some other world.

I Hired a Contract Killer and *Drifting Clouds* are unemployment films. *I Hired a Contract Killer* plays as comedy, however, where *Drifting Clouds* carries an elegiac tone. The latter film is dedicated to the memory of Matti Pellonpää, who was supposed to play the role of the *maître d'*, played by Kati Outinen in the film. Pellonpää died on 13 July 1995, just before the film went into production. *Drifting Clouds* signals its thematics and tone in the credit sequence by way of Shelley Fisher's performance of the song 'Lonesome Traveller'. The travel that occurs in the film is not physical, but psychological, as protagonists Ilona (Kati Outinen) and Lauri (Kari Väänänen) must recalibrate their self-understanding after they lose their jobs. The film is set in a sharp economic downturn that struck Finland especially forcefully between 1991 and 1993. Economic deregulation, privatisation, and new emphasis on the service economy had facilitated economic growth during the 1980s, but banks, companies, and individuals overextended themselves by taking large loans, many in foreign currency. When the global economic recession of the early 1990s and the loss of Soviet trade occurred, these companies, banks, and individuals could not pay their debts, causing credit availability to diminish and unemployment to rise. Lauri and Ilona are among the almost twenty percent of the population who lose their jobs. Bad luck and indifference to their struggle leads to a downward spiral. They must restructure their lives. They are finally delivered by a loan from Ilona's former employer, who invests in their new restaurant, which appears to be a success at the film's conclusion.

While also an unemployment story, *I Hired a Contract Killer* is a stylised repetition of the Ealing Studios films. The studio produced such films as *Whiskey Galore!* (Alexander Mackendrick, 1949), *The Lavender Hill Mob* (Charles Crichton, 1951), *The Ladykillers* (Alexander Mackendrick, 1955) and others, known for their rich dialogue and dry humour, low-key lighting, and quirky characters. In *I Hired a Contract Killer*, Henri Boulanger is laid off, and in despair attempts suicide, but fails. So he hires a hit-man to end his life. While waiting for him, he meets Margaret (Margi Clarke) and has his first whiskey. He falls in love with Margaret, and with life. But the hit-man won't be put off, leading to a chase through London. However, when the hit-man catches up with Henri, he pauses to contemplate his own mortality; he has been diagnosed with terminal lung cancer. He grants Henri a reprieve, and turns the gun on himself. Henri escapes with Margaret. While the unemployment story jabs at the Thatcherite UK, the film is a pastiche of references. Serge Toubiana plays a café patron, a tribute to his role as Georges Manda in *Golden Marie*. Jean-Pierre Léaud's role as Henri Boulanger pays tribute to the actor whose French New Wave roles gave Kaurismäki his ideas about acting; he tried to imitate Léaud in his performances as Ville Alfa in *The Liar*, *Jackpot 2* (Mika Kaurismäki, 1982), and *Arvottomat* (*The Worthless*, Mika Kaurismäki, 1982). And Joe Strummer makes his cameo. Henri is an exile from France, 'where no one liked him', and his unfortunate situation obviously makes him an alien.

If Henri is an exile in a foreign land, then M (Markku Peltola) of *The Man Without a Past* is an exile within his own land. His status as alien is established with a quick bat to the head in the Kaisaniemi Park, adjacent to Helsinki's Central Railway Station. Kaurismäki stresses the trauma more than usual. M's wound is physical and psychic, for the assault makes him an amnesiac. With no memory, he is stripped of his subjectivity, becoming an instance of what Georgio Agamben calls 'bare life' or *homo sacer*, as Thomas Elsaesser has pointed out about the film (2010; 2011). That is, M becomes an exile within his society, because he has been reduced to his biological existence, outside citizenship or politics, inassimilable to the law and political discourse (see Agamben 1998) – a point made comically when M is detained by police who do not know what to do with him, so transform him into a prisoner. Despite his inassimilable particularity, the state imposes its laws on him. M's zero-degree status finds visual expression in the sequence following his beating. In rare point-of-view moving-camera shots, we follow M into the railway station, the editing cutting him up into close-ups of a bloody hand, protruding legs, a leather jacket, but no face. M then appears to die, but sits back up and endeavours to begin anew. He lives in a shipping-container village and finds support and ultimately meaning and love in his interactions with Irma (Kati Outinen), who works at the Salvation Army. Finally, his identity is discovered, and he deals with the red tape of a finalised divorce, before returning to Irma.

The Man Without a Past epitomises Kaurismäki's loser melodramas in its use of a trauma experience to initiate a narrative of exile and dislodgement. While the literary adaptations stage exile, and the journey films use the narrative conventions of the road film, the loser films create their misfits through trauma that remains underplayed and contained, despite its centrality. *The Man Without a Past* also crystallises a utopian impulse that figures within these misfits' lives. Among the containers and the Salvation Army, outside the state, the corporations, and administrative and economic discourses, M finds a vital and inclusive community. Many of the characters in Kaurismäki's films aspire to such a community, often only catching a glimpse of it over the horizon, and taking off after it by ship. Yet if this aspiration is utopian, its vitality is also continually staged in Kaurismäki's films in the kind of subjective expression we saw earlier in the opening sequence of *Crime and Punishment*. Music, in almost Schopenhauerian registers, expresses a vital force in Kaurismäki's cinema. This is nowhere more evident than in the last category of films in his production, the concert films *The Saimaa Gesture* and *Total Balalaika Show*.

The Concert Films

Aki Kaurismäki's cinema might feature the most scenes of live musical performances of any filmmaker making feature films – and perhaps more than some making music videos. Every film he has made includes a live-music sequence, sometimes stretching to minutes. The fixation finds its fullest expression in Kaurismäki's two concert films, *The Saimaa Gesture*, which he made with his brother Mika, and *Total Balalaika Show*, which he directed and produced. Both films depict live concert performances. The former chronicles a summer-time tour of three bands on Lake Saimaa, Finland's largest body of fresh water. The latter features the Leningrad Cowboys performing with the Red Army Alexandra Ensemble before an audience of seventy thousand in Helsinki's Senate Square – the square built by Czar Alexander I and surrounded by neoclassical, Russian Imperial architecture, including the University of Helsinki main building, the Helsinki Cathedral and the Senate Building (Valtioneuvoston linna, which houses the Prime Minister's offices, the Ministry of State, and parts of the Ministry of Finance). These concert films show the importance of music in Kaurismäki's cinema, and in doing so raise the question: how do music and live performance relate to some of the concerns we have been tracing in Kaurismäki's body of work? The concert films would appear to privilege a notion of authentic performance, a perception which would correlate with views of Kaurismäki's cinema as one of musical nostalgia for an earlier, more innocent age of cultural and artistic expression. Such a reading finds support in a historicisation of Kaurismäki's films' production. They coincide with the rise of MTV (Music Television), yet where MTV pioneered rapid-tempo, lip-synced, musical fantasies, Kaurismäki embraces long takes of live performance. At the same time, however, the ostensible authenticity of the concert films (and other live performances in his films) is built on a complex historical and aesthetic contradiction. On the one hand, they embrace a notion of authenticity in musical presentation, which understands music and art in essentialist, non-performative terms. On the other, musical performance is part of a self-reflexive pastiche of aesthetic and historical role playing – the Leningrad Cowboys, no less – which disrupts any notion of authenticity and simultaneously mocks and exploits the commodification of music as entertainment. The live performances valorise a notion of vital cultural interaction, while eschewing commodification, expressing a doubtful, utopian aspiration. We might take this as an allegory of cinema's predicament, as well.

Kaurismäki's *The Saimaa Gesture* appeared in 1981, just before the emergence of the band Dingo, arguably the definitive mainstream band of 1980s' Finland. The film's style becomes clear when placed in contrast to the music, glamour, and artificiality that Dingo represented – drawing as it did on the mainstream of Anglo-American popular music of the 1970s. Dingo nationalised arena rock by adding melancholia and minor keys. It also fashioned itself as a glam-rock band, dressing in ruffled shirts and vests, bold prints, flowing scarves, tight pants, and other retro fashions. The band members also cultivated an androgynous image, wearing make-up and dyed, teased-up hair. Dingo might be thought of as a Finnish combination of Duran Duran's production values and The Cure's minor-key melancholia and neo-gothicism. If Dingo epitomised the 1980s, then the bands of *The Saimaa Gesture* can be seen as combining another set of key strands in Finnish popular music at the time, including the lyrical, literary Finnish Rock (*Suomirokki*) of Juice Leskinen's Slam, the punk energy and ethos of Eppu Normaali, and the hybrid of the two represented by Ismo Alanko and Hassisen Kone, a new wave band with a strong punk ethos. Critics writing on the film at the time all agreed that the concerts represented the best of the national rock scene, and belonged uniquely to it. 'It is hard to imagine California surfers digging the vitality of Finnish rock' (Yritys 1981). At the same time, this Finnish rock involves a dialectics. 'To reach their audience, and define themselves, the musicians draw on an Anglo-American form, which is transnational in distribution', but which enables them to attack a previous generation's popular culture and to define their own version of Finnishness (Yritys 1981). The speedy tempos of Eppu Normaali's performances and their anarchistic, rebellious lyrics give voice to the punk impulse of the 1970s, which is epitomised in the raucous and heretical rendition of Finland's national anthem. The abundance of live performance footage in *The Saimaa Gesture* emphasises the vitality and variety of performances and audience-engagement. In the context of 1980s' pop, the music in the film seeks contact with Finnish rock, punk, and new wave musical individualism, but *The Saimaa Gesture* also rejects the production values of an act like Dingo

A pivotal scene occurs towards the end when Aki Kaurismäki asks Ismo Alanko, 'what is rock-n-roll?'; Alanko answers that 'the majority of the public seems to think

Ismo Alanko being interviewed by Aki Kaurismäki in *The Saimaa Gesture*

it's some kind of show. It's not a show, or a performance. It's going out on stage and being yourself. You put yourself out there, in front of the audience. If you're pissed off, you show it.' Alanko loses his train of thought, and looks away, glances at the camera, then remarks that he forgot what he was going to say. The importance of the scene, and Alanko's point, is emphasised by Aki and Mika Kaurismäki's decision not to omit Alanko's troubled affect or glances at the camera. Aki coaxes him back. Alanko goes on to say: 'The audience thinks you're playing a role, which they have projected onto you. We're just living our lives.' *The Saimaa Gesture* is built around the notion Alanko expresses: rock-n-roll is a minimalist presentation of one's self and one's music, stripped of spectacle and roles, stripped of enhancing production effects. After Alanko's interview, we see primarily concert footage of a show at Tuusansaari near Punkaharju in southeastern Finland. In the images of the show, the film builds to a climax, with all three bands performing in order. This concert sequence places greater emphasis on close-ups than the previous concert footage, capturing the sweat and spit of the singers. The film then concludes on the final song of the tour, with all of the bands on stage together giving a raucous and dissonant performance of Finland's national anthem.

The notion Alanko expresses about music relates to *The Saimaa Gesture,* because in its simple structure, rejection of expensive production values, counterpuntal pacing, and silly humour it is minimalist and unadorned. The film begins on the ship *S/S Heinävesi*, with on-board shots of the vessel sailing across Lake Saimaa. This is a historical reference, for travel by steam ship across Finland's network of waterways was the key means of transportation and commerce before the combustion engine. The *Heinävesi*'s deck is scattered with debris and chairs are strewn around. Soon, the film moves to the first concert footage, introducing each of the bands' members in an outdoor concert in Lappeenranta. After the concert we return to the vessel, where toasts set the journey in motion. As the film moves between the performances and the *Heinävesi*, it captures images of the waterscapes the vessel passes, interviews band members about their music and outlook, and also captures images of the concert halls, backstage interactions and performances on the tour. It is a rock film, reminiscent of such films as *Don't Look Back* (D.A. Pennebaker, 1966), *Woodstock* (Michael Wadleigh, 1970), *Gimme Shelter* (Albert Maysles, David Maysles, Charlotte Zwerin, 1971), and *The Last Waltz* (Martin Scorsese, 1978) (see Noukka 1981).

The film was made on credit and a loan from Jörn Donner, as well as with prize money received from *The Liar*, and the production values are consequently those of an underground film. The intercut images of Saimaa and the concerts, interspersed with the interviews create a balance between quiet lyricism and energetic performance. The balance is important, for the film links its lyrical depiction of the Finnish east – canonised in the national epic *Kalevala* (1835) as the source of Finnish folk poetry – with a rebellious generational politics. Eppu Normaali frontman Martti Syrjä mocks the cherished narrative of Finnish masculinity, in which boys become men by ceding their independence and learning to follow orders in the Army. Syrjä refused mandatory conscription, and Kaurismäki for his part also left the army without completing the mandated period of service (see von Bagh 2006: 18). The iconoclasm is further expressed when Juice Leskinen ridicules the school system and Pantse Syrjä taunts the Finnish work ethic. Alanko and his bandmates get in jeers at small-town domesticity as well, when they visit a house in the northeastern town of Joensuu where they lived as squatters. Yet these jabs are balanced by silly humour that occurs in various group scenes, led by Asmo Hurula and the support crew of the tour, divided into the Squirrels and the Little-Squirrels by gender.

The gender politics of the film's music is evident in its omission of women as performers or narrative agents. With the exception of a few unnamed characters who figure in the background, no women perform, no women are interviewed, and no women participate in the shows. The iconoclasm, the struggle, and the rebellion expressed in the film, are coded male. As Kaurismäki's career develops, gender takes on more complexity, as we see, for example, in *The Match Factory Girl* and *Drifting Clouds*, as well as in *Take Care of Your Scarf, Tatiana*. Yet even in these later films, the highly important musical register is coded male. The definitive role of men as musicians in *The Saimaa Gesture* arguably continues throughout Kaurismäki's career. It is male tango singers, male blues players, and male bands that continually appear. There are some noteworthy exceptions. In *The Man Without A Past* the officer in charge of the Helsinki Salvation Army Chapter in which M finds succour is a woman, played by Annikki Tähti. The actress who is equally well known for her post-war musical career gives a powerful performance in the film of one of her most famous numbers, singing 'Do you remember Monrepos?' (*'Muistatko Monrepos'in?'*). Kirsi Tykkyläinen also makes a memorable performance of the 1972 hit by the Melodians, 'Rivers of Babylon', in *Leningrad Cowboys Meet Moses*. Yet these are two examples within scores of musical performances. Music, whether performed live or recorded, is associated with men in Kaurismäki's films. This association makes men the agents of authentic dissent, refusal, and alterity within the capitalist market and the rational state.

Total Balalaika Show differs from *The Saimaa Gesture*, acting as a counterpoint to it, even as to some degree it weaves together the same musical notions. Where *The Saimaa Gesture* sets performance within a lyrical trip across Finland's largest lake, *Total Balalaika Show* is a spectacular concert set in the most culturally privileged square of Finland's capital city. Where *The Saimaa Gesture* disavows roles, performance, and production values, *Total Balalaika Show* is all about self-reflexive performance, mixing of genres, epic music, and spectacle. Seen in combination *Total Balalaika Show* and *The Saimaa Gesture* epitomise the pastiche of elements that we saw in the posters with which the chapter opened, and help tie together the contradictions in Kaurismäki's cinema.

Total Balalaika Show resulted when the Leningrad Cowboys and Aki Kaurismäki invited the Red Army's Alexandra Ensemble and Dance Group, numbering one hundred singers and forty dancers, to perform with the Leningrad Cowboys at an outdoor concert in Helsinki. The Cowboys' predecessor band, the Sleepy Sleepers, had performed in the Soviet Union, and their sometime producer and operator of Love Records, Atte Blom, got involved in bringing about the performance. Such Finnish-Russian exchange has long been fraught with tension: after fighting against one another during World War II, Finland's friendship with the Soviet Union during the post-war period of Finlandisation was a foreign-policy compromise taken to enhance Finnish security, which forced widely-held Russophobia beneath the surface. At the same time, tourism, cultural exchanges, and economic ties united the two nations. Russophobia welled up after the dissolution of the Soviet Union, yet Kaurismäki's film gave voice to an alternative view, seeking to cultivate Russo-Finnish relations and cultural exchange

The Sleepers established a reputation during the 1970s for their 'WC-show' (see Bruun *et al.* 1998: 218). They performed with six to ten members on stage and violated many taboos, harassing the audience, and cultivating musical and social anarchy. Their show mocked the politics of left and right, embracing the show as event. Their tastelessness and punk-inspired assaults on their audiences were self-reflexive efforts at an aesthetic of spectacular disappointment: there is Dada in their effort to obliterate the band, and by extension 'popular music', with the mockery of the performance (see Bruun *et al.* 1998: 215–21). The spirit of the Sleepers continued in the Leningrad Cowboys, as we have seen, and this spirit is evoked in the introduction to *Total Balalaika Show,* presented by Kirsi Tykkyläinen. Welcome to this 'outrageous spectacle', she says. The open-air stage makes the spectacle clear. Inflatable palm trees stand as pillars on the wings, Day of the Dead '*calacas*' (figurines) are projected on a backdrop, alternating with images of airplanes. The stage is occupied by the massive Red Army Alexandra Ensemble dressed in formal uniform. A space at the front of the stage is reserved for the Leningrad Cowboys, where they perform with musical instruments decorated with images of their times in Mexico and at their collective farm. The artificiality and silliness of the juxtapositions creates absurdity, which works to heighten the spectacle at the same time as it diminishes it in self-mockery. The Cowboys' strutting, hopping, performance, coupled with the serious dancing of the Red Army dance troupe also contributes further to the absurdity. The combination recalls to mind the pastiche we analysed earlier in the film posters and other examples. If Alanko thinks performing is about stripping away roles, and putting oneself out there, then the aesthetic here could not be in greater opposition. The contrast between *The Saimaa Gesture* and *Total Balalaika Show* is another paradox of the many in Kaurismäki's body of films. It reminds us of the analysis of *Juha*'s 'Les Temps des Cerises', in which we saw an ambivalent, multiply constructed notion of beauty and innocence, formed by contrast and opposition, rather than by the expression of something defined in terms of purity or singularity. In the concert films and in Kaurismäki's use of music, then, we see a similar set of relationships to the ones we have been analysing in his body of work. In different ways, we continually find representatives of the 'outside' critically exploring and staging their ambiguous relationships to institutions, economically and politically empowered people, and places that represent such institutions and power.

Coda

The contrasts we have identified figure prominently in the layers of discourse that constitute Aki Kaurismäki's film authorship. They are part of the film texts themselves, and as such merit attention within a *politique-des-auteurs* framework. At the same time, they also contribute to Kaurismäki's role and status in cinematic discourses, as a producer who must finance his films, as a filmmaker who shows his films at festivals and makes contracts with distribution companies who must market the films, and as a cinematic and cultural figure who is an object of cinema-viewers' interest. Analysis of the films has indicated there is a tangle of paradox and contrasts present in Kaurismäki's films. These are the source, we will find, for a variety of coherent and divergent views of Kaurismäki among commentators and in the discourse about his cinema.

The structure of the book seeks to tease out the strands entwined in these paradoxes to create a fuller, richer, and more contradictory picture of Kaurismäki as a filmmaker. It makes sense to begin by looking at one of the main stories told about Kaurismäki and his films, that is, by analysing a biographical story which implies in a life-and-works way that his films find their meaning in the filmmaker's own life. This is the story of Kaurismäki the bohemian, an account of a man who lived as a bohemian in his early life, at home among the misfits, devoted to his art, and who proceeded to make films about bohemian artists and other denizens of bohemia. The second story is a somewhat related one, the story of Kaurismäki the nostalgic. One of the recurrent contrasts in his films is between images and objects of the past, which are implicitly and overtly set against images and things of the present. Commentators have argued that understanding Kaurismäki's cinema in terms of nostalgia helps us make sense of his films' aesthetics and their cultural politics. Yet what we find is that the contrasts are in some ways the point, as they provide a means of insinuating alternative discourses and ethical views into our notions of economy, politics, culture, and cinema – which is where Michel de Certeau becomes relevant. Finally, one of the recurrent points of reference in Kaurismäki's cinema of contrasts is Finland, the setting of many of his films, and the filmmaker's native land. Yet once again we find that the many contrasts in the Kaurismäki discourse generate rich complexities, which require thinking of Kaurismäki's cinema in terms of nation, or small-nation cinema, at the same time as such categories require qualification and revision in speaking of Kaurismäki. Kaurismäki thus provides a challenging and thought-provoking object of study, whose career is relevant to key categories and discussions in popular and scholarly discussions of European cinema, national cinema, and the globalisation of visual culture in late modernity.

Notes

1. Warhol 2006 [1975]: 31.
2. A noteworthy exception is the jazz opening of the 1996 film *Drifting Clouds*.
3. This is my translation of the following sentence, reproduced from my copy of the typescript held at the archives: 'Tein elokuvan "I Hired a Contract Killer" koska kymmenvuotiaana näin televisiosta Henry Kass's in elokuvan "Last Holiday" enkä sitemmin ole onnistunut karkoittamaan sen jättävää vaikutelmaa mielestäni...'
4. This notion of archiving makes a distinction from and builds upon the notion of archiving outlined in Satu Kyösola's article, 'The Archivist's Nostalgia' (2004b).
5. The opening image of *Crime and Punishment* has received extensive comment: the protagonist Rahkikainen slices a louse with a meat cleaver, in an apparent allusion to Luis Buñuel's *Un Chien Andalou* (1929), as Kyösola (2000: 292) and Toviainen (2002) observe.
6. *Grisettes* were young women recently arrived from the French countryside in eighteenth- and nineteenth-century Paris, who often worked as seamstresses or in other textile work, and were also fetishised for their ostensible sexual availability.
7. Thanks to Hanna Snellman (University of Jyväskylä, Department of History and Ethnology) and Heikki Hanka (University of Jyväskylä, Department of Art Studies) for their observations about the portrait.

CHAPTER TWO

The Bohemian

> I willingly consent to look back on the past, but it must be through a good bottle of wine and seated in a comfortable chair.
>
> Henri Murger, *The Bohemians of the Latin Quarter*[1]

Aki Kaurismäki's life and cinema find a source in bohemia. In the Kaurismäki discourse and films, the director and his characters often appear to opt out of their society, refuse many of its values, affirm itinerancy, disregard the mores and aspirations of the middle class, and inhabit and embrace the *demimonde* with its wild characters. Evidence of bohemia turns up throughout Kaurismäki's career. Most obviously, the director adapted a principal text of literary Bohemia, Henri Murger's *The Bohemians of the Latin Quarter* from 1852. Bohemian elements can also be seen in the itinerant 'losers', tricksters, and artists that make up the *dramatis personae* of Kaurismäki's films. Kaurismäki's musical choices also bear the mark of bohemia in their eccentricity, as is evident in the concert footage of *The Saimaa Gesture*, Harri Marstio's dissonant rendition of Schubert's 'Ständchen' at the opening of *Crime and Punishment*, the *Leningrad Cowboys*' gigs, or Elina Salo's sound performance of 'Les temps du cerises' in *Juha*.

Kaurismäki also tells the story of his life with bohemian tropes. He emphasises his itinerancy, he presents himself as an outsider, he expresses solidarity with the dislocated and marginalised (just as in his films), and he mocks the conventions and norms of middle-class society. Kaurismäki states his bohemian position in a polemical remark about Finland. 'It's a country in which silence and good manners conceal criminality, corruption, and violence. Its government is old, ossified, and outdated. There's not vigor, life force, or enthusiasm, and if there were someone would be sure to smother it' (in Anon. 1990). The state and middle-class conformity block any initiative. The only way out is exile in the *demimonde* or abroad. (Kaurismäki has lived part of the year near Porto since the 1980s.) The anecdotes and statements that fill out Kaurismäki's biographical arc show many features of bohemia.

The problem with the bohemian dimension of Kaurismäki's films and biographical narrative is that bohemia was already a cliché by Murger's time in the 1840s. Bohemia is largely a sentimental 'myth about the artist's life invented by artists and mediated, perpetuated, and reinvented by popular culture', writes historian and literary scholar Mary Gluck (2005: 15). The myth of the bohemian artist also touches the cinema. As 'cultural hero', the auteur often opposes the commercial cinema and confirms his membership in the cultural system, argues Thomas Elsaesser. 'Those who belong to a national cinema must strive after a certain status ... which is to say as either "artists", "bohemians", or "dissidents"' (2005: 48). What then is the relationship between the sentimental myth of bohemia and the many bohemian elements in Kaurismäki's films and biographical narrative? My answer to that question involves positioning Kaurismäki and his films in relation to what Gluck has called the sentimental and ironic traditions in bohemianism. Kaurismäki has been understood as a sentimental bohemian, and while elements of sentimental bohemia do figure in his cinema and biographical narrative, it is more productive to understand him as an ironic bohemian. When we understand Kaurismäki in terms of ironic bohemia, we can begin to see a gradual transformation of the films' aesthetic and political-economic dimensions over his career, which we can theorise as a staging of different identities and attitudes in critical dialogue with each other and their broader society. Further, approaching Kaurismäki in this way allows us to see the films and the authorship in relationship to political and popular culture, and to see this relationship as replenishing, provocative, and important to Kaurismäki's contribution to European cinema. Rather than seeing Kaurismäki as an exceptional figure, operating as a sentimental bohemian in a transcendent and autonomous artistic space, closer analysis of the bohemian aspects of his career and films allow us to see him in dialogue with political, economic, and popular cultural discourses, engaged in social struggle on many fronts.

Sentimental and Ironic Bohemia

The film scholar Satu Kyösola has placed emphasis on the sentimental bohemian dimensions of Kaurismäki's cinema, including a definitive article in the eleven-volume *Finnish National Filmography*, 'A Lost Par(ad)is(e), or Bohemia in Aki Kaurismäki's Cinema' (2004a). Kyösola argues that bohemianism in the films is built around an uncompromising opposition to bourgeois conventions and attitudes, equating Kaurismäki's position with a statement he made in an analysis of Luis Buñuel's filmmaking, entitled 'Luis Buñuel and the Death of God' (1979):

> The morality of the bourgeoisie is anti-moral, because it is founded upon the most unjust of institutions: religion, country, family, and the other pillars of society. I have always followed the advice of the Surrealists: the obligation to eat does not include the right to prostitute art. I oppose conventional morality, traditional ideals, society's entire moral malignance. (In Kyösola 2004a: 144)

According to Kyösola, the opposition to which Kaurismäki adheres finds its source in the work and lives of bohemian figures, in particular Henri Murger and Charles Baudelaire. They inspire an anti-conformist, creative energy in Kaurismäki, suggests Kyösola, which show him how cinema must liberate society from its middle-class perspective (2004a: 145). In this account, bohemia is a space in which art can be created whose energy overwhelms the philosophical, aesthetic, and commercial categories of Western middle-class culture. Kyösola sees this bohemian position most fully expressed in the adaptation of *The Bohemians of the Latin Quarter*, pointing out that Kaurismäki's largely faithful adaptation omits the last chapter of the novel. That chapter describes the four bohemians' successes: the painter Marcel has entered the salon and sold a painting to 'a rich Englishman', Rodolphe and Schaunard have become rich and famous, and Colline has come 'into an inheritance' and made an 'advantageous marriage' (Murger 2004: 390). The chapter concludes with a dialogue between Rodolphe and Marcel; Rodolphe observes to Marcel, that he has conceded his idealism. 'We have closed up, old man. We are dead and buried. Youth has but one time. Where do you dine tonight?' Rodolphe proposes eating at a bohemian café, to which Marcel replies.

> Not I. No … I willingly consent to look back on the past, but it must be through a good bottle of wine and seated in a comfortable chair. Ah, what do you want to say? That I am corrupted? I no longer care for anything but what is good and comfortable. (2004: 392)

In Kaurismäki's adaptation, the film ends a year before these sentiments are expressed, with Rodolfo leaving the hospital after his lover Mimi's death. For Kyösola, the omission of Marcel's sentiment in Murger's novel expresses an affirmation of the myth of bohemia as 'a utopia and a dream, an indivisible product of the imagination, a notion that requires speaking in the past tense' (Kyösola 2004a: 149). In this view, the film represents bohemia as an autonomous alternative that lies outside middle-class conventions and values.

This argument about sentimental bohemia belongs to the tradition of aesthetics dating back to Kant's philosophy, which regards art as the transcendent object of its own discourse. Mary Gluck (2005) points to three strands of this tradition. There is an argument that regards art, and in particular modernist art, in terms of its adversarial relationship to political and economic life. The artist is an oppositional figure. A second line of argument is Pierre Bourdieu's theory of the literary field (1996). Bourdieu maintains that art produces its autonomy by defining and operating according to a distinct set of symbolic practices, which distinguish the artist as a professional and furnish the context for his career. Finally, suggests Gluck, there is a psychological argument, that maintains that the artist turns away from the material world and into the psyche and subjectivity to produce his art – a notion familiar from *fin de siècle* decadence and symbolist art movements (see Gluck 2005: 4–6). Arguments about Kaurismäki's bohemia have tended to position him in interpretations of this sort.

In conceptualising Kaurismäki's bohemian themes as primarily an expression of opposition to convention, the middle-classes, commercialism, and bourgeois art, Kyösola's argument situates bohemia as a place outside space and time, a nostalgia for an earlier moment of bohemia articulated in Murger's writings. Her idealist emphasis resonates in many ways with Murger's account. His texts were set in the 1830s; Murger was already regarded as 'sentimental' and 'outdated' in his own time (Gluck 2005: 65). Looking back in time, Murger idealised bygone experiences just as, according to Kyösola, Kaurismäki idealises Murger a century-and-a-half later. Kyösola's argument makes a significant contribution to our understanding of Kaurismäki's cinema in demonstrating the significance of the history of Parisian bohemia for the filmmaker, yet her argument can be advanced even further by recognising another strand of bohemia.

An ironic attitude towards bohemia is also present in Kaurismäki's cinema and biographical narrative, which is evident in *The Bohemian Life*. The film begins with an overhead long shot of the philosopher Marcel scrounging in garbage to find enough to buy a glass of wine measuring ... five millilitres. He then shows the bartender the two-thousand-page manuscript on which he has been labouring. This scene is Kaurismäki's invention, and it is excessive in all its dimensions. Marcel's desperate scrounging, his miniscule portion of wine, and the small boulder of a manuscript are all exaggerations. The excess alerts us to the film's absurd and ironic humour. As viewers, we see the exaggeration, as does the bartender who serves Marcel, but Marcel himself does not, or ignores it out of pride. In this dramatic irony, Kaurismäki prompts spectators to think carefully about the appearances and experiences of bohemia. Indeed, one critic writes that Kaurismäki's adaptation of Murger is entirely ironic, except for its depiction of Mimi's death (see Taubin 1992: 11).

Irony causes the viewer to question the bohemians' self-understanding, and hence their perception of their relationship to the bourgeoisie. This is not the certain anti-conformism analysed by Kyösola, but a fluid, probing kind. The irony and related questions are unmistakable when Marcel is invited to become editor-in-chief of the fashion magazine *The Girdle of Iris* by its publisher Gassot (film director Samuel Fuller in a cameo appearance). Schaunard points out to Marcel that Gassot is a political reactionary. Taking money saturated with worker's sweat would contradict your moral and political ideals, asserts Schaunard. After some casuistry about Gassot's politics, Marcel points out that his employment by Gassot will also bring commissions for Schaunard and Rodolfo. Soon we see Gassot writing a cheque to the eager Marcel. What we witness is not a rejection of the attitudes and practices of middle-class society but rather a narrative that uses indirection (Marcel's pragmatism) to probe the conflict between such ideals and the appeal of middle-class financial stability and position. The combination of bohemian appearance and bourgeois expediency raises questions about the status of bohemia in *The Bohemians of the Latin Quarter*, and Kaurismäki's cinema as a whole.

What then is the difference between sentimental and ironic bohemia?

'Sentimental bohemia' ... was associated with realistic tales about the lives and tribulations of artists and tended to appeal to middle-class literary sensibilities. The second, less familiar version, I have called 'ironic bohemia', since it was concerned with the parodic gestures and ironic public performances of experimental artists and aimed to differentiate the artist of modernity from his middle-class counterparts. (Gluck 2005: 15)

The difference between sentimental and ironic bohemia involves divergent assumptions. Sentimental bohemianism assumes the autonomy of the bohemian identity, whereas ironic bohemia assumes that the bohemian identity is problematic and so requires continual reiteration. This continual reiteration destabilises both bohemia and terms related to it, for it troubles a notion of stable identity. If any identity can be performed in ways that question its premises and certainty, then even the most apparently stable identity can be seen as so many costumes, poses, and affectations, however naturally worn. Such an outlook does not see bohemia as a phase of life, the artist as a young person in bohemia, as Murger emphasises, but rather as a contingent identity, dependent on presentation, reception, and negotiation of perception and meaning. Premised on a notion of unstable identity, ironic bohemia sees identity as a series of disguises or masks and bohemia as one stance among others.

Gluck also suggests that the *flâneur* is a figure of ironic bohemia, and is typified by Charles Baudelaire, among others. The *flâneur* was the Parisian aesthetic participant, who took part in city life as he walked the city, read the newspaper, perceived and absorbed the people and images around him, engaging in many topics, entertaining many ideas and arguments, absorbed in the serial nature of modern life. The contrast to sentimental bohemia lies in a key assumption about the objectivity of social reality, and its availability to representation, as Baudelaire suggests in *The Painter of Modern Life* (1845). In his capacity to take on different perspectives as he moves through the modern city, the *flâneur* can imagine the city in divergent ways and see its many component parts in their changing relation to one another. It is not an objective reality that shapes the city, but a mediation of the *flâneur*'s imagination and a shifting perspective playing across changing urban space (see Gluck 2005: 102). In this view, the *flâneur*'s perspective intersects with ironic bohemia.

Gluck's argument about ironic bohemia also shares a good deal with Jerrold Seigel's definition of bohemia in his study *Bohemian Paris* (1986). The bohemian acts out 'the conflicts inherent in the bourgeois character', writes Seigel. Bohemia is the 'appropriation of marginal life styles by young and not-so-young bourgeois for the dramatization of ambivalence towards their own social identities and destinies', he continues (1986: 11). While Seigel's argument rests on a more stable notion of identity, like Gluck he posits that bohemia and its cultural production form a struggle within modernity, rather than a separate area of artistic life with their root in the Kantian tradition. The bohemian is the perceiver, participant and interpreter of modern life, in its political, economic, and cultural manifestations. He does not go outside modern life, but inhabits it, assumes diverse lifestyles, making them the medium of his art. This combination of ephemerality and embeddedness is evident in the bohemian elements in Kaurismäki's films and career, which show themselves to be a means of responding to the transformations of late modernity that have characterised Kaurismäki's lifetime.

The ironic dimensions of Kaurismäki's bohemianism are evident in remarks the director made in May 2008, when he accepted the title Artist of the Academy from Finnish President Tarja Halonen. Kaurismäki said: 'Only one sentence comes to mind. It's from the end of Henri Murger's book: "Youth has but one time"' (in Luukka 2008) – a sentence from the last chapter of *The Bohemians of the Latin Quarter*. This sentence is not a concession of having come in from the outside, or having 'sold out', but marks a shift in perspective, engagement of a different outlook. For if Kaurismäki has joined his heroes in a soft chair with a good bottle of wine, he also continues to see the world from the perspective of an itinerant. The film subsequent to the 2008 award, *Le Havre* (2011), tells the story of an immigrant boy helped by a shoe shiner in the French port city of Le Havre. The city provides the ubiquitous harbour of Kaurismäki's films, and also figured in many of the French poetic realist films of the 1930s – for example, Carné's *Port of Shadows* and Renoir's *La bête humaine* (*The Human Beast*, 1937). Youth may come but once, but the terrain mapped by Jean Renoir, Jean Gabin, and Jacques Prevert, all of whose work in Le Havre inspired Kaurismäki, provides another perspective. Let us examine the ironic and sentimental bohemian elements that give shape to the biographical narrative and cinematic work of Kaurismäki's career.

Ironic and sentimental bohemia are evident in Kaurismäki's biography, which the first part of this chapter explores. Ironic bohemia also helps us see more fully a dialectical shift that occurs in Kaurismäki's filmmaking; he begins with political critique of the Finnish state, but that gradually becomes an economic critique, as the Finnish state and Europe transform in the 1990s. An especially useful example of this shift is provided by the representation of alcohol consumption in the films. The chapter concludes by analysing the shifting economic dimensions of Kaurismäki's cinema, evident in analysis of his self-reflexive use of festival and awards-ceremony visibility.

Dislodged by Destruction

Aki Kaurismäki's account of his childhood furnishes a rich context for understanding the arc of the director's career and the films he has made in terms of bohemian tropes. In recounting his early life, Kaurismäki situates himself as a young witness to moral and material destruction wrought by the politically orchestrated modernisation and urbanisation of Finland. Bohemia becomes a means of critiquing this modernisation, as well as a means of situating oneself as its opponent. The story he tells about his youth recurs in different forms throughout his career. Kaurismäki describes himself as a nomad who affirms his dislocation as a social perspective – not unlike the characters in his films.

Kaurismäki grew up in many places. He was born in 1957 in Orimattila in south-central Finland – although in some interviews he has said he was born in Hyvinkää (see Nikkilä-Kiiski 1999; von Bagh 2006: 10). The Kaurismäkis lived in Orimattila at the time because of Kaurismäki's father's career, which caused the family to move frequently. Jorma Kaurismäki (1931–1991) earned a degree in business (*ekonomi*) and spent his career in sales and management in the textile industry of southern Finland. His mother Leena trained as a cosmetologist. In Orimattila, Jorma Kaurismäki worked in the financial offices of the textile company Villayhtymä. Later, the family relocated to Lahti, where Aki Kaurismäki began school. They then lived in Toijala and Kuusankoski, after which they moved several hundred kilometres northwest to Kankaanpää. Kaurismäki completed secondary school there in 1976 (see Leppä 1996; Pouta 2003).[2] The family also travelled outside Finland a good deal, which was exceptional for Finnish families during the 1960s. On one summer trip they drove through the USSR from Leningrad to Odessa. On another they drove from Finland to Spain (see Pouta 2003). Kaurismäki's recounting of his childhood underscores itinerancy. In a 1984 interview, for example, he sums things up by listing the places he lived as a young person: 'Hyvinkää, Orimattila, Lahti, Toijala, Kuusankoski, Kouvola, Kankaanpää, Helsinki, Tampere, Helsinki, Tampere, Helsinki...' (von Bagh 1984: 8).

Kaurismäki's memories also resonate with the fracture and change present in the national narrative, in which sacrifice and migration are common. The filmmaker's grandparents and his father were evacuated from the municipality of Lumivaara in Viipuri County in March 1940. They were among 420,000 citizens – 12 per cent of the nation's population at the time – evacuated from the Karelian Isthmus (see Nikkilä-Kiiski 1999; Soila 2003; Koivunen 2006). This evacuation of Karelia followed Finland's armistice with the Soviet Union, which ended the Winter War but cost Finland 10 per cent of her landmass, the city of Viipuri, and led to what Finns call the Continuation War (1941–44). The war exacted a contribution from Kaurismäki's family through his grandfather Petter Kaurismäki's service at the front (see Nikkilä-Kiiski 1999). Although Petter Kaurismäki survived, between 1939 and 1945 approximately 85,000 Finns died. The experiences of dislocation and sacrifice the Kaurismäkis underwent were thus part of a defining national experience. In contrast to such relocation and sacrifice, Kaurismäki's paternal grandparents' post-war home in Hyvinkää was an idyllic setting. Petter and Hilma Kaurismäki owned and operated a garden and nursery, where Aki Kaurismäki, and his brother and sisters spent weekends and several summers (see Nikkilä-Kiiski 1999; Pouta 2003).

Kaurismäki's anecdotes about his childhood usually connect it to his adulthood by characterising himself as witness to material and moral destruction set in train by politically guided modernisation. 'I am a defender of old Finland, the place where neighbours helped each other push-start their cars. I got the chance to live that time, but my sister, who is five years younger than I, did not. She was born too late' (in Leppä 1996: 10). Kaurismäki asserts that a change in moral outlook followed from the modernisation and urbanisation of the 1960s and 1970s, leaving 'smoking ruins' behind (ibid.). In 1945 about 65 per cent of Finland's population lived in rural settings and worked in agrarian occupations; by the 1990s, some 65 per cent of the population was urban. We will return to these changes in talking about Second and Third Republic Finland.

In Kaurismäki's polemic, objects and spaces that symbolise a moral 'old' stand in contrast to an amoral 'new'. We see this in the example of push-starting the car: people who help their neighbours share a moral outlook; but as people have followed work to the city and moved into urban apartment blocks, they have lost contact with their neighbours. Now you call the tow truck. This notion figures in the films as well. We often see alienated characters in the city, who discover that trusting others will harm them, as happens to Taisto when he arrives in Helsinki at the beginning of *Ariel* or Koistinen when he trusts Mirja in *Lights in the Dusk*. A similar narrative turn occurs in *The Man Without a Past*, when M arrives in Helsinki and is beaten. In each case, but especially the latter two, these characters suffer harm in a context of triumphant modernity. In *Lights in the Dusk*, Koistinen works, and meets Mirja in the Ruoholahti quarter, the old industrial West Harbour area that has been gentrified since the 1980s. In *The Man Without a Past*, the glass Sanomatalo building looms in the background as M is beaten by thugs; the large glass building is home to the tabloid *Ilta-Sanomat* and Finland's largest-circulation daily *Helsingin Sanomat*, both now part of a multinational media corporation. These milieus embody the smoking ruins mentioned by Kaurismäki. He asserts that when the moral framework in which objects existed is destroyed, the objects can no longer represent that framework, and the people that inhabit them lose their connection to one another. Ruoholahti and the Sanomatalo stand for moral lack.

In speaking of smoking ruins and other examples, Kaurismäki tells the story of his childhood and youth as one of moral erosion, in which the places and relationships that sustained people who helped one another out gradually fall apart, forcing people to fend for themselves in the amoral city. It is no surprise that the primary narrative of Kaurismäki's films is one in which the protagonist finds himself dislocated and alone, looking to put together a life, as we saw in chapter one.

On the Doormat: Entry into Filmmaking

Kaurismäki came to filmmaking after ceasing compulsory service in the army and breaking off his studies at the university. He recalled this period in his life in a 1982 interview he 'fled the army' in 1977 and 'went to sit around the university and figure out what to do', before moving back to Kankaanpää to work as a sandblaster (see Keskimäki 1982).[3] By contrast, successful completion of compulsory service in the army and voluntary enrolment in the officer corps traditionally provided young men legitimacy, reputation, contacts, and thus social mobility in post-war Finland. After the army, Kaurismäki studied journalism at the University of Tampere between 1977 and 1980. The university in working-class Tampere is the most politicised and leftist of Finland's universities. Kaurismäki also worked as an intern at the tabloid *Ilta-Sanomat* during summer 1978. He was still working as a student journalist in 1979 when he served as public relations representative for the Tampere Shorts Festival, a job that was traditionally given to students in the journalism department at the university (see Myllyoja 2007). Kaurismäki never completed the degree (see Leppä 1996). Since then, in his anecdotes the army, the university, and mainstream journalism have been associated with middle-class hegemony. His encounters with these institutions become moments of moral self-definition. Rejecting the status, relationships, and credentials provided by completion of army service and a post-secondary education, Kaurismäki finds a moral position in his departure from these institutions. Taking up a series of jobs 'was the act of a … morally uncompromising person', he says (in Keskimäki 1982).

And that morally uncompromising person tells of these experiences as moments in which he embraced bohemian impoverishment: 'When I was removed from the army and left in front of the Lasipalatsi in the fall of 1976, I began a noteworthy phase of my life. Since I was homeless and penniless, I glommed on to an old friend, who let me live on his doormat' (in von Bagh 2006: 18).[4] Implicit in this narrative as well is a moral and ethical link that holds Kaurismäki and his impoverished friends together. Their unstable lives bring continual change, which they handle by bonding together.

Between 1977 and 1981, says Kaurismäki, 'I worked for the most part in a variety of menial construction jobs, but also as a sandblaster, on a paper machine, as a hospital orderly, in a warehouse, as a painter, a reporter, and the like ... I also worked in Stockholm for about four months as a dishwasher...' (in von Bagh 2006: 18). These many jobs, Kaurismäki suggests, gave him the requisite diversity of experience to make films. As for George Orwell, impoverishment and comradeship on the margins evidently deepened Kaurismäki's commitment to those on the margins, and sharpened his critical perspective on society's function.

Living on the margins also integrated Kaurismäki into a group that shared a passion for the cinema and envisioned themselves as cultural heroes, not unlike the notion described by Elsaesser. Kaurismäki says:

> I got interested in making films in the spring of 1977. Pauli Pentti and Veikko Aaltonen were part of my crowd at the time. One Sunday afternoon we were walking down Mannherheimintie hungry and penniless. Somewhere around Erottaja we decided, let's make a goddamn movie about it all, since life was so miserable. (In Hämäläinen 1984)[5]

Kaurismäki's account of his entry into filmmaking turns on a cliché of sentimental bohemia, but this narrative also works to position him as cultural hero. He is at home with empty-pocketed deprivation; indeed it is the source of his creative energy. Yet while such an anecdote contributes to the myth of a cultural hero by echoing notions of sentimental bohemia, it would also seem to involve ironic bohemia. The clichés are so exaggerated that the reader wonders about their meaning.

Even if Kaurismäki characterises his entry into filmmaking in the clichés of sentimental bohemia, he also sought to follow a conventional institutional route into film. Yet again, his failure to follow such a path became a means of positioning himself as an outsider. Kaurismäki applied to the Helsinki School of Art and Design's Film School, then located at the Ateneum Museum. He also benefitted from his brother Mika's studies in Munich at the Hochschule für Fernsehen und Film (University of Television and Film) from 1977 to 1981.

Kaurismäki's application to film school was rejected. Admissions committee member Professsor Juha Rosma says: 'I got the impression that Aki had a good imagination, but that he was an introverted personality. He managed as a writer, but fared more poorly with cinema's visual elements and in working with actors' (in Hyvönen 1990: 21). Kaurismäki explains the rejection differently. 'I was so cynical and arrogant, and emotionally immature that they didn't want me there. It's of course true. The worst thing is to realise it yourself' (in Hämäläinen 1981). Once again, Kaurismäki's overstatement suggests a satirical tone that conveys a realisation about the institution's unnecessary role in his decision to become a filmmaker. Kaurismäki implies that it was good fortune to have been rejected from film school, for it placed him outside the institution of Finnish cinema.

A second and more important element in Kaurismäki's entry into professional filmmaking was his brother Mika. Aki visited Mika in Munich, acquainting himself with cultural and cinematic life there. Mika's studies in Munich also introduced him to figures of the New German Cinema, such as Wim Wenders, as well as rising names in German cinema, such as Toni Sulzman, who served as cinematographer for *The Liar* and later went on to work in Hollywood. These acquaintances helped develop a model for connecting with filmmakers abroad without the assistance of an official Finnish network. They also established a set of contacts who would be helpful in establishing the brothers commercially outside Finland later in their careers. Mika's studies also provided Aki with an opportunity to pursue filmmaking.

Mika's final project required help. He invited his brother, Pauli Pentti, and others in the Kaurismäki crowd in Helsinki to make *The Liar* with him during the summer of 1980. Mika returned to Helsinki to make the film, and shooting was completed in fifteen days during June that year (see Suvanto 1981). Aki co-wrote the screenplay with Pentti; Veikko Aaltonen is also credited in the Finnish Film Archives' database, although critics at the time only mention Aki and Pentti as screenwriters. The film also included Matti Pellonpää and Markku Peltola, who would later play leading roles in Aki's films.

The Liar was made on a small budget, with a small crew, following an impulsive Godardian production style and aesthetic. When it premiered in February 1981 at the Tampere Shorts Festival, it won the 50,000 Finnish-mark Risto Jarva prize for best film (see Hohtokari 1981). It later received 40,000 Finnish marks of post-production 'quality support' from the Finnish Film Foundation, money awarded by a committee decision based on institutionally defined criteria.

The Liar was received as a film that 'laughs at fundamental values' (Hämäläinen 1984: 52). It was almost universally seen as indebted to the early films of Godard, such as *À bout de souffle* (*Breathless*, 1960), but also Godard's first short *Charlotte et Véronique, ou Tous les garçons s'appellent Patrick* (*All the Boys are Called Patrick*, 1959),[6] as well as *Bande à part*.

Bohemianism is the key *topos* in *The Liar:* Ville Alfa (Aki Kaurismäki) is a down-and-out writer who lies about everything, mocking the polite intentions of his family and friends, and ceaselessly taking advantage of them. Critic Antti Lindqvist writes:

> You might call Ville a bohemian, if the term had not been debased by so many misuses. Living counter to all norms, he continually rattles off puckish aphorisms about supposedly fundamental experiences: life, love, death. Beneath the amusing appearance of this philosophical impertinence, however, resides a serious vision of an anguished humanity trapped in a cement dystopia, which continually grinds down the only thing that matters, dignity. (1982)

Lindqvist argues that *The Liar* is premised on a bohemianism that entails a philosophical position. His review stands in contrast to the twenty other reviews of the film published during the year that followed its release.[7] Every critic writing on the film likened it to the films of Godard and the French New Wave, and many differentiated *The Liar* from the intellectually serious, aesthetically ambitious, nationally oriented Finnish films of the 1970s; only Lindqvist put emphasis on the bohemian trope in the film. Lindqvist sees a twofold moral affirmation and repudiation in the film. In this *The Liar* calls to mind the poetic realist films of the 1930s, which presented the alienated and fatigued protagonist – often played by Jean Gabin – as advocating an alternative moral vision that also critiqued the moral devolution brought about by capitalist modernity, but also by other forces, as can be seen in the naturalism of *La bête humaine*, adapted as it was from Emile Zola. *The Liar* affirms Ville Alfa's pursuit of dignity, isolated and alone though he may be, and in doing so also rejects institutionally, politically, and aesthetically much of the Finnish culture of the 1970s from which the film emerged, thereby suggesting its ideological rot. Positioning this bohemianism will help account for the alienated relationship of Kaurismäki's cinema to the Finland of the 1970s and 1980s, from which it emerged.

Against the Paternalistic State

The importance of the moral critique in the Kaurismäki brothers' *The Liar* becomes apparent when we connect it to Aki Kaurismäki's anecdotes about witnessing material and moral destruction, and then situate that critique and *The Liar* in the Finland of the 1960s to the 1980s. Kaurismäki's critique emerges from a broad anti-institutional cultural politics of the late 1970s, which attacked state bureaucracies, party politics, and institutionalised organisation. These cultural politics affirmed vitality in social and cultural life, and were underpinned by an ethics of the kind we see in the nascent environmental and peace movements of the time. These movements rebelled against a period of deeply politicised daily life, and no less a politicised cultural life. Strikingly, Kaurismäki's recollections, and the early films, ally themselves with these anti-political movements, omitting discussion of political difference or struggle. *The Liar*'s casual regard for 'truth' mocks political orthodoxy and embraces a vague anarchism. Kaurismäki's trajectory differs from that of the radical left and the Social-Democratic mainstream, as well as from the national discourse that figured centrally in Finnish culture into the late twentieth century. Kaurismäki's anti-institutional intellectual lineage is best located in the emergence of anarchistic cultural and social movements that rejected the orthodox left that had dominated intellectual life during the 1970s.

The Finnish 1970s were shaped by political parties whose activities took place in co-ops with their retail outlets, unions, sports clubs, student groups, theatres, and other voluntary organisations – as was also the case in Sweden, Denmark, Norway, Germany, France, and the UK. In Finland the Marxist-Leninist 'class reform' movement, generally known as the '*Taistolaisuus*' (Militancy) movement, figured especially prominently in the Finnish Communist Party and more broadly in Finnish intellectual life. While it did not take up the extralegal tactics of the left in Germany or Italy, its radicalism sought to revise political, economic, and cultural life. The movement attacked the parliamentarian compromises of the Finnish Communist Party and sought to reinvigorate proletarian internationalism and commitment to Marxist-Leninist dogma as promulgated by Moscow. The movement attracted devoted students, intellectuals, and young people, gaining a foothold in the university system, the national broadcast service, and many other cultural institutions. The class-reform movement also figured in the film clubs in which Kaurismäki got his cinematic education. For example, Tampere's Monroe Film Club led a group of 74 students on a trip to Lenifilm Studios in Leningrad during 1974, a common type of pilgrimage for clubs and groups of the time.[8] Yet Kaurismäki's comments never explicitly engage the legacy of these radical politics, even though his films' moral positions entail leftist political convictions.

Filmmakers of the left and associated with the Taistolaisuus movement predominated in 1970s' Finnish cinema, exemplified by such directors as Jörn Donner, Mikko Niskanen, Risto Jarva, Jaakko Pakkasvirta, and Pirjo Honkasalo. Their films drew on Marxist aesthetics, were often anti-narrative in form, recuperated class struggle as the predominant force in Finnish history, and engaged in a serious, even humourless, examination of prominent figures in the national history (see Toiviainen 1981; Ylänen 2000). Film critic Helena Ylänen sums up the period in the words of influential film producer Jaakko Talaskivi – production manager of eight Aki Kaurismäki films: 'The hallmark of Finnish cinema is that it was made by communists, not gays and lesbians' (Ylänen 2000). In other words, according to Talaskivi, the minority position that defined the national cinema was dictated by ideological conformity and piety, rather than non-normative heterogeneity.

Kaurismäki's position distances him from the communist left, and also differentiates him from the mainstream of Finland's social democratic and national discourse, which have defined the centre-left and the right of Finnish intellectual and political life. Kaurismäki's embrace of narrative cinema differentiated him aesthetically from the filmmakers of the 1970s. His anarchistic politics positioned him in opposition to political parties. Kaurismäki's bohemianism is hard to reconcile with the institutional means used to execute consensus-based policy-making in Finnish institutions in general. Kaurismäki underscores his oppositional stance in interviews of the time: 'One of our aims in *The Liar* was to ridicule the social-democratic spirit and worldview. The film mocked norms of behaviour and constructive participation in general' (in von Bagh 1984: 6). This hostility to involvement in institutional action also distances Kaurismäki from nationalism, Finnish in particular.

Finnish national self-understanding places great emphasis on institutional action, the root of which can be traced to the philosophy of J.V. Snellman (1806–1881). Snellman's neo-Hegelian philosophical writings of the mid-nineteenth century delineated Finnish national identity in terms that remained definitive into the late twentieth century. For Snellman, the construction of state institutions created the sites in which the community in action could recognise itself as an expression of an indivisible, national spirit. Snellman's emphasis on institutional action and national identity differs sharply from Kaurismäki's position, whose anti-institutionalism and hostility towards identification with the mainstream or middle class distinguish him from the Snellmanian tradition. Kaurismäki has often spoken of the ambivalence of nation. 'I have a love-hate relationship with Finns, to whom I feel like I belong but don't belong' (in Alapuro 1983). The thorough influence of political and cultural institutions in Finnish history offer no place to an anti-conformist like Kaurismäki. 'The double standard in Finnish society is most evident in the highest ranks of its political and institutional culture. First politicians and officials screw everything up and lose everyone's jobs and homes, and then they take away any means of consolation or recuperation' (in Riihiranta 1982: 214). Institutional action, suggests Kaurismäki, is another word for cronyism. This observation is the premise of *Hamlet Goes Business*, in which a powerful family corporation enjoys shelter from the law. Because the state represents the interests of the few while speaking in the name of the many, it requires opposition in Kaurismäki's view. One never finds a positive representation of a state official in Kaurismäki's films, from the lowly police officer, to the presumptuous tax inspector, to the indifferent bureaucrats of the unemployment office. This view places Kaurismäki outside the main historical currents of national discourse in Finland.

Bohemians and Punks

Participants in the social movements of the late 1970s organised themselves outside the party infrastructure, embracing smaller-scale social forms instead. They focused on changing individual's attitudes and practices. This shift also impacted the arts, as can be seen in popular music and theatre, for example. Punk rock emerged as a movement in the late 1970s. Punk sought to maximise the energy in the rock-n-roll tradition through attacks on conformity and convention, stripping production values and tradition to yield a small band of three or four, playing short songs in the fastest possible time. Punks took pride in their do-it-yourself attitude, which encompassed everything from learning to play their instruments without training, rejection of musical convention or regard for skill to fashioning their own clothes. The same kind of critique is also evident in the theatre, where attacks on both tradition and the politicised theatre of the 1970s became prominent. Kaurismäki's entry into film took place in collaboration with musicians and actors involved in these movements.

The theatre of the early and mid-1970s was a fellow traveller with the class reform movement. Political commitment was evident in the Finnish National Theatre and the Helsinki Theatre, but also in explicitly political theatre led by such directors as Kalle Holmberg and Ralf Långbacka in Turku. Many productions took a revisionist approach to classical texts in Finnish literature. Plays by canonical authors such as Aleksis Kivi, Minna Canth, Teuvo Pakkala, and Maria Joutuni had been staged in ways that idealised the rural peasantry, a venerable mode in Finnish culture; but the political theatre of the 1970s shifted the idealisation, redescribing conflicts in class terms rather than in the idiom of an idealised and romanticised nationality. In a production of Kivi's *Seven Brothers* directed by Kalle Holmberg in 1974, for example, academic uniforms were used to distinguish between the brothers and their rivals from another village, making the uneducated brothers' struggle against their society a class struggle (see Paavolainen and Kukkonen 2005: 154).

This politicised theatre, and the culture it represented, was the target of a transformational critique in 1978 articulated through a production entitled *Nuorallatanssijan kuolema eli kuinka Pete Q sai siivet* (*Pete Q., or the Death of A Tightrope Walker*), produced by a student theatre company who called themselves The Finnish People's Theatre. This was a short-lived theatre, but the crew and actors were associated with the Ryhmäteatteri, which continued with similar projects. Actors from this theatre provided Kaurismäki with his casts. Casting for *Calamari Union* (1985), for example, involved Kaurismäki turning up at a rehearsal at Ryhmäteatteri and inviting everyone interested to shoot a film with him (see Kuosmanen 2007). In *Pete Q.* then, we find the lineage, and many of the intellectual and creative partners, around which Aki Kaurismäki's cinema subsequently took shape. *Pete Q.* attacked political and aesthetic authoritarianism, while affirming a mysticised, anarchistic notion of art. A conspicuous symbol in the play is a silenced painter whose painting calls to mind the anti-representational style and mysticism of Piet Mondrian. Art in the play involves a moral act, which cannot be reduced to political statement. The play gave voice to a critique of the Finnish radical left, construing it as a movement whose dogma had obscured and repressed the vitality and liberty of artistic activity. *Pete Q.* embraced an anarchistic anti-conformity.

Like the bohemians of the Latin Quarter, the artists who created *Pete Q.* fashioned an identity through a social group of artists, students, and youth, many of whom had met one another as students at the College of the Performing Arts in Helsinki. They included such actors as Kari Väänänen, Vesa Vierikko, Markku Peltola, and Matti Pellonpää. Their broader group also included Veikko Aaltonen, Pauli Pentti, and Aki Kaurismäki himself. Bohemianism was inherent in the social life of this group, which sought to define itself in contrast to an older generation of artists and intellectuals.

The signature of this group turns up in the acronym SHS attached to credits in Kaurismäki's early films. It stands for *Suomen hanaseura*, or Finland's (Beer) Tap Society, according to the actor Vesa Vierikko (see Kuosmanen 2007). SHS was a collective organised on the principle that whoever had money contributed it to drinks for all. Many of the actors and musicians who belonged to the group also acted, performed or contributed their skills to the production of Kaurismäki's films of the 1980s, expecting no pay for films that were made on a 'zero budget', as Vierikko points out. Vierikko does not recall being paid for his role as Aarne in *The Match Factory Girl*, although he does remember eating and drinking well during shooting (ibid.).

One way of getting a better sense of *Pete Q.*'s critique is by likening it to the emergence of punk as it impacted Finland and Western Europe during the late 1970s. The theatre and punk rock, which on the surface seemed to differ in their regard for institutions, shared a rebellious anti-institutional outlook. As *Pete Q.* sought to 'explode its viewers' consciousness' (Siikala 1978), so too the impact of punk through Ramones' gigs in Finland during spring 1977 and punk's influence on Finnish rock proved explosive. The historian Juha Sihvola captures the impact of the Ramones' arrival in Finland in a way that underscores its rebellious spirit:[9]

> I encountered the Ramones for the first time in 1976. *New Musical Express* had already been spreading the word for some time that the next big thing in music was four guys playing guitars in their basement, giving the finger to the dinosaurs of stadium rock like Zeppelin and the self-regarding progressive giants like Pink Floyd ... I found the Ramones' *Leave Home*. I bought it, brought it home, played it (in my room, where I didn't have much more than a turntable) at least eight times, and realised: this is it. (2008)

The Ramones' first concert in Helsinki was 16 May 1977, the first spring in which Aki Kaurismäki was living in the city. As Sihvola recalls, punk stripped away pomposity and self-regard affirming vital musical expression, just as *Pete Q.* sought to strip away the pieties of the political theatre to liberate a similar spirit. The Kaurismäki brothers' early films looked to do the same, although they came at it with different aesthetics than the punks and the thespians. But in each case, these expressions effectively 'gave the finger' to the lumbering political pieties and dogma of the 1970s, embracing instead condensed, vital, anarchistic forms of cultural expression. Sihvola's comment also indicates the extent to which young intellectuals, such as Kaurismäki and others, brought the rebellious attitude of punk to Finland – Kaurismäki through the casting of punk-inspired musicians in his early films. Punk in Finland was an attack on institutions of the middle class, but in its early form it came from within the middle class, in contrast to the movement's working-class constituency in England, for example. Nevertheless, a 'punk' attitude is clearly evident in films like *The Liar*, *The Saimaa Gesture*, *The Worthless*, and *Calamari Union*.

The Saimaa Gesture and *Calamari Union*, for instance, bear a strong connection to the Finnish punk movement. Eppu Normaali frontman Martti Syrjä appears in *The Saimaa Gesture*, *Calamari Union*, Mika Kaurismäki's *Jackpot 2* and *Rosso* (1985). Like Sihvola, Syrjä remarks that the Ramones' tour in Finland during spring 1977 changed his view of music, inspiring Eppu Normaali to adapt a punk aesthetic (see Bruun *et al.* 1998: 282–3). The cast of Aki Kaurismäki's *Calamari Union* is a combination of actors who played in *Pete Q.* and musicians playing in the rebellious Finnish rock scene of the time, including Syrjä, Juice Leskinen, and Tuomari Nurmio. Kaurismäki underscores the affiliation in a 1984 interview. 'I am an anarchist because Finland, just like other countries, is led by a herd of idiots, who make life almost impossible. Regular people don't have the opportunity to influence others, except by stabbing them at a midsummer celebration' (in Hämäläinen 1984: 53). Anarchism, bohemianism, and punk help explain the self-reflexively careless style and rebellious spirit of films like *The Liar* and *Calamari Union* as much as Godard's use of jump cuts and sloppy aesthetics.

In the avant-garde theatre and nascent punk movement that form the context of Kaurismäki's emergence as a filmmaker in the 1970s and 1980s, we see the antipathy to bourgeois convention, the anti-conformity, the emphasis on vitality of artistic expression, and an affirmation of small-scale, do-it-yourself artistic production. The political critique that is part of Kaurismäki's early career fits within this ethos, as well. At the same time, the do-it-yourself element of this context also figured in Kaurismäki's approach to the business of filmmaking. His early collaboration with his brother Mika took place through their company Villealfa Filmproductions Ltd. – in a tribute to Jean-Luc Godard's *Alphaville* (1965) – which helped define a business profile for Kaurismäki.

Kaurismäki Ltd.

When we see bohemianism as a contingent identity taking shape through participation in contemporary life, as Baudelaire does and Gluck and Seigel encourage us to do, then it makes sense to look at the way Kaurismäki participates in contemporary life. For example, is ironic bohemianism a relevant term in analysing Kaurismäki's film business? Commentators have often remarked on the bohemian character of Kaurismäki's business practice. Raimo Silius, the festival programmer for the Tampere Shorts Festival in 1979, recalls that 'Kaurismäki left a positive and sympathetic impression on me, although he was a true personality and a bohemian, indeed a little too bohemian to be PR representative in the opinion of some' (in Myllyoja 2007). The bohemian dynamics we have been tracing are also relevant to the business end of Kaurismäki's career, for as Silius suggests they motivate a distinctive approach.

Aki and Mika Kaurismäki formed their own production company Villealfa Filmproduction Ltd. in January 1981. This allowed them to control all aspects of production, which provided a means of defining the terms of their business. Villealfa was a participant in Filmtotal, a film production collective operating in Helsinki in the early 1980s – which also included Anssi Mänttäri's Reppufilmi and Markku Lehmuskallio's Giron Film. In 1986, Mika and Aki Kaurismäki founded the Midnight Sun Film Festival, which continues as an annual event at the time of writing. The same year, they also established the film-distribution company Senso Films, which owned a share in Finland's largest film distributor and exhibitor Finnkino. In 1987, the Kaurismäkis' Senso Films opened the Andorra Movie Theatre in Helsinki. Aki Kaurismäki is also co-owner of the bar Corona, and the hole-in-the-wall bar Moscow next door, both located in the same building as the Andorra Theatre. The Andorra Theatre was remodelled in 2007, becoming part of the Andorra Cultural Centre, which includes Corona, a night club known as Dubrovnik (after the restaurant in *Drifting Clouds*) and a movie theatre. Kaurismäki is also co-owner of the bar and restaurant in the Kiasma Museum of Contemporary Art. He opened the Oiva Hotel in Karkkila outside Helsinki in 1999, but closed it in 2007 (see Ylänen 1987; Hirvikorpi 1999; Anon. 2007). Villealfa also transformed in 1991, when Aki concentrated his production activity in Sputnik Ltd and Mika in his company Marianna Ltd (see Räihä 1991). Sputnik is now Aki Kaurismäki's production company. Villealfa continued until 1997, producing Veikko Aaltonen's films and serving as one of a number of co-producers of Lars von Trier's *Breaking the Waves* (1996). In all of Aki Kaurismäki's businesses we see a rejection of winner-take-all dynamics, and Kaurismäki's bohemianism: he describes his business as the mediation of an ethos of cooperation, which distinguishes it from other economic practice, calling to mind Gluck's argument about ironic bohemia and symbolic distinction. To be sure, what looks like cooperation from one perspective can be seen as an internalisation by employees of the boss's expectations from another perspective;

incidents lending themselves to an autocratic picture of Kaurismäki have also been reported (see Hyvönen 1990).

Villealfa's cooperation with Filmtotal impacted on Kaurismäki's career by helping him establish a low-budget, quickly produced, do-it-yourself method as his production practice. Filmtotal was initiated by Anssi Mänttäri, a filmmaker a generation older than Kaurismäki who had grown frustrated with the Finnish Film Foundation. Without the financial support of the foundation, it had been practically impossible to produce and release feature films since the failure of Finland's two main studios in the late 1960s. Filmtotal took the do-it-yourself, underground approach to filmmaking, its three companies producing a number of films without foundation support, including Kaurismäki's *Calamari Union*. The three film companies shared office space and personnel as a cost-cutting measure, and also coordinated their production and release schedules to minimise competition for resources. Most of the films associated with Filmtotal were made in Helsinki on short shooting schedules as part of the same low-budget approach (see von Bagh 1984: 4–5). Filmtotal's quick-and-cheap production method rejected the script development, storyboarding, shot-planning, and multiple-take shooting typical of mainstream cinema and required by the foundation, privileging instead on-the-spot scriptwriting, improvisation between director and actors, location shooting, and spontaneity in general. The production style became characteristic of Aki Kaurismäki's approach to filmmaking, and has continued since. In this practice we see a connection to punk.

The films the Kaurismäki brothers made in the early 1980s have proved to be their most successful Finnish releases, as measured by box office. *Crime and Punishment* sold 68,000 tickets. Among Kaurismäki's seventeen features, only the award-winning *Man Without a Past* at 176,000 theatre tickets eclipsed the sales for *Crime and Punishment*. In 1991, Villealfa publicist Erkki Astala said that the company's productions of the early 1980s such as *The Saimaa Gesture* and *The Worthless* had sold between '60,000 to 90,000 tickets' in Finland, before the company's films' sales figures dropped to '30,000 to 50,000 tickets sold' in the late 1980s (see Räihä 1991). These numbers do not include audience for broadcast of the films by Finnish state television (YLE), which typically numbers in the hundreds of thousands to around half a million for Kaurismäki's films.

Another example of the ethos on which Villealfa operated is evident in the way in which Kaurismäki has handled the international rights sales of his films. World Sales' Christa Saredi represented Aki Kaurismäki's films outside the Nordic region between 1986 and 2002. The Swiss Saredi has also handled the rights of films by such directors as Michael Haneke, Jim Jarmusch, Ang Lee, Bakhtiyar Khudojnazarov, and Thomas Vinterberg. Saredi became involved with the Kaurismäkis' distribution through Senso Films and the Andorra Theatre in Helsinki when Mika Kaurismäki contacted Saredi to acquire a print of Jarmusch's *Down By Law* (1986). Mika also used the discussion with Saredi to promote his and Aki's films, according to journalist Eero Hyvönen; Saredi would go on to help Mika and Aki get further connected with eminent filmmakers and actors who later appeared in their films, contribute to the organisation of a Kaurismäki Brothers' retrospective at the Museum of Modern Art in New York in January 1989, and establish festival premieres as a key tool in the international marketing of their films (see Hyvönen 1990: 23). Continuity in this relationship with Saredi helped Aki Kaurismäki establish a 'brand' in such important markets for his films as France and Germany. This branding is evident, for example, in the way in which the films have premiered and been marketed in these countries. Since 1990, four of Kaurismäki's eight features have premiered at the New York, Toronto, or Berlin Film Festivals, and all of them have been screened at one of these festivals or at the Cannes International Film Festival. In all cases, the publicity material of the films remained consistent, with press packets printed in antiquated fonts, films often represented by a distinctive image painted by the visual artist Paula Oinonen, and cryptic, parodic blurbs written by the director featuring centrally in the advertising copy. Even in films with prominent cameos, by such figures as Jim Jarmusch, Samuel Fuller, and Joe Strummer, Kaurismäki has not allowed their names to be used in the marketing of the films (ibid.). International sales, particularly those in France, Germany, and Italy have provided audiences, and helped attract upfront financing from such sources as French and German television channels. In short, an ethos of collaboration served to open doors, build loyalty, define Kaurismäki's films, and attract production funding. Foreign sales of Kaurismäki's films make up a significant majority of their total sales, dwarfing the economic significance of the relatively small Finnish market for Kaurismäki.

In this business practice, we see the mark of ironic bohemia, insofar as Kaurismäki is working within the film business to maximise the impact of his films, but putting principles such as artistic control, loyalty, and collaboration above profitability. These afford the symbolic distinction analysed by Gluck.

From the Second to the Third Republic

While Kaurismäki's early films and career take shape around a political critique of the nation-state, since the mid-1990s his films' critique and, as a consequence, the bohemianism have shifted their focus to an economic critique. This shift is not a change in kind, but one of degree, for one of the abiding features of bohemia is its antipathy towards the 'power of sheer wealth' in politics no less than in culture (Seigel 1986: 394). And politics, as legislation of the economy and the channelling of resources, also involves economics. The reasons for the shift in Kaurismäki's focus are interestingly evident in the representation of alcohol consumption in the films, the analysis of which helps create a picture of Kaurismäki's transforming bohemianism. What we see is that Kaurismäki's bohemianism does not transcend or create a position outside of the middle-class one he critiques, but rather contests and amplifies the conflicts and ambivalence within it – a view that echoes Jerrold Seigel's argument about bohemianism (1986: 11). Sketching out this transformation requires outlining the transition from Finland's Second to its Third Republic, and situating the representation of alcohol discourse in the films in relation to the transition.

Finland's Second Republic designates the period in which the Paasikivi-Kekkonen foreign policy towards the Soviet Union predominated, which also correlated with a domestic-policy regime. The policy was named for the two presidents of Finland who ruled the country between 1946 and 1982. This period stretches from 1944, when Finland signed an armistice ending its war with the Soviet Union, to the dissolution of the Agreement of Friendship, Cooperation, and Mutual Assistance (*YYA-sopimus*) in 1992, which had been put in place in 1948 and had governed Finnish-Soviet relations during the Cold War. The Third Republic can be said to be in place with Finland's affirmative vote to join the European Union in 1994. Although these mileposts are concerned with foreign policy, the Second Republic also involves the modernisation, urbanisation, and the construction of the Finnish welfare state. This Second Republic is crucial to understanding Kaurismäki's cinema, for the Second Republic established a middle-class perspective as fundamental in domestic politics, while linking this perspective to an acceptance of the state as a good actor working to better the lives of its citizens. Kaurismäki's early cinema can be seen in large degree to be a sustained critique of this perspective; as the state's role changes, his cinema also changes.

During the postwar period, Finland devoted itself to the production of industrial products for export – paper, metal, textiles – by which it could pay back its war debts, build a sustaining, non-agrarian economic infrastructure, and forge its five million citizens into a disciplined, productive, educated work force. In his book *Toinen tasavalta* (*The Second Republic*, 1996), the sociologist Pertti Alasuutari investigates the seminal discourses in the construction of the Finnish welfare state between 1946 and 1994. Alasuutari shows that a fundamental aim of Finnish post-war policy in a variety of areas was aligning ruling elites and the population around a middle-class vantage point (also, see Kosonen 1987). By elevating the population through education and well-paid work, an ideological unity was engendered, building on the unity forged in Finland's wars with the USSR between 1939 and 1944.[10] The Finnish state sought to universalise the benefits of this period of growth through the corporatist inclusion and egalitarian distribution policies that define the universal welfare state (see Esping-Andersen 1990). This project was also cultural, insofar as the state established an array of modernising and edifying projects aimed at moulding the population around a rational, cultured, self-reflexive perspective. Education, broadcasting, subsidisation of voluntary associations, and a state alcohol monopoly are areas where state control aimed to shape citizens into more enlightened, more productive, more capable, healthier workers. Alasuutari periodises this history into two phases. In the 1940s and 1950s, the state adhered to the moral task of national self-enlightenment, which dated to J.V. Snellman and his nineteenth-century national project. From the 1960s to the 1980s, the moral emphasis in the Snellman tradition gave way to a drive for rationalisation and planning, led by a state bureaucracy relying on the latest sociological and economic research. Alasuutari calls the first phase the moral economy and the second the economy of expertise. Both of these phases rested on the same foundational assumptions: the goodness of the state, the importance of a shared national perspective, the legitimacy of protectionism in domestic policy.

Kaurismäki's ironic bohemianism gives voice to ambivalence about the Second Republic. Such early films *as The Liar, The Worthless, The Saimaa Gesture*, and *Crime and Punishment* put explicit criticism of this system in the foreground. This is nowhere more evident than in the 'classless' status of the films' characters. They are below the working class, members of the lumpen-proletariat: they are symbolic outsiders in their own land, for they do not belong to the agrarian-, working-, and middle-class coalition that shaped post-war Finland. Such dissent is also explicit in the films. In *The Saimaa Gesture*, for example, the musicians interviewed mock symbolic national institutions such as the army and the state alcohol policy, drinking casually and happily. The Eppu Normaali frontman Matti Syrjä ridicules the Finnish army's clichés about 'making boys into men', asserting the army makes the thoughtful and impressionable into dolts. Kaurismäki's directorial debut *Crime and Punishment* articulates similar political criticism in Rahikainen's altered motive for murder. The commercial and political connections of the character Kari Honkanen, who accidentally killed Rahikainen's fiancée, implies a deep double standard in governance and law: the privileged may do as they wish without fear of consequences, while the masses must submit to the controls of the state. The film condemns the acceptance of state authority and ideological unity analysed by Alasuutari. Yet, as we will see, later films also embrace a middle-class perspective.

This embrace occurs as the Second Republic's political project loses significance. A shift begins to be visible in 1988 with *Ariel*, and finds full expression in the films that have appeared since 1996. The political emphasis of the bohemianism loses its urgency as the Second Republic gives way to the Third Republic, Finland as a member of the European Union, pursuing economic growth in high-tech industries, and gradually embracing neoliberal economic policy that makes economic growth, rather than full employment, the primary measure of economic wellbeing. Kaurismäki's bohemianism under the Third Republic takes on an economic dissent, and begins to challenge and work over the ideology and self-image of an *arriviste* consumer class. In a study of the shift from Second to Third Republic, Alasuutari and Petri Ruuska point out that referential Second-Republic categories such as 'work' and 'citizenship' are replaced by 'market' and 'consumer' in the Third Republic (1999). Beginning in the mid-1980s, Finland deregulated its economy, allowing direct foreign investment to pass in and out of the country, loosening banking regulations, and providing economic incentives aimed at diversifying the economy, so-called 'structural adjustment'. Rapid growth in the 1980s, and a catastrophic recession in 1991–1993 further transformed the economy, contributing to its restructuring around the hi-tech sector and in particular the telecommunications business of Nokia. The educational and technological expertise required to bolster this high-tech economy put new emphasis on education and competitiveness in the global economy. The old model of a nation that needed to be raised up around a shared project gave way to a nation of highly educated consumers, working, buying, travelling, and competing (see Alasuutari and Ruuska 1999: 215–43). The impact of these changes is easily visible in broadcasting and the alcohol monopoly. The national channels must now compete with an array of national and international cable channels, which has diversified the nation's audio-visual culture. The alcohol monopoly can no longer use tax and price controls to regulate consumption, for consumers simply import unrestricted amounts of less-expensive alcohol on trips to other EU countries.

The transition from the Second to the Third Republic has a large impact on Kaurismäki's cinema, insofar as the films show increasing interest in the middle-class perspective promulgated by the Second-Republic Finnish state, presenting it as an opposition to the market orientation of the Third Republic. Paradoxically, the Third Republic has completed the project of the Second Republic, generating a population of educated, middle-class consumers. Yet Kaurismäki's films remain bohemian insofar as they cast symbolic outsiders against this position by marking them with references to Second Republic Finland. The ambivalence of Kaurismäki's bohemian position in the films since the mid-1990s is most evident in the representation of alcohol consumption.

Drunkenness, Manners, and Kaurismäki

Alcohol consumption was a site of enormous contestation in Finland during the twentieth century – a fight Kaurismäki's cinema joins with relish. These struggles impacted Kaurismäki from his entry into filmmaking. In Mika's *The Worthless*, written by Aki, Manne (Matti Pellonpää) orders a calvados: at the time of production in 1983, the French apple brandy was not imported into Finland by the alcohol monopoly, and so was notably unavailable to Finns. Mika and Aki Kaurismäki were forced to remove an image of the rock musician Juice Leskinen drinking vermouth from their early film *The Saimaa Gesture*. 'When someone drinks stylishly, it's unacceptable' in the eyes of the state, said Kaurismäki about the censorship (in von Bagh 1984: 6). Kaurismäki's characters always drink with a certain humorous style. Reino drinks the Finnish national spirit Koskenkorva with zest and immunity to alcohol's effects in *Take Care of Your Scarf, Tatiana*. In *Shadows in Paradise*, Nikander seeks to initiate a romance with Ilona with carefully chosen wine. In *Drifting Clouds,* the alcoholic cook Lajunen (Markku Peltola) struggles with his disease, but does so with good humour and a sober outcome. These images differ strongly from the biological realism in such canonical national films as Mikko Niskanen's depiction of an alcoholic farmer's dissolution in *Kahdeksan surmanluotia* (*Eight Deadly Shots*, 1972), or the carnivalesque depiction of alcohol in such classic farces as *Lampaansyöjät* (*Sheep Eaters*, Seppo Huunonen, 1972). Such depictions circumscribe alcohol consumption within the disease model of alcoholism, or as an exceptional behaviour, which does not threaten the social order. Kaurismäki says: 'Finns approve of people getting drunk in the sauna, puking and rolling around in the bushes, having sex with the neighbour's wife. That's totally fine. But if someone drinks with some style, that's forbidden. It doesn't belong to the Finnish way of life' (in von Bagh 1984: 6). Drinking calvados sits disjunctively with the stereotypes that figure in the discursive history of Finnish drunkenness. 'Choice of beverage is a significant ... indicator of social status [and] imported or foreign drinks have a higher status than "local" beverages' observes the Social Issues Research Council Report *Social and Cultural Aspects of Drinking* (1998: 32). In 1983, lack of availability may have sent a message; in the context of the *de facto* deregulation of Finnish alcohol retail, Kaurismäki's message harmonises with Marcel's preference for a comfortable chair and good bottle of wine at the conclusion of *The Bohemians of the Latin Quarter*.

Alcohol consmption, and especially rural drinking, have long been a focus of Finnish state action, dating to Snellman and the civic-nationalist Fennomani movement in the nineteenth century. From the 1880s until the 1960s there was a prohibition on the sale of spirits in Finland's rural areas, as well as on beer from the 1900s to the 1960s (see Kuusi 1956; Alasuutari 1996). In the 1910s, prohibition movements began to advance biological and cultural theories of 'Finnish Drunkenness' (*suomalainen viinapää*), justifying state action to control and correct the problematic Finnish drinker, especially the putatively unsophisticated rural one (see Peltonen 1988; Alasuutari 1996; Apo 2001). National prohibition was legislated in 1917 and put into legal practice from 1919 to 1932. From 1932, local police and magistrates incarcerated problem drinkers routinely – as is evident in Niskanen's *Eight Deadly Shots*. In 1969, limited retail beer sales were legalised, and a discourse of moderation encouraging wine and beer consumption took shape. Alcohol laws were liberalised in the 1990s, making strong beer available in grocery stores – previously only low-alcohol beer had been. Beginning in 1995, the open markets policy of the EU forced Finland to give up restrictions on the importation of alcohol, as well as to change tax policy governing sales of alcohol. Further, the problem drinker model was challenged by the new model of the citizen as consumer.

The discourse of Finnish drinking has been contested by different quarters in line with diverse political agendas. Nineteenth- and twentieth-century conservative elites construed drunkenness as symbolic evidence of the rural masses' lack of development and sophistication, establishing drunkenness as a justification for coercive forms of social reform. Working-class movements affirmed similar theories of Finnish drunkenness, but formed their own prohibition movements to contest elite discourse and to take control of alcohol consumption. The working-class movement argued alcohol sales were a means of entrapping agrarian and factory workers and making them dependent on bourgeois purveyors. On both sides, however, a paternalistic relationship obtained between discursive actors and the objects of their discourse, the problematic masses. Consensus about Finnish drunkenness led to a policy emphasising restriction as a means of controlling consumption. A retail monopoly was put in place (*Alko*) in 1932, and a ration card system was used from the 1930s to the 1960s (see Alasuutari 1996).

Kaurismäki's generally happy drinkers contest the premise of these discourses, rejecting the construction of alcohol consumption as lacking sophistication, self-control, and middle-class manners.[11] Kaurismäki rejects the model of the problem drinker, replacing it instead with the stylish drinker. His characters drink in different ways, but alcohol is almost always represented as involving conventions of consumption and sociability that maintain control over alcohol intake – although *Shadows in Paradise* is one exception, involving a drunken outburst by Nikander after his colleague's death. For example, the alcoholic cook Lajunen in *Drifting Clouds* loses control, but his colleagues look out for him and protect him from himself. These representations reject the problem drinker model of the Second Republic. The mocking order of calvados in *The Worthless* is another instance of ridicule directed at the restrictive alcohol discourse. Yet if there is some sentimental bohemianism in this position, there is also significant irony, inasmuch as Kaurismäki's films in general, and especially since the mid-1990s, also affirm a bourgeois attitudes and settings.

Time and again, Kaurismäki's films feature scenes in tastefully appointed restaurants, with white linen and designer glassware on the tables, exuding a smart ambience. We see such settings in *The Worthless, Shadows in Pardise, The Bohemian Life, Take Care of Your Scarf, Tatiana, Drifting Clouds, The Man Without a Past,* and *Lights in the Dusk*. In these representations, Kaurismäki finds himself positioned within a minority discourse that challenged the restriction and regulation approach in Finnish alcohol discourse, arguing instead for an incrementalist approach that sought to model bourgeois manners as an ideal for rural and working-class Finns. The premise of this approach is mimetic action, rather than biological expression. Alasuutari offers a fascinating summation of this policy in a passage citing Alko's director from the 1930s to 1954, Arvo Linturi, who writes:

> Control and monitoring of restaurant alcohol service is of enormous significance to Finnish alcohol policy, since for the majority of restaurant customers licensed restaurants are the only place that they encounter proper manners and learn how to behave in public when drinking strong beverages. For this reason restaurant service is extremely important to Finnish alcohol policy. Under the current policy regime governing strong beverages, licensed restaurants have come to be like a national school system, establishing and disseminating model practices of consumption and behaviour. These practices ought to be broadened throughout the population and made more effective by working intensively on enforcement and control of the service culture in licensed restaurants. (In Alasuutari 1996: 154)

The restaurant becomes a site of *paedeia* in Linturi's view, an institution through which the agrarian and working classes can learn to view themselves as bourgeois subjects by engaging in the pleasures of restaurant service. This policy bleeds into the regulatory regime in many ways. For example, through the 1980s, customers who ordered strong beverages in tightly controlled licensed restaurants were required to order food along with their drinks – a legal requirement that in practice was often evaded through creative interpretation. Kaurismäki's stylish restaurant drinking echoes Linturi's perspective, valorising precisely the kind of institutions Linturi emphasises. In this sense, Kaurismäki's cinema embraces a bygone middle-class institution as a means of affirming an alternative to the problem drinker, but also to the alcohol consumer of today, importing trailer-loads of beer and vodka by ferry from Estonia. This contrast is seminal in *Drifting Clouds*: the dignified, old Dubrovnik is purchased by a corporate chain, planning to put something new in the space. Stylish drinking affirms the middle-class perspective that Kaurismäki wishes to reject in many other places in his cinema.

While alcohol consumption continued to be discouraged by way of restriction through the 1960s, Linturi's vision gained ground as the narrative of Finnish drunkeness as a class-based national phenomenon gave way to the disease model of alcoholism.

Since the 1970s, moderate drinking of beer and wine has been promoted. Since 1995, however, neoliberal notions of the customer have displaced the subject of Finnish drunkenness, leading officials to worry that the Finnish customer is just too thirsty. Opinion makers and politicians still do not trust the Finnish drinker. The discourse of Finnish drunkenness continues to surface in panicky discussions of growing consumption, which call for new means of controlling drinking.

The representation of alcohol in the films shows a transition in the orientation of Kaurismäki's bohemianism, while also showing its embeddedness in the political, economic, and cultural changes that have spanned Kaurismäki's career.

Kaurismäki's cinema also displays the ambivalence highlighted by Seigel: it mocks the discourse of regulation and restriction, while valorising strands of the Finnish drunkenness discourse entailing the model of bourgeois *paedeia*. Bohemianism is not a sentimental longing for a position outside of all discourse, but ambivalently shifts between diverse perspectives to engage in both ongoing and particular struggles. In this way, Kaurismäki's ironic bohemianism is not outside of the middle-class perspective, but situated within it, delineating positions and distinctions within its premises and attitudes. As the middle-class perspective changes, from a politically defined notion to an economically defined one, the bohemianism in Kaurismäki's cinema also changes.

Towards an Economic Critique

The shift in Kaurismäki's cinema can also be theorised as a dialectical transition from politically inflected aesthetics to economically inflected aesthetics (see Jameson 1998). Since the 1990s, Kaurismäki's cinema has become increasingly well-known and critically successful, as well as commercially so. Kaurismäki ascended to status of an internationally eminent auteur. This also made his cinema a model of 'global cultural export' within Finland's export economy. Kaurismäki contested this economic status with theatrical disruptions of the commodification of his cinema, and by construing politics as dominated by neoliberal economic discourse. This critique continued to mock the state, but increasingly asserted its moral premise by arguing that the neoliberal welfare state had abandoned any moral commitments. Kaurismäki has thus come to defend the morally and politically normative discourse of social-democratic universalism, which he criticised during the 1980s, for this discourse provides a means of resistance against the redefinition of the state and the citizen as primarily economic actors. The anarchist finds that social democracy has dialectically shifted to become the equivalent to an earlier anarchism. While the anarchist Kaurismäki attacked the normative order of the paternalistic welfare state, since the 1990s anarchism has changed, coming to look like a form of libertarianism. In this context, affirming convention, regulation, and egalitarianism against arguments for an unconstrained economy becomes an oppositional position.

It is easy to overlook these dialectical shifts in the bohemian story. The grey areas of transformation are visible in the ways in which cinema as an institution has itself changed, as it has once again come to be defined primarily as an economic entity. Cinema is promoted as a source of jobs, an economic export, and it is reported in headlines for its celebrity interests. The interaction of these dimensions can be seen in the reception of Kaurismäki's appointment as Artist of the Academy, as well as in the reception of *The Man Without a Past* at Cannes and its exposure at the Academy Awards.

When Kaurismäki received his title from President Halonen, one story about it was headlined 'Artist of the Academy Kaurismäki's Public Image Carefully Crafted'. The reporter pointed out the contradictions in the director's public image: 'In the course of his thirty year career Kaurismäki has given hundreds of interviews, ranging from Finnair's in-flight magazine to the communist newspaper *Tiedonantaja*. Yet in the opinion of most people, he avoids publicity' (Mäkinen 2008). Kaurismäki is a celebrity whose fame rests on his ostensible indifference to his status as a celebrity, which only makes his celebrity more valuable in a media context of ephemeral and empty fame vigorously pursued by everyone (see Nieminen 2007: D1). The real Kaurismäki is supposed to be a laconic, heavy smoking and drinking, left-wing intellectual, and friend of the poor, not a businessman who has skilfully tied together filmmaking and other enterprises in a savvy media strategy. The reporter's response to the contradictions is to surmise that a stable and unchanging stance underpins the appearances. Beneath the public image, what is Kaurismäki really like, he asks. This response to contradictions overlooks the extent to which these contradictions are part of a changing attitude and response to the conditions and ideas in which Kaurismäki's cinema and the discourse around it take shape. More broadly, the comparisons analysed by the reporter appear as contradictions when they presume that Kaurismäki is an outsider. When we take ambivalence as our premise and analyse Kaurismäki's ironic bohemia, we see that the shift from mocking the putatively moral, rational welfare state to critiquing the amoral, neoliberal welfare state is part of a response to a transition in the dominant political-economic regime in Finland, the Nordic countries and the West, rather than a matter of the outsider coming in, or selling out. The conflicts against which Kaurismäki has turned his bohemian stance have simply shifted.

The rising significance of economic shifts is also evident in the predominance of economic allegories in Kaurismäki's cinema, and especially in the films that have appeared since the late 1980s. Allegories of economic critique like the one we see in *Ariel* figure in the films after 1990, and centrally in Kaurismäki's cinema since *Drifting Clouds* in 1996. *Drifting Clouds* itself narrates the consequences of the banking crisis and deep economic recession of 1991–93. The protagonist couple of *Drifting Clouds* lose their jobs, and cannot get started again, as they are refused credit by comically malevolent bankers. The moral act of a former employer finally provides the couple redemption from their misfortune. An allegory of economic destruction and moral redemption is also part of Kaurismäki's *Juha*. The attraction of foreign wealth helps seduce the Finn into betraying her dignity. Economic downfall and redemption are also at the heart of *The Man Without a Past*. Unmerciful economic and state institutions ignore and persecute the protagonist. Only a non-economic and non-political actor, the Salvation Army, provides understanding and support capable of helping M. *Lights in the Dusk* also tells a story of economic exploitation. As in *Juha,* the protagonist betrays his dignity in pursuit of something too good to be true. As a night watchman, the protagonist also introduces a metaphor that has figured prominently in discussions of the rise of neoliberalism in Finland. The 'night watchman state' is a model of small government, which provides only the security necessary to ensure social order (see Löppönen 2008). Koistinen's occupation is no coincidence; the working title of the film was *Yövartija*, or *The Night Watchman*. His profession is also metonymic, in as much as security firms have taken over many police functions in Finland through subcontracting arrangements, for example maintaining order and enforcing laws in the Helsinki public transportation system. Each film can be read as an allegory of economic exploitation, in which the naïve and the vulnerable are exploited by the economically powerful, ignored and harassed by a 'night watchman' state, and only find redemption in relationships to others. The target of these films' allegorical critique is the aggressive individualism, amoral market dynamics, and wilful blindness to suffering commonly associated with neoliberal political positions. Indeed, the ambitions of the night watchman Koistinen to establish a firm of his own sum up the critique. His desire to represent the neoliberal state as owner-operator of a private security firm is destroyed by criminal economic actors, who are allegorically construed as the true owners of the neoliberal system. The moral and rational regimes of the 1940s–70s described by Alasuutari look quaint in the winner-takes-all world of globalisation that is the background picture of Kaurismäki's narratives of the 1990s and 2000s.

If the transformation of Kaurismäki's bohemianism is evident in the films, it is also evident in a shift in his relationship to the cinema. As the economic definition of auteur cinema in Finland and Europe has become more prominent in political-economic discussions, the ironic bohemianism we have been tracing also becomes relevant to the institution of cinema itself.

A Rising Tide Floats All Boats

Kaurismäki's breakthrough as an international auteur dates to the 1990s, as we noted in the Introduction, when his films reached new festival audiences, were programmed in prestigious institutions, reached a new popular audience in Europe, and received wide critical attention (see Connah 1991).[12] 'Kaurismäki's Laidback Attitude Sells in Europe' was the title of one reporter's article, summing up the consensus (Raeste 1990). While a change in critical regard was part of the story, 'selling well' was too. The dynamics underpinning commercial success, and struggles over its significance and relevance to Kaurismäki's cinema, have been a site of ambivalence in Kaurismäki's bohemian story since the 1990s. Ironic bohemianism comes to involve intervening in and inflecting the status of the filmmaker and his cinema as media and commercial entities. It is in this way the contradictions and ambivalences of the cinema as an institution – an aesthetic, political, and commercial form – are explored and worked out.

Since 2000, a number of commentators have formed their view of the significance of Kaurismäki's cinema by understanding it within the discourse of neoliberalism, construing Kaurismäki as a symbol of national success much like globetrotting

Finnish sports celebrities. Kaurismäki's cinema becomes a model of how Finnish film could emulate Swedish and Danish film, and become a small nation's global export. For example, Kaurismäki figures in arguments about the export potential of Finnish cinema advanced by Director of the Finnish Film Foundation from 1996 to 2006, Jouni Mykkänen (2002, 2004). He argues that Kaurismäki is an example of skilfully and strategically produced Finnish film, which also involves an original interpretation of national culture. This combination helps Kaurismäki reach a global niche audience. For Mykkänen, originality is synonymous with a commodification of Finland as strange and exotic, that is to say, Finnish cinema is fetishised as different from European and American cinema and therefore as potentially appealing to film audiences. In Mykkänen's argument we see the conventional narrative of Kaurismäki the bohemian – that is the original and dissident filmmaker – repurposed as an economic story. Kaurismäki's cinema takes a critical distance from the aesthetic mainstream of European and American cinema, yet draws on these same cinematic traditions, making it comprehensible as an 'export product.' Kaurismäki's rise to prominence becomes synonymous with success, but also stands as an economic model of niche marketing to global markets. Kaurismäki's difference is the commodity value in his films, suggests Mykkänen.

But if Kaurismäki's cinema has increased in prestige since the 1990s because of its economic success and global reach, the director and his champions expressed ambivalence towards the success story and the economic dynamics underpinning it, often by invoking a bohemian narrative. The central study of Kaurismäki's films in Finnish by Lauri Timonen (2006) distances itself from any analysis of the economic dimensions of Kaurismäki's cinema. In Timonen's bohemian story, Kaurismäki is the sentimental bohemian, who rejects the bourgeois values of the market in affirmation of his art and moral purpose. Such a story overlooks the extent to which such definition is premised not on ambivalence, but on black-and-white distinctions between economic and aesthetic discourses. To be sure, Kaurismäki often sought to define the economic status of his cinema by theatrically disrupting the economic story told by figures like Mykkänen and the institutions they represent. Yet to engage in such theatrical contestation requires participating in a mass media environment structured by intense competition for 'screen time' and attention. In other words, such self-definition requires a paradoxical double movement: one must engage in attention-getting action within a media field defined by the economic forces one is seeking to critique. The theatrical contestation is reabsorbed by media representations of it, and the attention generated ends up bolstering the economic value of the figure or text in question. What we see is the embeddedness of Kaurismäki in the very economic discourse he critiques, which he does by way of parodical performance within it. Such performances, of course, only increase his celebrity and economic value.

This dialectic is not lost in the Kaurismäki discourse, for the bohemian theatrics and distinctions focus increasingly on economic and institutional critique. This shift offers another reason for Kaurismäki's acceptance of the Artist of the Academy award. In allying himself with a politician like Halonen, who has defined herself through independent-minded commitments and moral stances that call Kaurismäki's positions to mind, he displays a pragmatism that implicitly acknowledges the impossibility of black-and-white distinctions. Kaurismäki's remark, 'Tarja Halonen is a good president' must be one of the only positive public statements he has ever uttered about a politician (Hammarberg 2002). But politics start looking good as a means of resisting arguments about markets and economic necessity.

The seminal examples of Kaurismäki's transforming bohemian stance are also evident in the reception of *The Man Without a Past* from 2002. Critic and film scholar Peter von Bagh sums up critical consensus, which uses textual interpretation to erect a barrier between Kaurismäki and the economic forces the film critiques. 'Kaurismäki has not forgotten things that are simple on their surface, but which have become stunningly unusual. Altruism. Solidarity. The notion that poverty is not evidence of stupidity. The conviction that every person is an end in herself' (2002b). Dissent defines *The Man Without a Past*, suggests von Bagh, construing Kaurismäki as carrying on the tradition of Charles Chaplin, Frank Capra, and Vittorio de Sica and rejecting the alienating relations of the market, the compromises of political institutions, and the commercialised aesthetic of mainstream cinema. A film about an outsider, told in a cinematic language no longer current, it is tempting to cast Kaurismäki in the film, interpreting it as a Manichean allegory of the bohemian outsider who rejects the superficial and the flashy to affirm a humanist morality.

This reading is credible, and was often repeated by critics, but it depends on treating the film as an autonomous object. The film's impact was not generated by the film alone, but by the discourse around it. Kaurismäki deftly used scandal to market the film and engage in a wide-ranging social struggle. In so doing, he embraced the commodified media he professes to disdain, making the scandals and events around the film equally significant to the film itself. In this we see the art of the event, a performance art, which foments social struggle in a way that calls to mind the surrealists and dadaists often praised by Kaurismäki, who figure in the bohemian tradition inasmuch as they ambivalently attacked not only the middle classes, but the art object and institutions established by the middle classes as the armature of modern art. In this connection the career of the dadaist artist Marcel Duchamp comes to mind. Duchamp replaced 'the production of objects with the self-dramatization of the artist, as the representative figure of a society unable to set clear limits for the identities and activities of its members' (Seigel 1986: 389). The many important differences of figure and period notwithstanding, Kaurismäki's use of scandal and media suggests a deep concern with the role of the artist as a negotiator of the significance of economic and moral identities and activities. We do not see this dimension when we position Kaurismäki as only a sentimental bohemian.

The Man Without a Past had its world premiere in Finland on 1 March 2002, but became a media event only in May of the same year, having been chosen for the competition series at Cannes. At the time of writing, only four films in the history of Finnish cinema have been selected for competition in Cannes: Erik Blomberg's *Valkoinen peura* (*White Reindeer*, 1952), Kaurismäki's *Drifting Clouds*, *The Man Without a Past*, and *Le Havre*. In addition to the intense international media attention focused on Cannes, the Finnish media and Ministry of Culture sought to present Kaurismäki as a representative of the national culture. *The Man Without a Past* had received a tepid reception in Finland. At the art-house Diana Theatre in Finland's 'second city' Turku, for example, sixty-eight spectators attended the film during one week in early May (see Suominen 2002). The film had received reviews that emphasised its significance in Kaurismäki's career and underscored its moral intervention (see von Bagh 2002a). Yet Kaurismäki's visibility at Cannes made him an important figure of public diplomacy. One of the key moments was the screening on the evening of Wednesday 22 May 2002. Kaurismäki vaulted to international attention on the red carpet when he twisted his way into the theatre in time to music from his film, and to the consternation of Finland's Minister of Culture Suvi Lindén. As we saw in the Introduction, Lindén scoldingly invoked the drunkenness discourse in responding to Kaurismäki's twist.

> I do not want to comment on Kaurismäki's behaviour. I will just say in general that it is fine to drink alcohol, but the premise must be that one maintains control of oneself and treats others with respect … Whether he represents culture or sport, anyone who appears in the international media should know that he creates an image of Finland. (In Tainola 2002)

Lindén overlooks the rationale for Kaurismäki's performance; the incident forces together national cultural expectations and 'success' stories, global cinema, and the status of the filmmaker in relation to his film. Kaurismäki's self-dramatisation on the red carpet worked to brand him as an eccentric, and hence an interesting, star, which is an economic category rather than one relevant to national representation. Such a performance challenges arguments like Mykkänen's, for it forces us to ask if the filmmaker when understood as an economic category continues to be relevant or valuable as a political or cultural category in a national discourse. Some argue no, as we will see when we take up Jörn Donner's contribution to this discussion in chapter four.

The debate caused by Kaurismäki as such a figure intensified following the gala awards ceremony in which *The Man Without a Past* received several awards. The awards ceremony was not broadcast on Finnish television, and the film's success was initially squeezed to the edge of the national news by reporting on events that coincided with Cannes: the disappointing performance of Finland's hockey team in the World Championships, a Finnish pop artist's failure at the Eurovision Song Contest, and the fortunes of Formula One driver Kimi Räikönen in the Monaco Grand Prix (see Näveri 2002c; Anon. 2002a; Lindstedt 2002). After initial confusion, however, Finnish commentators were quick to trumpet Kaurismäki's success, yet not primarily for the aesthetic or moral reasons that critics like von Bagh had identified, but for the reasons outlined by Mykkänen. Kaurismäki's cinema was a model of economic success, a cultural export story to be emulated by other quarters of Finnish culture. In telling Kaurismäki's success story as one of economic triumph, many commentators wondered what impact the film's success would have on the legislative session that would determine the Culture Ministry's budget for 2003–5 (see Anon. 2002a; Anon. 2002b; Anon. 2002c; Näveri 2002c). The international press also wrote about the economic dimensions of Kaurismäki's film, focusing on the many distribution contracts signed for it at Cannes, but also about its aesthetic and moral dimensions. By contrast, some commentators criticised the economic emphasis, arguing that Kaurismäki was misunderstood, that the story was one of aesthetics, originality, political opposition, and a unique achievement in the history of Finnish cinema (see von Bagh 2002b; Noukka 2002; Donner 2003; Valkola 2002; Sundström 2002). Such commentators ignored or criticised the economic arguments.

Kaurismäki continued to rise in prominence as the film circulated in festival and commercial release, culminating in a nomination for Best Foreign Film at the 2003 Academy Awards, which took place on 20 March 2003, three days before the US began its invasion of Iraq. Kaurismäki again engaged in self-dramatisation that probed economic, cultural, and political expectations about his cinema. Already in February, Kaurismäki initiated a mini-Oscar scandal by announcing that he would not attend the Academy Awards ceremony. He has routinely refused to allow his films to be chosen by the Finnish Film Foundation as its nominee for the Academy Awards, and has also said that he will never set foot in the state of California (see Luomi 2007: 94). Minister of Culture Kaarina Dromberg – who had replaced Lindén, after Lindén resigned in the conflict-of-interest scandal that followed Kaurismäki's prize at Cannes – sought to pressure Kaurismäki to attend, and newspapers published articles citing readers' support for Kaurismäki's attendance (see Blåfeld 2003; Asikainen 2003). Kaurismäki eventually responded by releasing to the press a letter he sent to Frank R. Pierson, then-director of the Academy of Motion Picture Arts and Sciences:

> I thank you for the invitation to the Academy Awards Ceremony. However I am sure that You and the Academy are well aware that we are not living the most glorious moments of the history of the mankind [sic]. Therefore I nor anybody else from Sputnik Ltd can participate the Oscar Gala event [sic.] at the same time the government of the United States is preparing a Crime against Humanity for the purpose of shameless economical interests [sic]. For these reasons we are not in a party mood. (In Roos 2003)

Kaurismäki's refusal to attend the Academy Awards, and his framing of it as a political-economic critique of George W. Bush's foreign policy, was widely reported, bolstering the director's image as a bohemian dissident. While the scandal can be read in terms of stark oppositions, it can also be understood within the ironic bohemian frame.

Kaurismäki's cinema and by extension the director have become significant economic values. The success of the film at Cannes, and the nomination for an Acvademy Award, led to more than a year in Finnish theatres, and commercial release and distribution in scores of markets. Total tickets sold for the film surpassed two million. The film's total theatrical gross of €9.5 million is the largest in the history of Finnish cinema; its estimated total gross (including DVD, video, television exhibition rights, and other rentals) reached an estimated €40 million (see Näveri 2003). The real and cultural capital Kaurismäki accumulated has provided him with a means of heightening his engagement in economic critique, as we see in the letter to Pierson.

The Ironic Bohemian

Kaurismäki's career is entangled with changes in the defining features of Finnish and Western society. The political activism of the 1970s gave way to social movements, which won certain gains, for example the successes of the feminist and environmentalist movements, but which have struggled to impact the rise of neoliberalism and globalisation. These latter have redefined the paternalistic state that Kaurismäki railed against in the 1980s as an economic facilitator, a 'night watchman' in the neoliberal utopia. We have tracked this shift from a politically defined state and society to an economically defined state and society in relation to Kaurismäki's bohemianism. The argument has suggested that the director is not an outsider to these discourses, a sentimental bohemian, so much as an internal resistor exploring and contesting shifting conditions, limits, and contradictions. Kaurismäki's project has drawn its material and inspiration from social movements, struggles, and popular culture: punk and the do-it-yourself cultural movement, new theatre movements, underground cinema, Finnish alcohol discourse. These have become material for Kaurismäki's cinema, but have also figured in his public statements and performances, which have also tested the premises and expectations that characterise late modernity in the West. Our picture of Kaurismäki is enriched by grasping the dialectical shifts that have animated the bohemianism that is a seminal part of his cinema and career. By thinking of this bohemianism as involving sentimental and ironic elements, we get a fuller view of the way Kaurismäki's cinema draws from 'modern life', as Baudelaire might say, to fashion a perspective on modern life that explores and tests its conflicts, sites of exclusion, opportunities for emancipation, and utopian aspirations.

Notes

1. Marcel speaking in *The Bohemians of the Latin Quarter* (2004 [1852]: 392).
2. A number of sources state that Kaurismäki completed his secondary education at the Kankaanpää lukio in 1973. In fact, in 1973 the Kaurismäki family still lived in Kuusa, where Kaurismäki's older brother Mika completed his secondary education in spring 1974 (see Pouta 2003).
3. In other interviews, he recalls 'being removed from the army in 1976' and ending up in Helsinki (von Bagh 2006: 18).
4. Kaurismäki gives differing chronologies of his activities between 1976 and 1980. He completed secondary school during June 1976 and served as a summer intern at *Ilta-Sanomat* during 1978 (see Niemelä 1978). He also studied journalism at the University of Tampere, presumably before he was summer intern at *Ilta-Sanomat*. This period ends in the summer of 1980, when he worked on making *The Liar* with his brother Mika and others. The differences do not contradict the bohemian narrative of this part of his life, however.
5. Mannerheimintie is the primary arterial road in central Helsinki. Its point of origin in the city centre is Erottaja (literally, the divider), which lies adjacent to Helsinki's Esplanade Park.

6 The Film historian Jari Sedergren connects *The Liar* to Godard's *All the Boys are Called Patrick,* noting that *The Liar* and Godard's first short are both built around an ironic, exaggerated Don Juan figure.
7 The film was shown on television in 1982, generating an unusual amount of coverage for a short film in the first year of its release.
8 See http://www.elokuvakeskus.fi/monroe/historia.html.
9 I am especially thankful to the late Professor Sihvola for sharing with me in several conversations his memories and thoughts about the arrival of punk in Finland, and possible connections to Kaurismäki. The argument that follows draws on his comments and observations.
10 Distinct from the post-war period, the inter-war period was a time of ideological division, suspicion, and instability, as the wounds of Finland's bloody civil war (1918) continued to figure in parliamentary and social conflict.
11 To be sure, alcoholism is also depicted in the films, embodied for example in Iiris Rukka's parents in *The Match Factory Girl.*
12 Fittingly ahead of the curve, the only book on Kaurismäki in English was published in 1991 by architectural critic Roger Connah, *K/K: A Couple of Finns and Some Donald Ducks.*

CHAPTER THREE

The Nostalgic

> Everything is not as simple as you assume.
> Antti Kalervo Rahikainen in *Crime and Punishment*[1]

Many critics have argued that Kaurismäki's cinema opposes the culture that surrounds it and that nostalgia defines the films' oppositional stance. One Finnish critic writes, 'a sharp oppositional attitude to mainstream films has been characteristic of Kaurismäki from the very beginning. That comes from Robert Bresson and Luis Buñuel. Kaurismäki's films are completely different from the mainstream...' (Koski 2006). In this account, a nostalgic affirmation of these idiosyncratic filmmakers positions Kaurismäki outside contemporary cinematic culture. The Finnish film critic Peter von Bagh makes a similar point about *The Match Factory Girl*, arguing that the film's minimalism is antagonistic to fashionable styles promoted in contemporary commercial media.

> During a time in which the diarrheic language of television series is repeated all over the place and with ever decreasing critical awareness, and the premise of understanding as a condition governing language and communication is continually disparaged, [*The Match Factory Girl*'s] expressions and attitudes express a certain militancy. When someone speaks in *The Match Factory Girl*, it means something, and speech can create fateful consequences. (2002c: 143)

Kaurismäki's cinema thus expresses a nostalgia for authentic communication, and in doing so attacks institutions of the present, television among others. Von Bagh maintains that 'out-of-touch, increasingly technocratic and forgetful' Goliaths use television 'to keep the people quiet, and in place' (ibid). In Kaurismäki's diminutive nostalgia, television meets its David, implies von Bagh.

These readings of Kaurismäki's cinema have proved influential; it is axiomatically taken to express nostalgia. Literary scholars Riikka Rossi and Katja Seutu sum up scholarly opinion in a fine collection of articles on Finnish literature titled *Nostalgia* (2007). Kaurismäki figures as the first example in their introduction – along with Proust. Rossi and Seutu write:

> Although the protagonist of Kaurismäki's *Man Without a Past* remembers nothing of his past, he is ensconced in a shared, secure-feeling past, which finds expression in the film through old music, cars, commercial items, and bygone urban and social images, in which a worker is paid in cash once a week. Desire for a unified community is a defining mark of nostalgia. (2007: 7)

This reading suggests that the film's nostalgia gives material form to a wish for belonging, which transcends the wealth and power of the banks, the corporations, and state. Nostalgia here positions the community outside capitalism. The old music, cars, and commercial items associate this community with the past, and differentiate it from what does not appear in Kaurismäki's films – the accoutrements of wealth and power: technology, glamour, eminence.

According to these observations, Kaurismäki's nostalgia is a means of creating an oppositional position exterior to economic and political discourse and institutions. In this view, the power of Kaurismäki's intervention lies in the position's temporal exteriority. Aligned with the forgotten past, Kaurismäki can supposedly see differently than the empowered of the present day. He does not depend on social networks or the rules of the system, and so can speak freely. And he is liberated from conflicts of interest, which might silence him. Nostalgia hence serves to vouch for the moral soundness of Kaurismäki's critique.

A key problem evident in such arguments about nostalgia, however, is that the temporally exterior position always remains unspecified. On the one hand, nostalgia invokes a longing for something not present, the 'past as foreign country': yet in being absent, the longed-for object is defined simply as an alterity, something other than what is present, something different than the current order. On the other hand, in fetishising the longed-for object of the past, nostalgia strips that object of a complex, potentially contradictory context. The nostalgic object can be longed for intensely because it figures against a whittled down background, before which it is simply an idealised goodness. If its context were specified, the nostalgic object could not sustain the idealising affective investment that makes it attractive in the first place. Aligned with such an object, the exterior position and the idealisation go hand in hand.

This chapter challenges such constructions of nostalgia and seeks to situate Kaurismäki's cinema and his nostalgia in relationship to some influential arguments about nostalgia and the representation of time and space in film studies. It then seeks to show that Kaurismäki's nostalgia is more complicated and embedded in mainstream cinema and culture than the definition of an exterior and oppositional position tends to acknowledge. Finally, it lays out an argument about the significance of Kaurismäki's nostalgia by likening it to the 'tactic' as theorised by Michel de Certeau. The argument seeks to demostrate the interest of Kaurismäki's cinema for film studies. At the same time, the argument contributes to Kaurismäki studies by bringing together arguments about a key theme in his cinema, and suggesting another perspective on them.

Nostalgia and Late Modernity

There are many examples in Kaurismäki's films that suggest his nostalgia fits within late modernity and its systems, rather than seeking to define a position exterior to it. These examples suggest that we ought to reconsider the rationale motivating Kaurismäki's nostalgia.

Kaurismäki's films continually construct relationships between objects, attitudes, and institutional practices that we often think of as belonging to discrete historical moments of the twentieth century. In *The Man Without a Past*, for example, the main character M arrives in Helsinki by train in a 'blue' passenger car dating to the 1970s, the oldest style of car in use on Finland's national railway (VR). VR has been replacing this equipment with Intercity and Pendolino trains. As film scholar Anu Koivunen astutely observes, M's costume includes a style of leather boots and work clothes associated with an earlier generation of men (2006: 135); and arrival by train in Finland's capital city also belongs to a historical narrative of the 1960s, not the 2000s. Yet M soon makes his home in a shipping-container village: the container was invented in 1956 and became the universal infrastructure for international shipping by the early 1980s (see Levinson 2006: 239). Containerisation has furnished the infrastructure for just-in-time manufacturing and the globalisation of consumer-oriented trade; the volume of goods shipped in containers quadrupled between 1980 and 2000 (ee Levinson 2006: 271). The container has transformed harbours around the world by providing a means of automation ten times less expensive than established bulk cargo loading, shipping, and unloading systems. The container can be read as a symbol of late modernity, that is the system of globalised capitalism involving broad, deep, and speedy flows of capital, deterritorialised relationships of production and distribution based on inexpensive labour costs, computerisation and automation, and a global consensus around economic policy tending to favour the interests of capital, that is, a neoliberal system. In featuring the container, *The Man Without a Past* includes images of Finnish modernisation and globalisation.

Another example of this symbolic combination is apparent in *Drifting Clouds*. Capital moves out of the Restaurant Dubrovnik, leading Ilona to lose her job and experience a humiliating chain of events, but the former owner of Dubrovnik agrees to finance a new restaurant when Ilona runs into her, reconstituting a utopian, nostalgic space and social configuration. When finance capital returns, the moral venture and crisp style of Restaurant Work (Ravintola Työ), becomes possible. The nostalgic restaurant is not outside modern capitalism or an alternative to it; it belongs to a strand within it, a combination of disjunctive elements.

A similar disjunction is evident in the way Kaurismäki's cinema symbolically combines disparate elements of the history of cinema. Kaurismäki's characters in *Drifting Clouds*, *The Man Without a Past*, and *Lights in the Dusk* recall Chaplin at work in *Modern Times* (1936), George Bailey (James Stewart) in Frank Capra's *It's a Wonderful Life* (1946) and Erin Brokovich (Julia Roberts) in the eponymously-titled film by Steven Soderbergh (2000). Kaurismäki's characters fall, they struggle, they come to understand themselves and the world around them more fully, and in some cases they even triumph. Kaurismäki signals the relevance of the Hollywood tradition, calling it to mind directly in *Leningrad Cowboys Meet Moses*, when the director appears as the little tramp working on the factory line. About this cameo, Kaurismäki remarks that he combined Buster Keaton and Charles Chaplin (in Nestingen 2007). The characters mentioned above and Kaurismäki's characters all share a defiant view of the capitalist system. It is not only Kaurismäki who has combined the history of the cinema with his own view. We can also see how other filmmakers intersect with Kaurismäki in their filmmaking, among them Jean-Pierre and Luc Dardenne, Jim Jarmusch, Dagar Kári, Mike Leigh, Quentin Tarantino, and Jia Zhangke. The interest of Kaurismäki's nostalgia and his cinema lies in their messy embeddedness in Euro-American and World society and cinema, and the films' representation of their history and transformation, rather than in their total opposition to other forms of cinema.

There is another way of avoiding the 'outsider' argument about nostalgia, which usefully points in a fruitful direction, and so lays in the background of the case I seek to make here. The films can be read as existentialist texts, not seeking an exterior position, but rather carving out a space of subjective authenticity. On one such account, this existentialist space is a variation of Freudian and Kristevan melancholia, in which the lost object of the past belongs to modernity, yet nevertheless exerts a pull on the subject, which keeps him shuttling between past and present in a bifurcated existence. By staging images of longing for a lost object, Kaurismäki's cinema prompts spectators to long for the past, allowing them to occupy a space of movement between the late-modern, capitalist present and a space of longing internal to it (see Kyösola 2004b). Akin to this argument is the claim that representations of nostalgia in Kaurismäki's cinema clear a space for Heideggerian *Dasein*. In this view, the nostalgic objects in Kaurismäki's cinema stage the construction of a dwelling that resists the instrumental logic of modernity, creating a space for authentic existence (see Vermeulen 2007). The strengths of these analyses notwithstanding, they depend on the premise that the past is out there and amenable to representation, rather than constructed through representations and claims that construct past, present, and future in contingent relations to one another.

A more convincing way of approaching nostalgia as a part of late modernity is suggested by the essay 'The Painter of Modern Life' by Charles Baudelaire. Kaurismäki has written about Baudelaire, mentioned Baudelaire's work in interviews, and he dedicated the film *Calamari Union* to the memory of Baudelaire, as well as naming the dog in *The Bohemian Life* after the poet. Baudelaire was hostile to nostalgia, for he viewed the contingent experiences of life in the modern city as the source of artistic originality. This was because the variety of experience could be synthesised by the modern artist, creating a vision of modern life. In 'The Painter of Modern Life', Baudelaire suggests that nostalgic representations can separate an artist from contact with the society surrounding him and thus diminish his originality:

> If a painstaking, scrupulous but feebly imaginative painter has to paint a courtesan of today and takes his inspiration (that is the accepted word) from a courtesan by Titian or Raphael, it is only too likely that he will produce a work which is false, ambiguous and obscure ... Woe to him who studies the antique for anything but pure art, logic, and general method! By steeping himself too thoroughly in it, he will lose all memory of the present; he will renounce the rights and privileges of circumstance – for almost all our originality comes from the seal which time imprints on our sensations. (2008: 14)

Gazing into the past distracts the artist from the people, spaces, institutions, and struggles surrounding him, causing isolation. Baudelaire's emphasis on contingency and 'the seal which time imprints' maintains that it is an observant sensitivity towards life in modern society, its changing people, spaces, and images, that is the artist's chief faculty. The artist must recognise the relevance of the past, but not be distracted from the present.

As a post-Romantic thinker, Baudelaire's double vision negotiates the problems of idealisation and realism. The artist must not be seduced by the past as the putative idealisation of some entity of interest, but finds his originality in depicting the contingencies of modern life. We see the way Kaurismäki does this in his representation of shipping containers and capitalist dynamics in *The Man Without a Past* and *Drifting Cloud*, but also in his contemporary adaptations of Dostoevsky, Shakespeare, and Murger, as well as in his films' citations of TV news and newspapers. It is also wise to avoid placing too great an emphasis on the existentialist elements in Kaurismäki's cinema. As a subjective philosophy, existentialist thinking has trouble with the social awareness and observation we see in Baudelaire and in his impact on Kaurismäki. Kaurismäki is not a patient and scrupulous filmmaker who seeks to depict a contemporary worker by modelling him or her on the work of Teuvo Tulio or Robert Bresson, Valentin Vaala or Jean Renoir, Frank Capra or Yasujiro Ozu. We should not take Kaurismäki's use of nostalgic representations to depict contemporary life by way of images of the past, or as a subjectively oriented existentialism, but instead ask about the films' relationship to 'the seal which time imprints on our sensations'. What is the aesthetic and cultural political relationship between Kaurismäki's representation of contemporary Europe and the use of nostalgic images, sounds, and styles?

Nostalgia and History

Kaurismäki's cinema has the potential to contribute to discussions of nostalgia in film studies and cultural studies. The films' multiple temporal registers encompass American and European inter-war and post-war culture and cinema, especially the latter's formal elements, its narrative styles, and many of its moral assertions, making it aesthetically and culturally suggestive material. Further, these references seem to concern history less than they insistently link up with present-day issues and debates. Given these features, it is no surprise that only one of Kaurismäki's films is explicitly situated in the past: the TV film *Dirty Hands*, the Sartre adaptation. Kaurismäki has distanced himself from the film over his lack of production control (see von Bagh 2006: 73–5). Despite Kaurismäki's reputation as a nostalgic filmmaker, his films are neither heritage films nor costume dramas, the genres most strongly associated with nostalgic cinema in Finnish, Nordic, and European film since the 1980s. The critical tone, minimalist style, and pastiche features of Kaurismäki's cinema do not mesh with the middle-brow sensibility and production values commonly associated with nostalgic genres like the heritage film.

Kaurismäki's films do include diverse temporal registers and objects belonging to different historical moments; this combination causes them to seem timeless in some ways. Yet at the same time the films are often specifically situated in their moment of production by way of topical references or diegetical dating. In *Take Care of Your Scarf, Tatiana* and *Juha*, for instance, the *mise-en-scène* of 1960s' rural Finland figures centrally and certain aesthetic features conjure a sense of the past, for example the black-and-white image track and *Juha*'s production as a silent film. Yet the films also include narrative events and images that tie them to the present. In *Tatiana*, Manne spontaneously returns to Estonia with Tatiana, but without a visa, a journey not possible before Estonian independence from the USSR in 1991. In *Juha*, a microwave oven and a plastic package of meatballs roughly locates the diegesis historically. In *Drifting Clouds* and *The Man Without a Past*, a television broadcast and a newspaper masthead nail down specific dates, which heighten the clash with some of the older elements of *mise-en-scène*. This temporal mixing raises questions about how to approach Kaurismäki's work in the context of some predominant theories about cinema and nostalgia.

Discussions of nostalgia often argue that it is a mode or representation that critiques history, but such arguments do not necessarily help unpack Kaurismäki's cinema. In her influential and suggestive book *Screening the Past*, for instance, Pam Cook (2005) reads film texts' nostalgic representations of the past in relationship to history. Cook makes the case that analysis of nostalgia is necessary to understand changes in notions of media culture and spectatorship. Shifts in the theorisation of media culture and spectatorship help make visible a variety of spectatorial relationships to history. Cook contrasts such arguments with apparatus theory and psychoanalytic film theory of the 1970s, which maintain that film texts overpower docile spectators, constructing a uniform relationship to history for them. Nostalgia, argues Cook, involves active viewers' diverse uses of films to do memory work. Analysis of nostalgia allows us to discern the spectator's historical self-construction in ways that link up with counter-narratives and critiques of canonical historiography. The richness of Cook's argument notwithstanding, its concern with analysing nostalgia as a form of historiographical critique can distract us from the other kinds of nostalgia less concerned with history, such as Kaurismäki's. Furthermore, the focus on history tends to emphasise the particular, or in Kaurismäki's case, national history, which would only reinforce arguments about his exterior and distinct cultural position.

Another way to tackle nostalgia in Kaurismäki's films is to approach it as melancholia, as Satu Kyösola and Anu Koivunen have done. Koivunen has suggested that Kaurismäki's films give voice to a sense of the 'loss of an ideal, be it the political project of the welfare state or the leftist revolutionary dreams' (2006: 144). This melancholia finds seductive expression in nostalgic images and music, which Koivunen situates within a discussion of Fredric Jameson's (1991) and Vera Dika's (2003) related notions of the nostalgia film. Kaurismäki's eclectic musical choices, 'technicolor-inspired, carefully planned frames...', as well as the immobile camera, and 'lighting and setting produce elaborate compositions for the spectator's pleasure' (ibid.). The image track and soundtrack create a sensual experience, which generates a seductive, emotional register through which melancholic loss can be experienced. For Koivunen, however, the nostalgia and melancholy are only part of the picture. Kaurismäki's films are an eclectic pastiche also combining sentimentality, irony, and political critique.

One of the points implied here is that nostalgic representations also use images of the past to create affective relationships to institutions and figures in the present. A compelling framework for this line of analysis is David Harvey's argument about the consequences of time/space compression in his classic study *The Condition of Postmodernity* (1989). A defining feature of late or post-modernity is its systematic control of temporality – the capacity to make things happen rapidly by moving money, goods, commodities, people, and images around the world in short time spans. Time/space compression, impacts the temporality of social relations. Objects, relationships, and experiences become ephemeral, obsolescent, and disposable, because change can be brought about easily and inexpensively through resupply, replacement, realignment, or recontextualisation. As a consequence, the capacity to appear to resist change, to project durability, rises in value. In this context, the nostalgic image and the heritage industry gain cultural capital, in their capacity to create the appearance of durability. Harvey's argument stands in contrast to Cook's, for Harvey is concerned with the way images of the past are used instrumentally in political and economic discourses of the present, rather than to engage in historical debate. Kaurismäki is working within Harvey's frame of reference.

Harvey's argument about time/space compression bears directly on the production and marketing strategies of national cinemas in an era of globalised cinema, which is part of its relevancy to Kaurismäki. In *Film History: An Introduction,* David Bordwell and Kristin Thompson point out that small-nation cinemas have long used location shooting and narratives drawn from national history and literature to differentiate their films from mainstream American and European productions (2003: 78–9). Such an argument echoes Harvey by maintaining that nostalgia can generate distinction in the marketplace. At the same time, Bordwell and Thompson's formalist account of nostalgia can overlook the dynamics created by asymmetries of history, business, aesthetics, and cultural politics, which distinguish Hollywood production and distribution from national and small national cinemas. The Hollywood majors and boutique producers have also registered the value of national nostalgia, which is visible in such films as *The Lord of the Rings* trilogy (Peter Jackson, 2001–2003), the *Harry Potter* films (various directors, 2001–2011), *Chronicles of Narnia* (various directors, 2005–2008) or nominally art-house hits like *Babel* (Alejandro González Iñárritu, 2006) and *Slumdog Millionaire* (Danny Boyle, 2008). An earlier instance of the same phenomenon is Sydney Pollack's adaptation of Isak Dinesen's (Karen Blixen) memoir

Out of Africa (1985), as Mette Hjort has argued (2005). Nostalgia is a key aspect of national cinema, as Bordwell and Thompson suggest, but also an overdetermined and contested element in a globalised film culture.

What we need then is a frame of reference for situating Kaurismäki's nostalgia within the present, and in relation to the debates and critique his cinema involves, but also a framework that includes movement between multiple registers, as Koivunen argues.

The Temporality of Double Occupancy

Theories of nostalgia assign different roles to contemporary discursive actors. While some minimise their role in shaping our notions of the past, other maximise their role, making the past the construction of present-day actors. The latter approach is relevant to Thomas Elsaesser's arguments about identity politics. In *European Cinema: Face to Face With Hollywood* (2005), as well as in an article on Kaurismäki's *Man Without a Past*, 'Hitting Bottom' (2010; 2011), Elsaesser develops a notion he calls 'double occupancy'. All European social identities involve displacement and multiplicity, because of Europe's violent and migratory internal history. As the metaphor of two people holding or contesting one space indicates, double occupancy works in Elsaesser's analysis primarily to discuss spatial relationships in film concerning identity discourse – the term is also a critique of 'Fortress Europe' and multiculturalist arguments (2010: 109–10). Elsaesser does not explore the temporal dimensions of the term, but developing an account of double occupancy's temporal dimension helps illuminate Kaurismäki's nostalgia and its relevance for film studies.

Kaurismäki's *Man Without a Past* can be read as an allegory of double occupancy inasmuch as it depicts a community of citizens within the state, who are nominally bonded to the state by the social contract, but in practice living a citizenship under erasure. The protagonist M is governed by the laws and obligations of the Republic of Finland, yet is also a non-citizen, unable to receive any, which challenges recognition let alone benefit from his status as citizen. In this character, the political notion of citizenship is in conflict with the neoliberal economic discourse that has recast the citizen as consumer. In Elsaesser's account (2010), Kaurismäki's critique of citizenship is an instance of double occupancy, for it shows the emptiness of political and economic categories of citizenship at the same time as it elaborates an ethics of tolerance and humility that seeks to displace the political and economic discourses of citizenship. This argument places great emphasis on double movement, contestation, and ambivalence. Different concepts of citizenship are involved in a contest that will alter all notions involved, and will not produce a singular winner.

In speaking of double occupancy, Elsaesser discusses similar dynamics to the temporal and aesthetic ones theorised by Baudelaire, when the latter argues that no pure aesthetic models are available in the work of the masters of the past, but that the artist must shuttle between past and present, general and particular. Past and present are involved in a relationship of double occupancy within the artist's creative practice. The allegory of double occupancy Elsaesser identifies in *The Man Without a Past* is also relevant to nostalgia in Kaurismäki's films, for it gives us a way of recognising how nostalgia also works as a form of temporal double occupancy that disrupts – or to use Elsaesser's term, interferes with – notions of homogeneity and singularity, and prompts us beyond the usual identity categories.

The categories and identities involved in double occupancies always have a history; a symbolically significant identity or place often carries importance precisely because of its temporal status, its salience justified by temporal claims. A place has always been the home of this or that ethnic group, creed, or language. Yet such histories are always fraught, subject to multiple claims. Institutions and cities take shape through histories of gender, class, ethnicity, construction, and inclusion, but also destruction and exclusion. The dynamics are evident in the built environment. To take a classic example, the financial operations of capital cities concentrate capital flows into specific areas, which require infrastructure and tertiary services facilitating capital flows. The investment bankers not only need their Bloomberg monitors, but the infrastructure, real estate, and amenities that define their social status. These latter often push older forms of culture and commerce out of the way, which alters the cultural and symbolic ecology. The present and the past make competing claims on the same urban space. In a different vein, the 'smoking ruins' of postwar Finnish modernisation – the brutalist cement apartment blocks of eastern Helsinki, the Pasila district, or the town of Lahti, for example – seek to generate equality into the future by erasing the uneven development of the past, and its wooden construction. This is a version of double occupancy that bears on the definition of the nation as 'modern': old and new both make their claims on the same space. Nostalgia in Kaurismäki's cinema stages such conflicting claims of past and present, and in so doing engages in double occupancy. Double occupancy, then, must also be understood to involve multiple and contested temporal claims on subject positions, spaces, and institutional status. Kaurismäki's nostalgic images arguably interfere with or disrupt the temporality of the national and European narrative promulgated by officials, in which the Finnish welfare state, and the European Union, grow and enrich themselves, having moved from the welfare-state phase to successful competition in the global economy, according to the officials.

The temporal dimension of double occupancy is important, for it shows the perishability of national and supranational narratives of progress. In this case, the Finnish state and the EU continually present themselves as durable, whether because of their history or because of the institutional consensus on which they rest. Yet as they continually repackage their self-presentation, to respond to the issues of the news cycle, they also highlight their vulnerability. This temporal dialectic has been analysed by Andreas Huyssen. Huyssen writes that 'as the more the present of advanced consumer capitalism prevails over past and future, sucking both into an expanding synchronous space, the weaker is its grip on itself, the less stability it provides for contemporary subjects ... There is both too much and too little present at the same time...' (2000: 33). If the leading edge continually razes the past to make room for new buildings, networks, lifestyles, images, and consumption, this tendency is also a kind of self-cannibalisation. The present attacks itself, because it gets old too quickly. Even a present-day expression of nostalgia for some past object or moment does not preserve the past in the present, but is an ephemeral representation in a present that quickly erases itself. Because 'there is no pure space outside of commodity culture, however much we may desire such a space ... [m]uch depends, therefore, on the specific strategies of representation and commodification and on the context in which they are staged' (2000: 29). Nostalgia is also haunted by its contingency in relation to the past and the future. Discourses of nostalgia must struggle with the issues of durability, historical justification, and obsolescence typical of late modernity, and accordingly develop strategies of representation.

A good example of the temporal double occupancy in question is evident in fashion photography, and more broadly in manipulations of body image by way of powerful beauty products, plastic surgery, and other medical interventions. Kaurismäki rejects the standards of beauty promoted by the fashion industry and Hollywood. 'People ask me, "Why do you use such ugly actors?" For me, they're beautiful. I don't know what people mean by beautiful actors. Bruce Willis, maybe?' (in Romney 1997: 13). The notion here is one of authenticity in contrast to manipulation. The images of celebrities and models that appear on the covers and in the contents of fashion magazines are routinely manipulated with image-processing software to correlate with idealised and presumably impossible notions of beauty. These images entice consumers to aspire to a future appearance, but undermine one's foothold in the present, which is defined by its lack and its possibility for transformation in the future. 'Heartless retouching ... has taken a much too big part in how women are being visually defined today', says a fashion magazine art director commenting on a controversy created by several French magazines that rejected image manipulation (Wilson 2009). In other words, the present is too powerful, for the fashion magazines establish an impossible standard; but at the same time the present is too weak, continually inadequate in relation to the standards it projects into the future or nostalgically conjures from the past. Yet if this contested present results in nostalgia for authenticity, we can immediately see that nostalgia, too, is contested by multiple claims. Producing nostalgic and authentic-looking images leads to alternative forms of image manipulation and presentation, for example lighting and colour design, or layout and font, which of course also result in defining the present in terms of lack, inviting other, more fashionable representations. Nostalgia can be seen as simply another available tactic for product differentiation, and so subject to the same contradictory claims on its status.

Kaurismäki's nostalgia provides a means of studying nostalgia as an intersection between a number of cinematic and cultural discourses. It stages a contestation of the present via the past in ways that arguably bolster several cultural-political outlooks. Arguments about nostalgia in Kaurismäki's work have nevertheless tended to circumscribe his cinema in narrowly national terms, overlooking the multiple claims possible. Yet when we look at the struggles over this cinema, we will find that such limiting arguments continually run up against a disruptive aspect within the nostalgic articulation, a staging of double occupancy, if you will. By outlining three varieties of nostalgic stories told about Kaurismäki's cinema – archivist, anachronistic, and ethical nostalgia – an alternative view of nostalgia in Kaurismäki's cinema comes into view, what I call everyday nostalgia. Everyday nostalgia brings us back to the issue of double occupancy, which can be elaborated further to show the way Kaurismäki's cinema calls for a category of national cinema, but also disrupts and undermines such a category.

The Stupid People

The name of this model comes from the book *Tyhmän kansan teoria* (*Theory of the Stupid People*), a thought-provoking 1994 study by the folklorist Seppo Knuuttila. In his critique of folklore, anthropological, and cultural theory, Knuuttila identifies a version of colonialist theorising that works by way of the critic identifying the text on which he's commenting with a stigmatised yet also potentially positively valued representation of the past, at the same time as the critic designates himself as representative of that past. Knuuttila's argument is reminiscent of Gayatri Spivak's arguments about the subaltern. Elites can see the people as ignorant, static, parochial, and pre-modern. A romanticised view of the same people finds in them originality, custom, devotion, and authenticity. In Finnish national discourse, the Finnish-speaking, land-owning peasantry functioned as the central symbol and constituency for the construction of a national culture during the nineteenth century. Folklore studies were crucial in attributing this identity, for scholars of folklore could produce a folk and nation capable and worthy of bringing together the Swedish-speaking elites and the Finnish-speaking peasantry in a unified nation. Finnish-speaking academics and writers often sought to encourage identification with the folk by way of the 'stupid people' argument. The argument rests on the notion that the 'ordinary people', sub-alterns, left behind by modernity and stuck in the past, need an intellectual advocate to make their case to the elites. The people are too simple, or stupid, to represent themselves. Elites, for their part, need to learn from the ordinary people, for ordinary people's connection with the past is not a liability, but in fact a connection to authenticity and tradition, which can be seen as a moral source for the nation. Because elites cannot fully appreciate the ordinary people, the latter's champions must make elites see the masses' inherent genius. This relationship is always tense in its normative aspirations.

The sociologist Pertti Alasuutari (1996) has analysed a similar phenomenon in discourses of Finnish national identity, although he places more stress on the power differentials involved. He argues that '*suomalaisuus puhe*', or Finnishness talk, works in a twofold manner. Commentators define national characteristics in ways that essentialise the object of their discourse while elevating themselves to a position external and implicitly superior to the ordinary people. The power differential makes assuming the role of commentator highly valuable, for the commentator can speak in the name of the people to the empowered, while positioning himself outside both formations.

Stupid people arguments about Kaurismäki's nostalgia became prominent during the 1990s, and in particular with the road film *Take Care of Your Scarf, Tatiana*. Such arguments can of course be made about his early films. One critic called a 1983 article '*Crime and Punishment* in Helsinki: The Past in the Present', a title that indicates the extent to which what critics now call nostalgia was evident in Kaurismäki's first films (Montonen 1983).[2] Yet the archive of Finnish and international criticism on Kaurismäki from the 1980s treats him not as a nostalgic but examines his aesthetic and philosophical agenda. Analyses focused on the films' intertextuality, the links to the French New Wave, Kaurismäki's prolific production pace, his films' connections to Finnish rock music, existentialist themes, the paternalism of the Finnish state, and the poor quality of Finnish cinema, among others. Stupid people accounts of Kaurismäki's nostalgia correlate with the shift to the Third Republic, discussed in chapter two. This shift also correlates with Kaurismäki's rise to international prominence on the film festival circuit. Suggesting that Kaurismäki spoke for the people, but that Finnish elites did not recognise this genius who had been recognised abroad, lent emotional force to stupid-people arguments.

The stupid people argument is strikingly present in a 1991 conversation between Kaurismäki and Peter von Bagh:

> PvB: Your films' characters, as well as the milieus, have a sort of ineluctable innocence, which is in no way a phenomenon of today's Kingdom of Esko Aho.[3] We don't find the perverse types we find everywhere else nowadays.
>
> AK: The most modern figures are from somewhere in the 1960s or 1970s. It's figures from the 1970s who are the workers in my films, and that's probably about right for today, too. Workers don't change in the workplace, although that doesn't apply to what they do in their leisure time. Workers still wear their coveralls, and happily they still do not use plastic in the production of industrial equipment, which means we can shoot on the factory floor. It seems pretty much impossible for me to put a computer terminal in the frame. I don't know where I picked up my hate for contemporary design, including lived environments, buildings, cars, and clothing. Maybe it's not hate for modernity so much as love for the past – which I've only seen in the movies anyhow. (1991: 10)

Von Bagh's sarcastic political contextualisation of Kaurismäki's cinema reveals several registers that recurrently turn up in the stupid-people arguments. Von Bagh's comment asserts that Kaurismäki's films transcend the political circumstances of the day – vouching for their aesthetic status. Second, von Bagh suggests that the source of the films' transcendence is their guileless characters, who stand in sharp contrast to the politician and the perversity he represents. Finally, von Bagh stakes out an outsider position for Kaurismäki and himself by implying that appreciation of the films' characters' innocence is unusual in society at large. In the remark then we have an aesthetic argument, a political critique, and a discursive positioning as dissident. In these we find a link to a 'foundational fiction' of Finnish national culture, that elite and people are separated but should be united (see Koivunen 2006).[4] By positioning the humble characters of Kaurismäki's films against the ascendant politician and the narrative of erosion in which he figures, von Bagh asserts that Kaurismäki's films are the corrective to the perversity. Von Bagh and Kaurismäki invoke a set of associated oppositions that structure their position and related nostalgia: metal versus plastic, artisanal craft versus automated production, labour versus capital, materiality versus abstraction, locality versus globalism, perversity versus moderation, past versus present.

Such a chain of associations also figures prominently in the work of critic Lauri Timonen, an associate of von Bagh. Timonen wrote the first book in Finnish on Kaurismäki's cinema, and has written numerous articles on the director including several in *The Finnish National Filmography*, arguably defining the canonical view. He has also made a short film, produced by Kaurismäki's Sputnik Ltd. Timonen puts nostalgia at the heart of Kaurismäki's cinema, making him both outsider and spokesperson for the ordinary people; 'The distinguishing mark of Aki Kaurismäki's cinema is its "double-vision", which seamlessly juxtaposes present and past, in which the latter stands as the measure of the former. Once things were better in the world and among people, and since things have declined, maybe forever' (2005: 57). Timonen argues for a different double-vision than the kind analysed by Baudelaire or Elsaesser. Timonen maintains that what is at stake in Kaurismäki's cinema is not only love for the past, but a pure and unsullied past, which stands as an opposite to the present. Such a view associates the past with an exterior discursive position, because it implies that that position in the past is characterised by harmony and wholeness. It is also an example of the theory of the stupid people, or 'Finnishness talk'.

The Archivist

An interesting argument about the aesthetics of Kaurismäki's nostalgia, which also involves some of the weaknesses of the stupid people theory, is evident in what Kaurismäki scholar Satu Kyösola has called 'archivist nostalgia'. Cinematic authorship here is understood as a tool for expressing a personal outlook, which values conserving and preserving a disappearing past, which would otherwise be destroyed. 'Archiving what will soon disappear is an attempt to refashion irreversible time, to master the ephemeral, to preserve the vanishing, to keep in memory what one is destined to forget, even if the task is condemned to failure' (Kyösola 2004b: 47). Kaurismäki has spoken about his films in this way, as Kyösola shows. This argument links to the stupid people argument, for it supposes that the archivist must act on behalf of the people to identify and collect what would otherwise be lost, because the people would not preserve it.

The argument about archivist nostalgia understands nostalgia as a variety of realism. Cinematically, the argument is a version of André Bazin's theory of film, and culturally it is a variety of what Svetlana Boym calls 'restorative nostalgia' (2001). In the cinematic dimension, the argument maintains that Kaurismäki fills the frame with outdated objects because he wishes to freeze the decline incurred by capitalist modernity's creative destruction. This claim de-emphasises the aesthetics of representation and focuses on the way Kaurismäki ostensibly records objects and spaces on film, employing depth of field and long takes that allow spectators to register and contemplate objects and spaces, and the people using and inhabiting them. In its cultural dimension, the argument implies that the films 'musealise' as a way of compensating for loss; that is, the filmmaker collects and records as a means of creating an alternative cultural space in which values of the past are preserved and can continue to speak.

The plausibility of this argument is made plain in the films. In the opening sequence of *Ariel*, for example, we see the *keskiolutbaari*, the jukebox, Taisto Kasurinen's cardboard valise, the transistor radio, and an old Cadillac. Indeed one of the recurrent settings in Kaurismäki's films is the *keskiolutbaari* or *ruokabaari*, an institution associated primarily with rural Finland of the 1970s, as discussed in chapter two, but now largely gone. One book on the institution construes such beer bars as 'the people's living room' (see Numminen 1986). Ilona works in such a bar in *Drifting Clouds*, Rahikainen eats lunch in one early in *Crime and Punishment*, Iiris has a beer in one in *The Match Factory Girl*, and M and Nieminen visit one in *The Man Without a Past*. As a 'low' cultural site, stigmatised by the alcohol regulatory discourse, such bars connote authenticity, suggests Anu Koivunen (2006). Not only are these places, things, and curiosities old, they carry an indexical realism: someone had to find them, register them, collect them, before they disappeared.

Kyösola puts emphasis on the combination of temporal, national, and cinematic discourses in Kaurismäki's films. In a reading of *Juha*, for example, Kyösola argues that the silent film's intertext introducing Juha and Marja as figures defined by their 'childlike happiness' uses the Finnish countryside and material culture of the 1950s and 1960s to indicate that the past is a moral source of innocence and happiness (2007: 178). Home within the national past can be preserved by the cinema, even if the cinema can only substitute for this lost object. Kyösola emphasises the collecting practice necessary to Kaurismäki's films' *mise-en-scène*, linking the director's project to the Snellmanian Fennomani collectors of the late nineteenth century, who sought to collect folklore and material culture as a means of documenting the richness of, and preserving, the national past (2004b: 47–8). This realism makes Kaurismäki's cinema a sort of indexical representative of his nostalgic mentality: his films are the smoke which bears witness to the fire of the past. Kyösola points out that the dedication of a film like *Ariel*, to 'the memory of Finnish reality', or *Tatiana*, 'a personal farewell to old Finland', indicate the significance of the archivist project for Kaurismäki. *Ariel, Take Care of Your Scarf, Tatiana,* and *Juha* preserve a national innocence, which though lost continues to provide an aspirational ideal (see Kyösola 2007).

The story of archivist nostalgia also involves a problematic notion about the stability of the past, that overlooks the ambivalence we highlighted in discussing temporality and double occupancy. When we take for granted that the past can be represented through indexical realism, we assume that the past is given, unchanging, and uncontroversial. The past is reduced to a fetishised object: a jukebox, a Cadillac, a valise, which communicates a simple meaning. An old-fashioned beer mug in the *keskiolutbaari* stands for authentic community. But, as we saw in our discussion of the history of alcohol discourse in Finnish history, that beer mug and the context in which it is drunk from has been fraught with conflict. Such debates continually change in meaning as they are used in diverse contexts towards different ends. What, then, does a nostalgia premised on indexical realism show us? We cannot take present or past for granted, Elsaesser and Huyssen argue, for the past is a subject to double occupancy.

Anachronistic Nostalgia

Anachronistic nostalgia sees Kaurismäki's films' nostalgia as constructed through *mise-en-scène* and formal principles that are purposely disjunctive in their representation of past and present. The disjointed temporal representation in the films works to question the historical narratives of triumph and progress told about Finland's modernisation, Europeanisation, and globalisation between the 1940s and the 2000s. The anachronistic nostalgia story implies a similar claim to the one Pam Cook makes about nostalgia, maintaining that the aesthetics of Kaurismäki's cinema critique historiographical constructions of post-war Finland. This understanding of Kaurismäki's cinema might also be compared to Svetlana Boym's (2001) concept of reflective nostalgia, which constructs self-aware gaps in its representation of the past, allowing for the pleasure of nostalgia but also providing the intellectual distance that putatively fosters critical examination of the relations between past and present. The argument has been advanced by the sociologist Ilpo Helén, and echoed to some degree by film scholar Anu Koivunen (2006). A version of it has also been elaborated by Henry Bacon (2003) in an analysis of the anachronistic representation of urban space in Kaurismäki's films, which he speaks of as a poetics of displacement. Pietari Kääpä (2008) has also contributed to this view, arguing that the disjunctive spaces of Kaurismäki's cinema cannot be reconciled in a single national space.

The evidence for the anachronistic nostalgia story is particularly clear in images that appear to date Kaurismäki's films in a historically specific manner. *The Match Factory Girl* includes television images of the demonstrations at Tiananmen Square in June 1989, *The Man Without a Past* shows a dated newspaper. In *Drifting Clouds*, we hear a television news broadcast from Finland's public TV1, which relates news of Typhoon Angela's landfall in the Philippines and the execution of Ogoni author Ken Saro-Wiwa and eight other Ogoni activists by the Nigerian government. Included as diegetic sound, the news broadcast is an ostensibly authentic one which dates the film's narrative precisely to TV1's reporting of these events in November 1995. Yet this apparently specific dating also includes a disruptive anachronism. Presented as a single report on historical events that have occurred within the film's diegesis, Typhoon Angela and Saro-Wiwa do not actually belong together, or in the same news broadcast. Typhoon Angela struck the Philippines on 2 November 1995, killing 882 people and resulting in damages worth 9.33 billion Philippine pesos before the storm dissipated in the Gulf of Tonkin on 7 November 1995. Saro-Wiwa was executed on 10 November 1995. In other words, the documentary referent has been constructed through editing, yet is presented to imply historical specificity. On the anachronistic nostalgia account, this construction shows us Kaurismäki's method in microcosm. By constructing the film through disparate temporal units of meaning, which invite a realist reading and assumption of continuity, the films create apparent unities from parts that under analysis reveal clashes. The contradictions among the images and units of meaning disrupt the reality they appear to represent, thereby raising questions about the relationship between representations and their referents, signifiers and signifieds.

A useful elaboration of the argument is offered by Ilpo Helén in a reading of *The Match Factory Girl*. He argues that the representation of time in Kaurismäki's films questions the possibility of community, which the films construe in quasi-Marxist terms as the construction of the ruling class:

> The milieu inhabited by Iiris Rukka, her mother, and her stepfather appears as a working-class home from the late 1960s and early 1970s (albeit with a television broadcasting news broadcasts from the 1980s). Aarne, for his part, is a 1980s' yuppie. These contradictory strata are tied together in the figure of Iiris. Yet the contradictions that constitute the ahistoricism contrast sharply: the 1960s and 1980s are not tied together by historical change and development, but by exploitation and alienation. (1991: 18)

For Helén, the films put emphasis on anachronistic contrasts that show how national elites have constructed the nation as a unified, historical agent. The contrasts make clear that the historical discourse of unity and collective agency is in fact built upon and sustains exploitation that secures the interests of the elite. The many anachronistic juxtapositions, suggests Helén, disrupt national historical narratives, raising questions about the narrative of national advancement, progress, and self-understanding. Helén's argument can be compared to Harvey and Huyssen, for Helén argues that Kaurismäki stages a 'failure' of heritage-industry principles to show the way the state uses heritage-industry stories to create a narrative of national progress.

Yet if the purpose of Kaursimäki's anachronistic nostalgia is to stage an interpretive dilemma, the dilemma created can easily lead to other construals of the nostalgia when we put greater emphasis on the aesthetics, and less on cultural politics. One aesthetic route is to note that the anachronisms contribute to a recurrent representation of isolation, which suggests an entirely different kind of nostalgia than we have discussed so far. A second route sees the anachronisms as constituting an aesthetic entirety that in sum gives proof of the artistic genius of Kaurismäki as a modernist filmmaker.

Nostalgia is a collective emotion, one which conjures shared experiences of the past. The Latin roots *nostos* and *algia*, points out Svetlana Boym, literally mean a longing for a home most often connoting a homeland, people, or ethnos (2001: 3). Desire for a unified community is a seminal feature of nostalgia in Kaurismäki's cinema, suggest Rossi and Seutu (2007). Yet does the nostalgia express a desire for community? The films formally chop up and isolate their characters, often depicting social groups and institutions as the enemies of the isolated characters in the films. Henri Boulanger does not long to return to France (they did not like him there), the Leningrad Cowboys do not long to return to the plains of Ostrobothnia, and many of the films conclude with escape rather than reunion. This anti-communal dimension is evident formally in the films. Over and over, editing is used to depict characters as cut apart and cut off. In *The Match Factory Girl*, the composition of the shot depicting Iiris's stepfather's visit to the hospital cuts off his head, creating an image of separation and alienation – in addition to a cinematic pun.[6] After M is beaten in *The Man Without a Past*, we see discrete images of his hand, his back, his feet sticking out in the bathroom, each of which emphasise his dismembered, dehumanised abjection. Nikander's lonely execution of his daily routine in *Shadows in Paradise* – driving the garbage truck, shopping at the grocery store, preparing dinner for himself – use composition and lighting inspired by film noir to underscore the character's isolation. In examining these themes and formal elements, it begins to seem that the object of nostalgia is not community, togetherness, or fullness, but loneliness, alienation, and exile. The disjunctions of anachronistic nostalgia can thus be seen to stage isolation formally, as a means of giving emphasis to the experience of men whose principles cast them 'out of time', hiving off their existence, the Raskolnikovs and Rahikainens.

In this version of anachronistic nostalgia, it becomes comprehensible in aesthetic terms as the articulation of a longing for the cinematic representation of isolation prominent in some American and European inter-war and post-war cinema, and in particular the auteur cinema, in which Kaurismäki finds his inspiration.[7] We see this detachment in French poetic realism, for example. Isolation defines the characters of Jean (Jean Gabin) in *Port of Shadows*, as well as Gabin's roles as the title character in *Pepe le Moko* and as Jacques Lantier in *La bête humaine*. Similar disconnection figures in the protagonists of Hollywood film noir too, for example Roy Earle (Humphrey Bogart) in the early noir *High Sierra* (1941), or Philip Marlowe in the adaptations of Raymond Chandler's hardboiled fiction. Godard's characters are also often deeply isolated, from Michel Poiccard (Jean-Paul Belmondo) to Lemmy Caution (Eddy Constantine). Truffaut's Antoine Doinel films are a study in isolation. We find similar representations through the canon of the European art film. In this view, then, the formal gaps and disjunctions that comprise anachronistic nostalgia can fetishise isolation as it figures in the history of cinema.

When we put the emphasis on the aesthetics of anachronistic nostalgia, yet a final and different account emerges. Film critic Markku Koski argues that the anachronisms are the mark of modernist, aesthetic originality. He draws on Georg Simmel to make this case, recalling how Simmel argues that art stands in contrast to design and craft, inasmuch as design is defined by consistency of stylisation and hence can be understood to represent the style of its times. The artist invents his own inimitable idiom, which attracts attention because of its comparatively exceptional and transgressive qualities. Koski writes:

> The office of a large company, a government agency, or a furniture company's display at a design convention must be carefully stylised; comparable unity of stylisation in a home would betray bad taste or social striving. A stylised home is not a home; it is a representational object … The images in Kaurismäki's films, full of anachronisms and stylistic blunders, are realism that has been coloured in a unique way. Our homes, surroundings, and clothes are full of similar anachronism. (2006)

The problem with this account is that cinema is here reduced to a question of personal style by way of a metaphor that equates the film artefact with the home or one's wardrobe. By finding an equivalence between decorating one's home or choosing one's clothes and making and putting into circulation hundreds of prints of a film, Koski reduces a broad cultural dialogue into an instance of personal expression. In so doing, the anachronistic nostalgia in question loses its social or political interest.

By creating gaps and disjunctions, Kaurismäki's films can be seen to open holes that invite filling, that is to say dialogue. That process results in multiple claims and instances of double occupancy. The many layers of Kaurismäki's films at least stage a problem of dialogue, which cannot be reduced to the singular statement or style attributed to the director. In making visible the rich layering of these films, the anachronistic nostalgia view pushes us beyond the kind of formalist reading advanced by Koski, and towards the open-ended questions raised by Helén, Koivunen, Bacon, and Kääpä. The issue is whether the questions made possible through anachronistic nostalgia are present for their own sake, or whether they figure in some broader project. In turning to a further account of nostalgia, the ethical nostalgia view, we find one description of what such a project may be.

Ethical Nostalgia

Ethical nostalgia is well illustrated by an anecdote Kaurismäki tells about the Arriflex camera he purchased from Ingmar Bergman:

> I still make films on Bergman's old camera. When Bergman quit directing films with *Fanny and Alexander* I bought his old camera. I still make films with it, although I have a more modern camera. The one I bought from Bergman is just more beautiful. That is, I do not film with it because it is Bergman's old camera, but because it is simply a beautiful camera. (In Puukko 2000: 474)

On one level, there is an ethos of craft in this discussion: the beautiful tool facilitates the craft by inspiring the artist. Mastery of the tool involves a quasi-feudal continuity of craftsmanship, as the apprentice dutifully learns his trade from the master.

In a second dimension, Kaurismäki's comments on Bergman's camera can also be understood as a nostalgia that contests contemporary filmmaking practice. By using Bergman's camera, Kaurismäki creates a material link between his films and a specific tradition of visual expression, which Kaurismäki suggests differs from what he alleges is a contemporary decline of visual expression:

> The trend has gotten to the point where during the last two decades there has been a conscious effort to cultivate generations of viewers who will only watch certain kinds of films. The film clubs were destroyed so that no one could inadvertently demand anything but what is being offered. Viewers are no longer aware of cinema's magnificent history. (Ibid.)

Bergman's camera serves as an object of dissent, a way of using nostalgia to claim a history that challenges viewers' assumptions about the cinema, and proposes alternative modes of filmmaking. The tool of the filmmaker introduces an alternative, by which visual culture can be revitalised to undermine its predominant form of production.

Finally, the 'beauty' of Bergman's camera also involves an ethos of intrinsic value. Bergman's camera is not only a means of establishing continuity and unity with a craft tradition or history of visual expression; in providing no justification for its use other than its beauty, the camera expresses a self-reflexive opting out of discursive justification. It is simply beautiful. As a consequence, it is not only an affirmation of beauty, but dialectically a rejection of technological choices motivated by marketing agendas and audience tastes. Such choices are construed by Kaurismäki as cynical, soulless, and destructive of film culture. Films like *Star Wars: Episode I – The Phantom Menace* (George Lucas, 1999) illustrate the target of Kaurismäki's critique – a conceptually conservative text whose value arguably rests on its status as a brand and potential return as an investment instrument.

An argument about ethical nostalgia which takes as its premise some notion of opting out of commerce must confront Huyssen's claim that there is no outside to the commodity culture. As we saw in the Introduction, Kaurismäki's visibility in the domestic and transnational media has been built on the critical and commercial successes of his films primarily at the A-List European film festivals of Berlin, Cannes, and Venice. The festivals are crucial to the financial success of the films in the many markets in which they are distributed. The ethical nostalgia rejects the economic success that makes possible the visibility. But an art film that grosses €40million, as did *The Man Without a Past*, generates broad media attention (see Näveri 2002a, 2003). While Kaurismäki and his cinema advocate for simple values of the past, the platform for such advocacy, Kaurismäki's cultural power, derives largely from his success and visibility.

Everyday Nostalgia

Halfway through *Ariel* a Finnish judge unjustly puts Taisto Kasurinen in prison for appearing to commit assault with a deadly weapon. The sentence ends the laid-off miner's search for a job in Helsinki, and also disrupts his new relationship with Irmeli, who is working four jobs to repay multiple loans. One of the jobs is as a slaughterhouse worker, a metonymic occupation for a dehumanising capitalism in Kaurismäki's cinema. Made with Bergman's camera and adhering to Kaurismäki's idiosyncratic aesthetic, *Ariel* might also be understood in terms of ethical nostalgia. There is another dimension of nostalgia in this film and in Kaurismäki's filmmaking practice, however, which has gone unremarked but which enriches the account of nostalgia in Kaurismäki's cinema. We can call it 'everyday nostalgia'. The adjective everyday connotes an attitude, affective stance and set of practices motivating the nostalgic elements in the films and the filmmaking practice. Focusing our analysis on the attitude, its cinematic representation, and associated filmmaking practice helps capture the double occupancy and immanence in Kaurismäki's nostalgia. Everyday nostalgia involves an attitude that leads to a many layered negotiation between past and present.

Everyday nostalgia is evident in Taisto's entry into prison in *Ariel*. When Taisto arrives at the prison, a processing officer's questions elicit the matriculating prisoner's name and former occupation, while revealing he has nothing else: no religion, no place of residence, no home or address, no living family, no spouse, no children, and worldly possessions ironically comprised of a watch, a cigarette lighter, and a Finnish social insurance card in a wallet empty of cash. Is Taisto as a representative of the past, a melodramatic victim of the present? Should we read this scene as an allegory of an all-powerful capitalist system crushing a diminutive citizen? No, for Taisto is a scrapper and a survivor, rather than a lumbering monument of the past. There is a level of entanglement and negotiation between present and past in *Ariel*, also evident in the other films. Moreover, this negotiation points towards an analysis of Kaurismäki's relationship to cinema. As a filmmaker, Kaurismäki can be seen as something of a Taisto, too.

The images, sounds, and dialogue that depict Taisto's entry into prison are a portrait of stubbornness, but also stupid adherence to principle. Taisto lands in prison because he repeatedly does *the wrong things*, just as he drives across a snowy landscape from northern to southern Finland in a Cadillac convertible with the top down, because he cannot operate the roof. He gets mugged and robbed. He gets swindled. He gets arrested and thrown in prison. He allows his friend Mikkonen to take a risk that leads to Mikkonen's death. *Why does Taisto do all the wrong things?* It is not a matter of naïve innocence and misplaced trust, for Taisto knows how to work, how to get up from a knockdown, and fire a handgun. What we have is inertia, a displaced man whose habits and ways are ill-suited to the world he inhabits, but who slowly refashions himself to inhabit a new social world. This conflict between habit and inhospitable social world recurs in Kaurismäki's cinema thematically, through the director's typically displaced characters, but also aesthetically, through Kaurismäki's particular interpretation of the history of cinema aesthetics. His films are continually concerned with adaptation and coping. The negotiation between habit and social world also figures in the mode of production of Kaurismäki's films, from their circumscribed budgeting practice to the stylised anachronisms of the films' marketing material. Kaurismäki has stubbornly stuck to a filmmaking practice that is at once readily recognisable in its connections to underground filmmaking and auteur filmmaking, yet distinct in its adaptation of principles from these. These elements and practices engage in dialogue with current cinematic, cultural, political, and not least economic discourses, but use the past to resist assimilation to these discourses, seeking to push them in alternative directions – an argument already developed in our discussion of ironic bohemianism. This stubborn attitude creates a remainder, something which cannot be absorbed or assimilated by the discourses critiqued. We see this remainder in Taisto's blank but animated look, his hunching gait, his clumsiness, and dumb luck, as well as the characters Nikander in *Shadows in Paradise*, Henri in *I Hired a Contract Killer*, M in *The Man Without a Past*, and Koistinen in *Lights in the Dusk*.

A compelling account of the remainder as relevant to nostalgia is suggested by Michel de Certeau's notions of everyday life as practice, poetics, and tactics. Certeau's abiding question is similar to the one raised continually in Kaurismäki's films: how do subjects persist within social systems that aspire to determine subjective identities and practice? In asking this question, Certeau's thought differs from theorists like Marx, Freud, and Foucault, and their many interpreters, whose theories emphasise how social forces and relationships constitute modes of control, determination, and subject formation. In contrast, the fundamental outlook in Certeau's thought concerns resistance, as aptly described by historian Nathalie Zemon Davis:

> Certeau developed a distinctive way of interpreting social and personal relations. In contrast to those who described societies by evoking what he called homogeneities and hegemonies – what unified and controlled them – Certeau wanted to identify the creative and disruptive presence of 'the other' – the outsider, the stranger, the alien, the subversive, the radically different – in systems of power and thought. He found it not only in the ways people imagined figures distant from them ... But also in behaviours and groups close to home, in the ever-present tensions at the heart of all social life, whether in schools, religious institutions, or the mass media. (2008: 57)

The 'ever-present tension' Davis identifies arises from practices like walking through the city, narrating, reading, and ultimately decaying and dying, all of which resist and transform engineered systems, technologies, and institutions that constitute modern forms of social order. Within everyday life, Certeau famously argues, there are many ways people adapt and repurpose determinative forces such as market and state, and it is through these practices that past and present intertwine. Certeau's analysis focuses on the notion of contested spaces that are also part of Elsaesser's analysis.

One of the dangers in Certeau's thought is its amenability to exaggeration and romanticisation of quotidian forms of resistance. In a book on Certeau's poetics of the everyday, Ben Highmore writes that 'for the most part, responses to Certeau's work have opted for a limited focus, considering only those aspects of his work that evoke daily practices of guerrilla-like and subversive opposition, ignoring those practices perhaps more "everyday", that connect with memory, stubbornness, and inertia' (2006: 103). Highmore goes on to point out that there are several overlapping categories through which Certeau distinguishes between everyday practices: the hidden, the multiform and extensive, the devious, and the stubborn. The hidden and stubborn character of everyday life practices in Certeau's theory figure all too little in most discussion, suggests Highmore, yet it is in these dimensions that Certeau's analysis is most subtle, and most relevant to Kaurismäki's nostalgia. The hidden and stubborn practices involve the adaptation and modification of quotidian ways to function in capitalist modernity. The shopkeeper who runs a for-profit enterprise, but does so as a means of engaging with a particular group within a city. The adaptation of fast-food restaurants, airports, and office spaces to serve their employees' needs, rather than customers. Taking these practices as an object of study avoids assuming a binary opposition between capitalist modernity and community (see Highmore 2006: 111). The restaurant, the store, and the family meal cannot be separated from the late-modern capitalist system and its conflicts, but can also sustain signifying practices which obdurately differentiate and sustain these activities. In these hidden and stubborn practices we see the interpenetration of competing claims, which are hybrid and subject to negotiation. So, for example, the store is both a for-profit enterprise and

Taisto (Turo Pajala) finally gets an industrial job while in prison in *Ariel* (1988) (used with permission of Sputnik Ltd.)

community gathering point. Or to turn to the films, the restaurant in *Drifting Clouds* involves business, fantasy, nostalgia, style, and humour, which cannot be parsed into singular, homogeneous units of past and present, mainstream and unique. Here again we also find Elsaesser's double occupancy, which concerns the ongoing negotiation over such competing claims. In capturing hidden and stubborn aspects of quotidian practice, Kaurismäki's films render nostalgia an affective node of agonistic claims and questions, rather than reducing nostalgia to an object to be depicted or a narrative to be disrupted.

A good example of everyday nostalgia, the attitude it involves, and the relevance of Certeau are made evident in Taisto's fashioning of a ring for Irmeli while in prison. Why does Taisto make a wedding band from scrap metal? What in his past causes him to take such risks to complete this symbolic task? It is a strange choice, insofar as the diegesis suggests that Taisto's only family life has been difficult. Taisto witnesses his father's suicide without a tear, and he doesn't hang around for the funeral. The film tells us nothing about his mother or family. Taisto resembles Iiris in *The Match Factory Girl* to a degree, for Taisto's wedding band calls to mind Iiris's response to her bleak family life. In response to crushing family circumstances, both cling to romantic fantasies. There are no happy families in Kaurismäki's films. Yet his families believe they can bend institutions like marriage, prison, the law, and the market to their needs – and they usually do, just a little. They adhere to these beliefs through habit, material practices, and the fashioning of objects – like Iiris's taffeta dress – which maintain a modicum of hope.

In Taisto's case, the ring is nostalgic, for it gives form to an idea of love which has no place or image in the narrative of the film, which is dominated by the legal order of the state. The ring defies the state in an appeal to an extra-legal, moral order, yet Taisto and Irmeli's marital aspirations also depend on the state's recognition of their union. They go to the magistrate to marry them after Taisto escapes from prison. In this tiny struggle we see precisely how nostalgia matters: memory and habit contest new or current practices by raising questions about the latter's rationale, thereby calling for alternatives. Yet these questions are introduced within the practices and institutions of the system. To be sure, while heterosexual couplehood as narrative closure can be read allegorically as a new beginning, the hero going off into the sunset, it can also be seen as 'confirmation of social exclusion of those not empowered by romance and compulsory intimacy', as Anu Koivunen has pointed out (2006: 141).

Another way to see this episode unpacks another allegorical layer, concerning Kaurismäki's relationship to cinema. Certeau would arguably describe Taisto's fashioning of the wedding band in terms of '*la perruque*', or the wig. By this term Certeau means neither theft nor malingering, but workers' covert use of their employers' tools or surplus resources in symbolically important projects.

> The worker who indulges in *la perruque* actually diverts time (not goods, since he uses only scraps) from the factory for work that is free, creative, and precisely not directed toward profit. In the very place where the machine he must serve reigns supreme, he cunningly takes pleasure in finding a way to create gratuitous products whose sole purpose is to signify his own capabilities through his *work* and to confirm his solidarity with other workers or his family through *spending* his time in this way. (1984: 24–5; emphasis in original)

In *la perruque*, suggests Certeau, resistance occurs when the worker uses time in a way that has no motivation in the economic logic that commodifies workers' time as labour power. In using his time for non-economic relationships, whose rationale is not profitability, the worker finds motivation for his activity in a contrasting moral order. Just as the beautiful camera cannot be explained as an economic choice, 'the wig' cannot be explained by economic relationships. By juxtaposing Taisto's fashioning of the ring with his unhappy search for work and imprisonment, *Ariel* establishes a contrast that makes evident coexisting moral and legal orders, which make divergent claims on social spaces and institutions, which in their turn find their rationale in discrete temporalities. The contrast also finds a particularly clear expression in the later film *The Man Without a Past*, when the guard Anttila says, 'the state does not sin'. Indeed, sin belongs to the moral order to which Taisto and other characters in Kaurismäki's films appeal, and the state is premised on a legal order. Yet they coexist, and we understand Anttila's humorous metaphor. These films stage precisely the conflicts of double occupancy we have been tracking.

Narrative instances of *la perruque* and everyday nostalgia recur throughout Kaurismäki's films, often creating contrasts that put the focus on practices and objects that exist within orders to which they have ambivalent yet tenacious relationships. The characters in the films continually duck company rules and state laws in the interest of helping friends and confirming solidarity with others. In the early films written by Aki Kaurismäki and directed by his brother Mika – such as *The Liar* and *The Worthless* – Ville Alfa disrupts not only employment situations, but rule-bound settings of all kinds. The relationship between the manager Vladimir and the band members of the Leningrad Cowboys stages

Taisto surreptitiously fabricates a ring for Irmeli, in *Ariel's* instance of *la perruque* (used with permission of Sputnik Ltd.)

the same sort of resistance. We see a recurrence of *la perruque* in *Drifting Clouds,* in which spouses, siblings, and friends understatedly disobey workplace rules to help one another out – giving free rides, free meals, and free passes to the movies. The *topos* returns in *Lights in the Dusk,* when the security guard Koistinen seeks to impress a romantic interest by defying workplace rules, bringing about his own misfortune in a way that suggests the dubious status of morally motivated action in a market-driven society.

Certeau helps us see the extent to which these instances of *la perruque* are in fact subtle conflicts over a socio-political ethics and the moral order that underpins it, which also carry a temporal dimension.

> Into the institution to be served are thus insinuated styles of social exchange, technical invention, and moral resistance, that is, an economy of the 'gift' (generosities for which one expects a return), an esthetics of 'tricks' (artists' operations), and an ethics of tenacity (countless ways of refusing to accord to the established order the status of law, a meaning, or a fatality) … The practice of economic diversion is in reality the return of a sociopolitical ethics into an economic system. (1984: 26–7)

By withholding cooperation in the workplace, a worker differentiates his activity by justifying it with an alternative ethos to the one that predominates in the workplace. He opts out of the economically motivated measure of his subjectivity in terms of time. The economy of the gift depends on relationships premised on memory and future acts, rather than on measurement of value in terms of time spent.

Everyday nostalgia and *la perruque* are not only figurations in the films, but also a way of understanding Kaurismäki's filmmaking practice. Kaurismäki's filmmaking responds to historical conditions, in which the predominant narratives and institutions are those which produce and sell images, things, and experiences. In terms of filmmaking practice, the ambivalence of Kaurismäki's everyday nostalgia responds to a similar dilemma to the one Jean-Luc Godard described in 1963, talking about the Hollywood studio system and the *Cahiers du cinéma* canon of auteurs: 'When we were at last able to make films, we could no longer make the films which had made us want to make films. The dream of the *nouvelle vague* – which will never come about ñ is to make *Spartacus* in Hollywood on a ten million dollar budget' (in Hillier 1986: 63). Godard is not speaking of making a big-budget film, which he of course did with *Le mépris* (*Contempt*) made the same year he made this remark. Rather, he articulates a dream about working within the old Hollywood system, which had of course become an impossibility historically and aesthetically following the Paramount decision in 1948, which broke up the studio system. The inspiring films of the past, and the system that produced them, was gone, and one could only dream of making them. As for Godard, so too for Kaurismäki: making films involves a paradoxical and ambivalent situation, in which making the films he would wish to make is impossible, but making them is a means of engaging inspiration while transforming the film culture that has come down to him. Stubbornly persisting, Kaurismäki's cinema introduces into the middle-class perspective of the West an alternative ethos, creating a thought-provoking double occupancy by way of nostalgia.

Coda

The multiplicity of Kaurismäki's everyday nostalgia suggests that temporal representation can involve a subtle cultural politics. By avoiding the pitfalls of idealising the director's nostalgia to position him as a *sui generis* outsider, we are able to see a far more complex and provocative nostalgic discourse in his films. To be sure, in some ways Kaurismäki's nostalgia lends itself to being read as a localist critique of deterritorialised capital and the 'perverse' elites who manage its flows. There are some conservative dimensions to the nostalgia, which sit in contradiction with some of the more utopian elements. What is certain is that Kaurismäki's nostalgia requires a contextualisation that gets at issues of double occupancy, for it is through this term that we see how temporal disjunction involves disparate claims on the institutions, subject positions, and systems of the present. My claim is that when we attend to the textures of everyday nostalgia in the films, we begin to see a more multilayered nostalgia in the films. In this, the archivist, anachronistic, and ethical stories come together, in tension to be sure, but in a productive tension. When we take nostalgia as a prompt in dialogue, we can begin to see and hear the multiple claims, temporal registers, and stories involved. Kaurismäki's multilayered cinema prods us to engage in such dialogue, then, rather than to draw hard and fast conclusions.

In prodding us to listen and ascertain temporal double occupancy, Kaurismäki's cinema also encourages film scholars to regard nostalgia as a far more contested site of meaning-making than we tend to regard it. Even in a suggestive book like Pam Cook's, nostalgia too easily becomes past versus present, history versus memory, theory versus cultural studies. In bringing the past into the present, Kaurismäki's nostalgia stubbornly and transformatively produces contrasts and juxtapositions that generate different perspectives on discussions of nostalgia. Kaurismäki helps us see that nostalgia involves attitudes and affective stances that are far broader and varied than we often assume. And in this his films invite further attention, as well as further comparison with other filmmakers who have been concerned with the cultural politics of temporal difference and changing attitudes, from Ang Lee to Wong Kar Wai, from Todd Haynes to Mike Leigh.

Notes

1   Kaikki ei ole niin yksinkertaista kuin te luulette.
2   *Rikos ja rangaistus Helsingissä: Menneisyyttä nykypäivässä* (Montonen 1983).
3   Centre Party politician Esko Aho was Prime Minister from 1991 to 1995, leading the first centre-conservative coalition (*porvarihallitus*) in Finnish post-war history, with the exception of one coalition government formed for a few months in the late 1970s.
4   Anu Koivunen (2003) uses the term 'foundational fiction' to speak of the performatively constituted scripts in national discourses which are at once taken as 'givens' yet which have been constructed through ongoing power struggles. Within such struggles, she argues, film is a critical lever and powerful multiplier.
5   A literalist translation to the American context might be the '3.2-beer bar', referring to the percentage of allowable alcohol content for off-sale beer in gas stations in many states.
6   The word for stepfather in Finnish is *isäpuoli*, literally ' half father'. The image can thus be read as a pun on the Finnish word.
7   This thought-provoking argument about 'nostalgia for cinematic isolation' was suggested to me by the film scholar Kimmo Laine (University of Oulu), to whom I wish to express my thanks.

CHAPTER FOUR

The Finn

Over the centuries Finns have moved around the world. Some have succeeded, some haven't. We can only congratulate them for their success, and acknowledge that our country has been too confining for them. But I want to stress that understanding such lives within a national framework – which is the underlying ideology of the Commission to Develop Finland's National Brand – is a notion that belongs to the past.

Jörn Donner (2008)

How does nation, or more specifically Finnishness, figure in the cinema of Aki Kaurismäki? Finnish and non-Finnish commentators routinely understand Kaurismäki and his films as figures of nationality. Indicative titles include *K/K: A Couple of Finns and Some Donald Ducks* (Connah 1991), 'Do the Right Finn' (Floyd 1991), 'Original Finn' (Andrew 1997), 'The Mighty Finn' (Andrew 2003), 'Finnish Character: An Interview With Aki Kaurismäki' (Cardullo 2006), and 'The Finnish Touch' (Coslovich 2003). Finnish critics sometimes employ the same frame when writing about Kaurismäki: 'Suomi-elokuvan suuri hiljainen puhuu' ('Finnish cinema's silent man speaks', Sallinen, 1998), 'I melankolins finska ruinlandskap' ('In a landscape of Finnish melancholy', Sundström 2002), 'Aki Kaurismäki ja suomalainen todellisuus' ('Aki Kaurismäki and Finnish reality', Von Bagh 2002c).

An exemplary construction of Kaurismäki as 'Finn' is the journalist Wille Hammarberg's interview with Kaurismäki, which appeared in the provincial Finnish daily *Satakunnan kansa* in September 2002. The article demonstrates how commentators attribute a Finnish identity to Kaurismäki by positioning the filmmaker within a series of opposite pairs and related associations. For example, Kaurismäki does not care about money, but about friends. He disdains the film business, but loves cinema.

He makes univerSCal films, not particular ones. On the other hand, the 'opposite term' in such pairs also tells us a good deal. Kaurismäki can denigrate the film business, since he is successful. He can display indifference to the film festival network, because he has been involved in hundreds of them. Universal stories matter, because Kaurismäki's reputation is for national stories. Analysis of such examples points towards key concerns in this chapter by showing how nation causes us to ignore 'opposite pairs' and oversimplify the layers and relationships that make up an auteur's cinema. While Kaurismäki's cinema coheres with some representations of Finnishness, we see the complexities of his cinema more fully when we recognise him as a participant in ongoing, multiparty debate over the status of nation, a discourse I will call *multinational*. Further, Kaurismäki's cinema often ironically subverts and disperses conventions of national identity, at the same time as it finds its audience primarily outside of Finland. In analysing Kaurismäki's relationship to a transnational audience, it becomes clear we can understand the director as a small-nation auteur for whom transnational distribution and exhibition at film festivals is crucial. His example helps us advance understanding of the category small-nation cinema.

Other Reporters' Agendas

Hammarberg interviewed Kaurismäki at the Hamburg Film Festival, where the director was scheduled to receive the Douglas Sirk prize at the festival's gala on the eve of *The Man Without a Past*'s theatrical release in Germany. The picture and director had been in the spotlight at Cannes the previous spring. With fifty prints scheduled for the German market, one hundred and thirty for France, and the film's rights sold in forty-four total markets, the Hamburg event furnished a timely marketing opportunity for European distributors of the director's films and for Kaurismäki's production company Sputnik Ltd. What is more, the journalists awaited humour and maybe scandal from Kaurismäki. And so, Hammarberg writes, 'a representative of the Finnish press who happened to show up before the gala did not seem to stand much chance of an interview. "Well, as you took the trouble to come all the way here, you may have some of his time, since he seemed to want to talk to you. But ten minutes max,"' conceded Kaurismäki's handlers. Kaurismäki gave Hammarberg an hour. The wide-ranging interview includes many of Kaurismäki's most frequent tropes: 'I don't give a shit about money' (Hammarberg discovers Kaurismäki had given the award money from a recent prize to a film and video club for the disabled in the Finnish town Ulvila); Kaurismäki sees himself as trying to tell universal stories 'anyone can understand'; that 'love and death are life, just like planting potatoes'; that in Hamburg the director was reading a novel by early twentieth-century Finnish neorealist and ironist Joel Lehtonen; that Kaurismäki plans to go into exile if Finland joins NATO; that he thinks Social Democrat Tarja Halonen is 'a good President' for Finland; and that Kaurismäki has a busy travel schedule: 'I am leaving Hamburg for New York, then France, Italy, Japan, Portugal, and Belgium.' By the time an hour has passed, the handlers are in a rage. Hammarberg concludes: 'Since they didn't dare say anything to the director, and lacking a better target, they turned on the reporter. Although he had just sat and listened' (Hammarberg 2002). An anonymous remark is scribbled in the margin of the copy of Hammarberg's article, which is on file at the Finnish Film Archives: 'The other reporters NOT the company...'.[1]

Hammarberg's interview with Kaurismäki constructs an opposition between the business of cinema being transacted in Hamburg, and Kaurismäki the Finn. Following the prelude describing the struggle among journalists and PR representatives over access to the director, Kaurismäki is introduced as being disgusted by money.

> When he arrives, Kaurismäki makes a gesture that representatives of the European press have awaited. 'Should we have something to drink?' he says gesturing to the waiter. 'Two beers for me, and one for the reporter.' Kaurismäki does not look comfortable amid the opulence of the five-star hotel ... 'So this is it. I haven't had any chance to choose this year. But believe it or not, I don't give a shit about money. What matters most is remembering your friends.' (In Hammarberg 2002)

Hammarberg's account of Kaurismäki's behaviour and remarks differentiate the director from the hotel, the journalists, and the commercial context. The entertainment business is synonymous with rapacious pursuit of profit; in Hollywood, according to another stereotype invoked by Hammarberg, your friends are the people who can make you richer. Kaurismäki stands in an opposing camp. Friends, not money, matter to him. Further, by juxtaposing the director's beer order with remarks about money and friends, Hammarberg invokes a familiar national stereotype, which we have already seen. The honest Finn drinks his fill and gets drunk. For their part, the press exoticises Kaurismäki's drinking, hoping for the colourful or scandalous moment that might heighten sales of their publications and shows. Hammarberg presents himself as intuitively understanding Kaurismäki, identifying with the director amid the hotel lobby, content to sit over beers. The interview underscores Kaurismäki's violations of convention in the transnational art-film business, but implies that the explanation for them is to be found in the director's 'Finnishness' – a rather different notion of the national cultural export than held by Jouni Mykkänen or Suvi Lindén.

Another strand of this interview becomes evident when we ask, who wrote the note in the margin of Hammarberg's interview held at the archives? Finnish production companies and publishers maintain their own archives and also provide copies to the national archives. Read as a note scrawled by a Sputnik employee, the comment in the margin tells a story about clashing agendas. The note in the margin rebuts the reporter's supposed identification with the director, suggesting that Hammarberg failed to observe professional convention, angering the other journalists. Hamburg is an important market for Kaurismäki's films, for he is 'more than a cult director in Germany, where his most popular films will exceed 350,000 admissions' (Jensen 1994: 30). That is more than six times the admissions of Kaurismäki's best-performing films in Finland, excepting *The Man Without a Past*'s numbers. The note in the margin raises the question, what is the purpose for Kaurismäki of such a media transaction? He is deeply experienced with film festivals, having attended hundreds, and having founded the Midnight Sun Film Festival. The latter has included scores of eminent filmmakers and actors, including Samuel Fuller, Abbas Kiarostami, Chantal Akerman, Francis Ford Coppola, Carrol Ballard, Amos Gitai, Fatih Akin, and Thelma Schoonmaker, among others, while also screening Finnish films and providing a forum of conversation about contemporary Finnish cinema. In general, the film festival as an institution concentrates media attention, making it an overdetermined and crucial event for film workers, journalists, companies and investors who form networks and transact business at such events. Film festivals have little to do with categories of nation, art, or auteur, argues Marijke de Valck, despite the fundamental contribution festivals make to the perpetuation of these terms in cinema discourse; such terms as nation 'often result in thinking in binary oppositions and do not offer any starting points for considering the transnational dynamics, the multiple agendas, nor the complex spatial and temporal dimensions of the international film festival circuit' (2007: 206). In such a context, Hammarberg's story misses the point. He tells the wrong story, and crowds aside others with agendas different than his. The margin note reminds us of his error, and thereby of the complex transactional nature of an appearance by Kaurismäki at the Hamburg, Berlin, Venice, or Cannes film festivals. Hammarberg takes a niche story and tells it to a tiny general audience in Finland, the readership of his newspaper. In Hamburg, Kaurismäki is indeed a niche story, but framed and addressed to a large niche audience – and perhaps a general audience at the height of the festival – which far surpasses in size the total audience of Hammarberg's paper.

Kaurismäki's role as filmmaker and public figure involves presenting himself in different ways at different times, and in this sense Kaurismäki continually co-authors his self-presentation with the many journalists, critics, and writers who interact with him. This entails an address of a variety of audiences, but also shifts in the tone of address. Sometimes Kaurismäki plays the straight man, sometimes the ironic joker, and sometimes (if rarely) the good citizen, as he does when he remarks on President Tarja Halonen. Some interviews provide a means of heightening interest in his films. Others have taken up politics, or ethical stances held by the director. For example, one prominent story bubbled up when Kaurismäki was chosen to receive an honorary doctoral degree from the Helsinki School of Industrial Design (known as Aalto University since 2010). He refused the degree privately, but ultimately explained publicly that he objected to sharing the stage with the chief executive of a Finnish design company, that also owned a large fur concern at the time (see Kaurismäki 2001). Kaurismäki's multilayered public image recalls Richard Dyer's theory of stardom, which we have touched on over the course of this study. Layers of stardom and celebrity, argues Dyer, work to address a diverse audience in varying ways. This variance in audience address makes it necessary to move away from some of the usual categories for considering national cinema, and to approach it via an alternative framework, which I do by developing a discussion of multination and transnationalism, and by analysing Kaurismäki's cinema through the prism of Mette Hjort's theory of small-nation cinemas and Valck's discussion of film festivals. It will also prove useful to situate Kaurismäki in the niche and general audience dynamics mentioned above, which prove highly relevant to the role of the film-festival in Kaurismäki's cinema.

The multinational and the transnational

Film scholars and cultural studies scholars use the term national cinema to invoke a sense of homogeneity and cohesion, whether in speaking about continuity within a certain tradition or, by contrast, in critiquing exclusions of gender or ethnicity, for example, from an ostensibly homogeneous national culture or cinema. Yet closer analysis of any national history or cinema will lead one to qualify significantly claims about homogeneity and to come to see national cinema as 'multinational', insofar as multiple groups contest the cultural and political identity of a nation, even if there are moments of national unity as well. For instance, participants and publics involved in debates about immigration, class, and gender construct the nation in strikingly differing ways. Similarly, debates over European national cinemas since the 1960s and the advent of the state funding model have involved competing constructions of national cinema. Industry participants argue that cinema is an economic entity, maintaining the state should support films with large audiences. Some officials believe that national cinema is a political entity, and that national films should project a certain image at home and abroad. For their part, intellectuals often argue that national cinema is a cultural and aesthetic category, and that state support should go to film artists with something to say, whether they are young and promising or established; the favour of artists' films among audiences should not be relevant to the funding of national cinema. These arguments construct national culture and cinema in multiple and sometimes non-reciprocal ways. These arguments take on even greater complexity as visual culture has globalised and the materiality of cinema has changed through a proliferation of new media and distribution platforms – digital video, DVD, Internet, streaming video, digital television, on-demand television, and so forth. Such changes have fostered aesthetic transformations, from the emergence of the global martial arts film, to the rejuvenation of realism (as evident in Dogme 95) and documentary cinema, to a renaissance in national cinema, evident in the efflorescence of, among others, Danish, Mexican, and Romanian cinema since the 1990s. We have also seen a sea change in audience dynamics, as there is at once more audience for events and texts able to command national or global attention; more audiences for a cornucopia of micro-cinemas, subnational, and transnational cinemas; and less audience for traditional theatrical-release cinema, which must now compete with proliferating digital platforms – from MP4 files, to cable television, to on-demand streaming media. National cinema is at once defined by larger audiences, bigger films, and more effective release and marketing strategies, at the same time as it involves a more dispersed and fragmented audience, viewing a greater variety of cinema on a wider variety of platforms. We need to question fundamental categories to help us better fathom their relevance, at the same time as we need new categories and theoretical models to guide analysis. Studying Kaurismäki's cinema can contribute to the reconfiguration of the theoretical and analytical practices by which we study national cinema in times of globalisation.[2]

The terms 'multinational' and 'transnational' that provide the subtitle for this section designate a continuum of production, distribution, and aesthetic practices. We return to the term transnational below. Multinational here denotes the contested multiplicity of any national arena, its heterogeneity – not a commercial operation across national territories, as in the multinational corporation. A nation is never homogeneous, for even the smallest national arena consists of multiple, changing political positions and associated institutions, which find diverse allies within and beyond the borders of the state. These positions and alliances of course change over time, leading to new alignments. The theoretical impulse here is Ernesto Laclau and Chantal Mouffe's poststructuralist arguments about social identity (see Laclau and Mouffe 1985; Laclau 2005) rather than Benedict Anderson's 'Imagined Communities' argument (1991). Laclau and Mouffe argue that no representation can ever be self-sufficient, for there is always a signified which cannot be encompassed within a signifier's representation. When the nation is represented by the image of the self-sacrificing soldier, we must ask in what ways men, women, children, and groups distinct from the militarised representation of the nation are encoded in such an image. There can never be a perfect homogeneity, or identity, in questions of representation, making struggles over representation highly important to the formation of a notion of national identity, at the same time as such an identity will always be the contingent and exclusionary outcome of struggles. By contrast, Anderson famously argues that consumption of print culture constitutes a communicative space, which inculcates assumptions about strangers' identity with oneself within that space. Representations of the nation matter less in Anderson's analysis than practices and markets that cultivate and delimit imaginative interconnection. For cinema studies today, the relevance of Anderson is insignificant, for the local and transnational distribution and exhibition of cinema does not correlate with the discrete reading publics and print cultures on which Anderson's theory is premised.[3] Multinational is a term that places emphasis on the contested and changing character of any nexus of national discourse, which contributes to representation of a nation.

This argument about multinational cinema finds theoretical support in Philip Rosen's elegant argument that national cinema takes shape around cohesive and dispersive arguments, texts, and other dynamics. 'The discussion of national cinema assumes not only that there is a principle or principles of coherence among a large number of films; it also involves an assumption that those principles have something to do with the production and/or reception of those films within the legal borders (or benefiting capital controlled within) a given nation-state' (2006: 18); yet at the same time, Rosen observes, coherence is in tension with 'countervailing, dispersive forces', for example, critique of the national cinema, audience address going beyond the nation, or transnational financing of production, among others. So while commentators may stress the historical continuity and homogeneity of a national cinema – in the history of Finnish cinema the importance of natural lighting, summer-time location shots, midsummer celebrations, staging designed to make the actors 'glow' with summer enchantment, as Antti Alanen has pointed out (2005: 619) – homogeneity is a construction that always exists in tension with dispersive forces – for example the long historical preference for Hollywood imports, rather than national scenography, among Finnish audiences. When conceptualising the national in Kaurismäki's cinema, this dialectics of coherence and dispersion helps us think about his cinema as a multilayered, contradictory, and disputed body of work.

Dispersive qualities are evident in what Kaurismäki omits from his films and in their audience address, even though there are strong coherences to national convention, as we will explore shortly. In the context of Alanen's point, we can see a dispersive quality in Kaurismäki's construction of nationality. Despite critical consensus about the national character of visual expression in Kaurismäki's cinema, on the few occasions Kaurismäki includes the conventions mentioned by Alanen – as for example in *Juha* or in images of the potato garden in *The Man Without a Past* – there is a strong charge of irony, creating a tone of ambiguity in what on the surface appears to be a nod to tradition. The dialectic of coherence and dispersion is also plainly evident in questions of audience address. Kaurismäki could seek the favour of national audiences by valorising nationally coded elements in his films. But he constructs his films around one of the least symbolically privileged figures in Finnish culture, the *lumpen prole*, a small urban aggregate which does not belong to the working classes, does not belong to the intelligentsia or administrative classes, and stands a great distance from the Finnish-speaking, land-owning peasantry, around which Finnish national identity took shape. The author Kaurismäki was reading in Hamburg, Joel Lehtonen, created one of the most famous literary analogues to the lumpen prole, Juutas Käkriäinen, a landless agrarian worker who figured in Lehtonen's highly ironic critique of the Finnish intelligentsia's self-understanding at the time of the Finnish Civil War (1918). Kaurismäki often treats nationally coded elements in the films ironically or even parodically. The *Leningrad Cowboys* films, for example, mock the national audience's notions about Finnish culture in circulation outside the country – as is evident in the opening sequence of *Leningrad Cowboys Go America*. Jean Sibelius, Alvar Aalto, Lasse Virén, and Ville Valo (HIM) triumphed on the world stage, while remaining true to their roots – or at least living most of the year in Finland. The Leningrad Cowboys leave home, fail abroad, and return to a collective farm in the Ukraine, after the fall of the Soviet Union. Such parody attacks the representations and narratives that a national audience views benignly or even prizes, questioning the elements that ostensibly appeal to the national audience. 'The comic, ironic and violent tones of the narration create a distance, blocking and hindering rather than encouraging national sentiments and nostalgic pleasures', writes Anu Koivunen (2006: 134). Omissions and the ambiguous tone of the films question the status of national convention, suggesting it is not natural or necessary, but subject to irony, parody, and humour from diverse perspectives.

Issues of representation and audience address are also relevant to viewers beyond Finnish borders, which brings us to the discussion of transnationalism. In a thoughtful criticism of the term's use in cinema studies, Mette Hjort observes that transnationalism is often taken as self-evident. 'The term functions as shorthand for a series of assumptions about the networked and globalised realities that are those of a contemporary situation, and it is these assumptions, rather than explicit definitions, that lend semantic content to "transnational"' (2010: 13). It also enjoys a positive semantic charge, as transnationalism entails the 'welcome demise of the ideologically suspect nation-states and the cinematic arrangements to which they gave rise' (2010: 14). My notion of transnationalism draws on Rosen, for I see it as tending towards the construction and maintenance of non-national coherences and tending towards dissipating or making less significant national and state-based ones. Transnationalism is significant for Kaurismäki's films, for like many other auteur cinemas, his depends on crossing borders. Kaurismäki's films are a niche product in all their markets, but that niche audience can total millions when cobbled together through festivals and art-house distribution. Kaurismäki's films address a multi-local, transnational audience far more than a national one. For example, just nine percent of the theatrical admissions of *The Man Without a Past* occurred in Finland, although the film is also Kaurismäki's most successful film on home soil; admissions in France accounted for some thirty-five percent, Germany eighteen, and Italy fifteen.[4] The Lumiere Database on Admissions of Films Released in Europe shows that France, Germany, and Italy account for sixty to seventy percent of the director's admissions. Yet even with France making up thirty-five percent of the admissions for *The Man Without a Past*, one percent of the French population purchased a ticket to the film – the cinephile audience in large cities. Given this niche audience, the importance of film festivals is obvious: festival impact and related publicity help put a film on the cinephile's viewing agenda, for the media attention focused on a festival performs a 'value adding' function, as Marijke de Valck argues (2007: 210). It momentarily elevates a collection of largely niche-audience films to a general interest story – a notion we will return to below. Festivals act as transnational multipliers, generating notoriety that translates into distribution, word of mouth, enhanced reputation, and so forth. We would miss these dimensions completely, if we failed to consider the transnational dynamics of Kaurismäki's cinema.

Transnationalism in Kaurismäki's cinema is an instance of globalisation, rather than internationalism, to draw on terms from a relevant discussion to further develop the point in question. The political scientist Peter Katzenstein writes that

> globalization [is] a process that transcends space and compresses time. Internationalization [is] a process that refers to territorially based exchanges across borders. It refers to basic continuities in the international state system. Globalization highlights the emergence of new actors and novel relations in the world system, internationalization, the continued relevance of existing actors and the intensification of existing relations. (In Hjort and Petrie 2007: 14)

Katzenstein's distinction between internationalism and globalisation complements our approach to Kaurismäki's cinema, in which we have sought to track a dialectic of cohesion and dispersal. Globalisation disperses the formations around which the nation-state system coheres, internationalism shores up the political, economic, and cultural cohesion of the nation-state system. We see echoes of these dynamics on many levels of Kaurismäki's cinema, inasmuch as repeating images of summer light, location shooting, and agrarian life in *Juha* and the *Leningrad Cowboys* films can be read as instances of internationalism, projecting abroad a repertoire of Finnish iconography, even as Kaurismäki's ambiguous audience address and distribution patterns indicate that he belongs to a globalised auteur cinema – comprised of festivals, rights representatives, boutique distribution, and associated forms of narration, tone, audience address and so forth.

The multinational and the transnational are entangled, for the auteur can work in multiple locations and address diverse audiences, making films with national dimensions that also speak to a broader, larger, more diverse audience. Whether we frame Kaurismäki's cinema in a national and international framework or transnational and global framework, forces of cohesion and dispersal push and pull his cinema, making clear that it cannot be reduced to a singular identity. This ambivalence brings us back to Laclau and Mouffe's argument that signifiers, or symbols, of identity always involve a relationship between a part and an impossible whole. What matters are the parts chosen to represent the whole, and the arguments we make about what these parts represent. Symbols can be chosen that connote cohesion, in Rosen's sense. By contrast, symbols can be chosen that connote dispersion and heterogeneity. While Kaurismäki's cinema tends to be framed in terms of national cohesion, seeing his cinema in multinational and transnational contexts make evident the dispersive dynamics.

Ambiguous Identities

By turning from a theoretical emphasis to closer analysis of some symbolic and often discussed elements of Kaurismäki's films we find confirmation of the ambiguity we have noted. In its resistance to categorisation, Kaurismäki's cinema prompts us to specify further the categories under discussion, a project that correlates with Hjort's argument about the necessity of elaborating more carefully terms such as transnationalism. In so doing, we find that Kaurismäki's cinema shows the persistence of national and multinational cinema, at the same time as it shows pervasive and significant dimensions of transnationalism.

One of the oft-cited aesthetic elements taken to express national sentiment in Kaurismäki's cinema is the silence of the characters and the films' sparse dialogue. The characters are laconic, bordering on the catatonic. The director Kaurismäki is also often described as silent. The characters and the director's silence are supposed to express a national trait. This conjunction of elements has coalesced since Kaurismäki came to the attention of the festival circuit in 1989, and it has become one of the typical narratives for treating Kaurismäki's cinema. Swedish critic Gunnar Bergdahl makes clear the cohesion between the films, the silence, the director, and the nation in a 1990 interview with Kaurismäki. 'Should we see *Ariel* as a depiction of Finnish reality?' asks the journalist. 'I take out a cigarette. I light it. Then the police arrive, and it's over. That's why I keep making my films shorter and shorter. Do you understand what I mean?' replies Kaurismäki (in Bergdahl 1989). Here Kaurismäki advocates narrative and visual concision; by showing very little, and including little dialogue, one empowers the spectator to read the film's omissions and silences. Yet he also implies that the concision comes from a national mentality premised on the notion that verbal expression is a relatively weak form of social interaction, and moreover one ill-suited to social struggle, such as when the police arrive. *Helsingin Sanomat* critic Helena Ylänen, who has commented on Kaurismäki's career and films since the director appeared on the scene in 1981, sums up the consensus: 'Everything is laconic and minimalist.

One speaks of overpowering feelings with few words and almost imperceptible expression. Eroticism is absent, since Aki makes films about the enchantment of feeling, not meat' (in Siistonen 2006: 28). Feature magazine articles in the Finnish press often tell the same story, as their titles make clear: 'The Quiet Man of Finnish Cinema Speaks'; another says 'Chairman of the Quiet and Small' (Sallinen 1998; Leppä 1996). But how to situate this silence? Does the quiet of the films and the director embody the quiet Finnish nation? Or is it more complicated, an ironic signifier? Does silence necessarily involve cohesion, given its privileged place in Finnish self-understanding? Might it also involve dispersion?

The silence of a film or filmmaker can be interpreted as failure, as an aesthetic choice, as an existential expression, as an ironic gesture. Perhaps the films and the director have little of substance to say? Such a critique has been levelled at *Hamlet Goes Business* as well as the *Leningrad Cowboys* films. Or perhaps the silence is an affilliative aesthetic gesture towards the silent cinema or the melodramatic tradition. Kaurismäki has for example remarked that cinema died when sound was introduced. The melodramatic strand in French poetic realism relies on silence, as Jean Gabin's pregnant silences in films such as *Les bas-fonds* (*The Lower Depths*, Jean Renoir, 1936), *La grande illusion* (*The Grand Illusion*, Jean Renoir, 1937), and especially *La bête humaine* show. In the poetic realist film *Golden Marie*, Georges Manda delivers just eighty-seven lines (see Andrew 1995: 340). Perhaps the silence in Kaurismäki's films is an existential one, that is to say, it expresses a stoic worldview. Then again, perhaps the silence is ironic, working by indirection, saying nothing in order to say something else, negating speech in order to convey meaning. Let us focus on the last two of these readings, as we have touched on the others in earlier chapters.

The silences, sparse dialogue, and the dramatic stress these receive in Kaurismäki's films arguably give expression to a range of emotions that are coded Finnish. Given symbolic emphasis as a metonymy for Kaurismäki's cinema, it is easy to see the films' silence cohering with a Finnish worldview in which silence tends to be regarded as a dignified expression of authentic emotion, of respect for others' boundaries, of longing, but also as an expression of durable stoicism. When Iiris sits while others dance in *The Match Factory Girl*, the unfulfilled longing evident in her silence might be seen as an expression of the evocative Finnish word *kaiho*. Likewise, Rodolfo's silent departure from Mimi's deathbed at the conclusion of *The Bohemian Life* might be seen as a similar forlorn expression. *Kaiho* also captures the feelings evoked in *Drifting Clouds*, when a photograph of the late Matti Pellonpää is examined by Ilona.[5] *Kaiho* is also called to mind by the images of Koistinen eating alone at a Hopperesque kiosk in *Lights in the Dusk*, by Irma's goodbye to M on his departure to find his wife in *The Man Without a Past*, and by many other silent images of loneliness in Kaurismäki's cinema. *Kaiho* is a brooding nostalgia, often associated with a feeling of longing for the community of the agrarian village and its society, which largely disappeared through the urbanisation of the post-war period. Music critic Ilkka Mattila (2009) points out that *kaiho* and national-romantic themes help explain the relatively high popularity of Finnish-language albums in the domestic market. Finnish recording artists sell more albums in their home market than domestic music sells in many other national markets, where English-language pop tends to receive a higher market share. At the same time, these albums and the acts that record them have not been exported or have performed poorly in export. Identifying a combination of silence and *kaiho* as a seminal theme in Kaurismäki's films provides a means of identifying a coherence with national culture and national cinema.

Yet the silence can also involve painful ambivalence, when silent longing mixes with shame. This occurs when longing is placed in a cultural context, as well as when the longing involves a triangular relationship, in which the subject of longing identifies with others like her, at the same time as she identifies with an ego-ideal or 'social eye', who sees the subject longing for something possessed by the ego-ideal, as the scholar of visual culture Tarja Laine has argued (2004: 92–101). Silent longing in such a case still involves coherence with a positively coded national sentiment. Yet it also includes a painful lack, inasmuch as being seen as a subject of longing means that the subject does not have that thing, which the ego-ideal possesses. In a number of Kaurismäki films, the ego-ideal or 'social eye' possesses work, and the subject of longing does not. Such relationships are key features of *Shadows in Paradise, Ariel, Drifting Clouds, The Man Without a Past,* and *Lights in the Dusk,* for example. As Laine points out, work is a constitutive feature of Finnish national identity, and everyone is supposed to have it. As a constitutive national myth, enduring, silent work figures prominently in the texts of such canonical authors as J.L. Runeberg, Aleksis Kivi, and Väinö Linna. The idea is that through long-suffering and tireless labour Finns can transform their boggy soil and northern forests into a nation among nations. 'The place of the "ego-ideal" has been defined by the features of an honest, hard-working subject', writes Laine (2004: 94). When the unemployed subject longing for work recognises herself among the unemployed at the same time as she identifies with the ego ideal, ambivalence is generated and shame results. While the narrative of *Drifting Clouds* can be understood in terms of universal experience, Laine suggests that the experiences of ambivalent longing and shame in the film draw emotional force by situating them historically and culturally in a Finnish context. The representation of silence in *Drifting Clouds* and other films helps explain the relevance of a national context to Kaurismäki's cinema, at the same time as it shows the complexity and multivalence of a national myth like silence. It can involve coherence, but also ambivalence that diminishes certainty about what exactly silent longing means.

The openness of silence in the national context entails the possibility of varying responses to representations of silence. Silence can be linked to shame, as in *Drifting Clouds,* but as we have seen it can also be charged positively, associated with stoicism and doggedness. These different perspectives often turn up in ironic ways. Consider for example the scene in *The Match Factory Girl* in which Iiris's love interest Aarne (Vesa Vierikko) comes to pick her up for their date. Aarne and Iiris's stepfather sit silently at the coffee table, neatly set with a lace tablecloth and china. The scene's exaggerated silence mocks Iiris's mother and stepfather, saying something more about them than the images convey literally. In this case, the excess would seem to speak not of an alignment with a positively valued national feeling. Rather, it evokes bitter laughter that implicitly attacks the parental silence that conceals Iiris's suffering.

The link between silence and irony has been analysed by the critic Jonathan Romney, who argues that in combination they lend the films openness and undecidability. It's hard to describe the response Kaurismäki's cinema calls for, writes Romney:

> Kaurismäki's humour – except for the surreal farce of the *Leningrad Cowboys* – is characteristically deadpan in the extreme ... a humour that is so acute and economic that laughter seems a superfluous extravagance. As a result, many have walked out of his films uncertain whether they have seen a comedy at all ... His detractors may think he's a joke, but then so do his fans – they feel he's the best joke the art cinema has to offer at its own expense. These films are jokes about the seriousness of the art-house tradition by a man who reveres Robert Bresson, Carl Dreyer and Yasujiro Ozu; and jokes about the stereotype of the national character by a man who has made a career out of presenting himself as a the gloomiest of Finns (his own lead actors excepted) who ever stared into a glass of Koskenkorva, the national tipple. (1997: 10)

The silence forces spectators to suspend their judgement, prompting them to reconsider the status of the film, the filmmaker, the art cinema, and the discourses it invokes, nationality among others. Laine makes a similar point, suggesting Kaurismäki can be understood within the tradition of the 'cinema of irony', which uses self-reflection and emotional detachment to prompt critical responses that prod viewers to try and square the absurd depiction of national stereotypes in the films with widely-held notions about the same stereotypes (see Laine 2004: 93–4). Such arguments lead Romney to place Kaurismäki in the modernist tradition of the art cinema, wherein humour and absurd self-presentation discourage identification and accentuate distance, prompting spectators' self-aware response to the films and the director.

The tension between a sympathetic reading and an ironic reading of the national discourse also raises some productive questions about the cultural politics of gender, which once again show how contested a national stereotype like silence can be. When critics laud the beauty of silent expressions in Kaurismäki's films, their praise is usually directed at men's silence. To be sure, films such as *The Match Factory Girl* and *Drifting Clouds* are notable for their dynamic and comparatively unusual working-women protagonists. Yet still, what do we talk about when we talk about longing, nostalgia, *kaiho*? We talk about the men who express these feelings: the performance of Matti Pellonpää in *The Bohemian Life*, Markku Peltola's role as M in *The Man Without a Past*, the feelings expressed by Koistinen in *Lights in the Dusk*, and so forth. Yet, praising these male characters for their stoicism also genders silence or *kaiho*, making it an experience controlled by and especially relevant to men. The erasure of women can be seen in *The Bohemian Life*, especially when set in contrast to Sally Potter's well-known feminist adaptation of Murger's text, *Thriller*. Potter's film shifts the perspective of the Rudolphe and Mimi plot from the vantage of the painter to the seamstress arrived in Bohemian Paris from the countryside. Like Kaurismäki's *The Bohemian Life*, Potter's film also screened at Berlin in the festival's Forum for New Cinema.[6] Noting this institutional connection, film critic Amy Taubin compared the cultural politics of gender in Potter and Kaurismäki's films:[7]

> as easy as it is for me to be moved as a 'human being' by ... the devotion of man and, yes, dog ... as a woman I just felt left out. *Thriller* poses and answers the powerful question, 'Why did Mimi have to die?' ... Potter's answer was that Mimi died so that Rudolfo could be transformed by loss and so that we could identify with him in his loss. What's disturbing about *La vie de Bohème* is not only that Kaurismäki (whose *The Match Factory Girl* is a great feminist text) seems totally unaware of Potter's intervention, but that he ironises every aspect of the original novel *except* Mimi's death, which he accepts as a given. (1992: 15; emphasis in original)

While Kaurismäki eschews the objectifying male gaze that often accompanies an implicitly masculine narrative perspective, his films are often premised on the equation of male, lower-class experience in post-war Finland with national experience, which is arguably represented in the silent, stoic man. The film scholar Sanna Kivimäki points out that few critics and scholars have commented on the issue of gender in Kaurismäki's films. Yet she argues that even in a film with strong feminist aspects such as *The Match Factory Girl*, the film's many clichés of the silently suffering woman, driven by her emotions and body, also require critical attention. The representation of gender in Kaurismäki's films replicates images and narratives that have often been criticised by feminists, yet the films' irony and their status within an auteur cinema have forestalled criticism, suggests Kivimäki (2010; 2012). Here questions related to multination and representation arise.

Beyond silence, the gender politics of Kaurismäki's films can also be seen in the typical structure of their narrative. Time and again, the films are built around the experience of a lower-class man. His alienation furnishes a motivation for his longing, melancholia, or hope for love and acceptance. His emotional stance is then taken by critics to be an expression of national experience and sentiment. The typical narrative of Kaurismäki's cinema overlaps with the narrative of Finland's industrialisation and urbanisation – and is typical as a 'narrative of education'. In the Finnish context, the story tells of men (re)building Finland and its industry after the wars. This connection is underscored by the privileged status of industrial work in Kaurismäki's cinema. In such connections, we find a powerful force of cohesion between Kaurismäki and the national history and cinema. But whose national history and cinema? These categories and the narratives that underpin them involve gendered perspectives. This perspective is emphasised in Anu Koivunen's analysis of masculinity and nostalgia in *The Man Without a Past* (2006), which shows how the film equates nostalgia and a nationally coded, working-class masculinity. Koivunen's argument resonates with a body of scholarship which has documented and challenged the gendering of national experience as male in Finnish social discourse (see Gordon *et al.* 2002). Scholars such as Mia Spangenberg (2009) have pointed out that even as growing gender equity pressures the privileged male and induces a 'crisis of masculinity', such films as *The Man Without a*

Past and *Lights in the Dusk* maintain men's status as the privileged representative of the Finnish nation (if not urban late modernity) by presenting male experience as symptomatic. By minimising or downplaying gender difference within national discourse, they code as male such privileged symbols of nation as silence, stoicism, and longing. While appearing to cohere with national discourse, they replicate a gendered exclusion, which in fact diminishes the inclusiveness, legitimacy, and emotional resonance of the national culture they invoke. In this point we see the relevance of studying cohesion and dispersion of national discourse within the context of Laclau and Mouffes's argument about the politics of identity and representation, and the notion of multination. Who and what stand as representatives of the nation?

What we have seen is that nation in Kaurismäki's cinema is multiple and contested, insofar as diverse elements of national discourse are put into dialogue in the films. The characters are not simply expressions of the laconic reality of Finnish experience, or a stoic worldview, but representations constructed in ways that stage questions about national discourse. While there is clearly good reason to analyse nation in Kaurismäki's cinema, it is also clear that the self-aware, ironic status of his work raises questions about the premises of such analysis. Might we better understand Kaurismäki by seeing him as a Socratic figure, who uses indirection and humour to drive home existential questions and dilemmas, as Søren Kierkegaard suggested about Socrates? The irony is so pervasive and open that it becomes necessary to ask whether the body of work might be considered an ironic critique of national discourse, among other targets. When coupled with Kaurismäki's frequently blunt remarks about nation – 'Finland is run by idiots' (Jutila 1999) – this imperative becomes even clearer.

Ironic Nationality

'Jätä kaikki ja tule kanssani Eiraan' ('Leave everything and come with me to Eira') says one of the Franks in *Calamari Union*. The film chronicles the odyssey of thirteen Franks and one Pekka, as they make their way from Helsinki's working-class neighbourhood Kallio south across the 'Long Bridge' (*Pitkä silta*), past the University of Helsinki and into Eira, where lie Helsinki's *jugendstil* (art nouveau) apartment buildings, foreign embassies, and the city's premiere park (*Kaivopuisto*), nestled against the water. The men's journey might well be construed in picturesque terms, as other filmmakers have done. Such a depiction of Helsinki and the Eira neighbourhood characterises *Kaivopuiston kaunis Regina* (*Beautiful Regina of Kaivopuisto Park*, T. J. Särkkä, 1941), one of Finnish cinema's all-time most popular domestic productions. This costume drama set in the mid-nineteenth century seeks to enchant the viewer by presenting the park and Eira as a surprisingly pastoral space, alive with the beauty and romantic charge of nature. Other films have adopted the tourist's gaze in approaching Eira, glamourising the wealthiest corner of the city to portray it as an appealing space, which the average viewer cannot fully access. This approach structures the hit film *Kuutamolla* (*Lovers & Leavers*, Aku Louhimies, 2002), a Bridget Jones-style romantic comedy, which associates the cultural geography of Helsinki with characters to distinguish their moral status. Eira and the characters living there exude elegance, caché and inaccessibility, for which the protagonist Iiris (Minna Haapkylä) yearns, but which she ultimately discovers are confining and disingenuous. *In the Moonlight* thematises the conflict between appearances and reality by making Iiris a film buff, which also motivates intertextual references to images of romance and Helsinki in Finnish cinema. The spectator is positioned as a tourist and consumer. *Calamari Union,* by contrast, eschews the picturesque and the touristic gaze. Shot in black-and-white and occurring diegetically in the course of twenty-four hours, its low-key lighting, noir costuming, and location choices make the city and Eira look gritty, rather than picturesque or appealing – like the London of *I Hired a Contract Killer*. *Calamari Union*'s framing avoids recognisable landmarks, or severs their usual framing. We see similarities in Kaurismäki's urban images in general. London, Paris, New York, and New Orleans are depicted with realist location shots, yet deterritorialised and stripped of landmarks, familiar architecture, and markers of place. While Kaurismäki's cinema latches on to some of the cohesive forces within Finnish cinema, lending the films to national understanding, we can also see how *Calamari Union*'s aesthetic distances the film from historical and contemporary conventions by which Finnish visual culture has defined its status in national terms. Kaurismäki's style can be understood in terms of irony, for in differing from the conventions by which Helsinki and other cities are represented, the films take a position about the visual construction of city and nation. This irony can be likened to 'the wig', as explored in chapter three, drawing on Certeau. Kaurismäki's ironic nationality insinuates a competing socio-ethical position into the consumerist and touristic image of city and nation.

One of the chief ways by which Kaurismäki's cinema ironically disputes the conventional means of representing nation is by unmasking the images and narratives promulgated by state institutions. The premise beneath such a project is that the mode of communication, rather than the mode of production, figures most prominently in the ways that people produce meaning in their lives and communities. It goes without saying that in late modernity electronically mediated images and narratives help shape quotidian perceptions, experiences, and hopes. They make visual culture a charged arena of competition over which images and narratives will take and hold sway in defining cultural, economic, and political outlooks and agendas. This struggle is not about signs, but about images whose relationship to their apparent referents is tangential. The issue is how images can create chains of associations that engender ideas, affects, and attitudes. Such a task involves public diplomacy for the state. In contrast, critique of the state can be accomplished by twisting tropes of national self-representation, thereby modifying the images and associations the state affirms.

The power attributed to the mode of communication in defining Finland as a nation was made particularly overt in the country in a pivotal moment during autumn 2008, but the fabrication and modulation of the national image goes back to the nineteenth century. One key moment in this history is the artistic contributions of composer Jean Sibelius and visual artist Akseli Gallén-Kallela in 1899 and 1900, seeking to resist Tsar Nicholas II's exertion of strong Russification pressure on Finland. Sibelius composed the symphonic poem Finlandia, and Gallén-Kallela created four *Kalevala*-themed frescoes for the Finnish pavilion at the Paris World's Fair of 1900. The pavilion played an important public-diplomacy role, seeking to define the legitimacy and autonomy of the Finnish nation before European eyes. Another key instance is the 1952 Helsinki Olympic Games, in which Finland sought to project an image of modernity and neutrality, erasing the stain of its cooperation with Nazi Germany during World War II. The recent pivotal moment in this history occurred in September 2008, when Finnish Foreign Minister Alexander Stubb appointed a commission to research and propose a 'national brand' for Finland. Art and sport were no longer sufficient; corporate strategy needed to be used to burnish the national image. Stubb chose former Nokia CEO Jorma Ollila to lead the commission. The purpose of the national brand is 'to support the business activities of Finnish enterprise, enhance Finland's influence abroad, develop interest in Finland as a site of investment, and increase tourism to Finland' (Finnish Foreign Ministry 2009). As filmmaker and public intellectual Jörn Donner pointed out in a number of comments on debates over this commission and the national image, Sibelius, Gallén-Kallela and the 1952 Olympics are but several instances of a long-lived obsession with the national self-image. Donner should know, as he and Martti Häikkiö had written a book on the topic entitled *Finland's Image, Year Zero,* published by the Finnish Foreign Ministry one year after the fall of the Berlin Wall and on the eve of the dissolution of the Soviet Union (1990).[8] In recent writing, Donner (2008) disparages the national-branding project for seeking to engineer a brand, rather than encouraging the development and competition that would foster success and consequent global visibility. What is clear is the extent to which the iconography, images, and indeed vision, are *multinational,* objects of struggle between many quarters, including the state. In the context of such debate, Kaurismäki's irony and his conscious refusal to repeat conventions of nationalised visual culture helps us see the way his films embrace disseminating and pluralising forces that diminish the hold of national cinema, more so than they embrace cohesive forces.

Kaurismäki's thinking on this issue is visible in an interview with a Swiss magazine published just before the Hamburg Film Festival in 2002 – one of the stories that heightened the excitement over Kaurismäki, according to Hammarberg in his interview. The Swiss journalist says: 'You're a hopeless nostalgic ... Was everything really so much better in the past?' Kaurismäki replies:

> It's purely a question of aesthetic values. Old cars, old cameras, old radios, old glasses, and old ashtrays are simply more beautiful than new ones ... My films have never included what [mainstream Finnish critics] want: no reindeer, no new cars, no computers. The Finnish Tourism Bureau has considered taking legal action against me. Every film I make apparently sets their efforts back a decade. (In Stecher 2002)

One way of reading this remark is to understand it as an ascription of subjective value to old objects, which would support a nostalgic reading of the films as an expression of *kaiho*-like longing. These objects are beautiful 'in my eyes', so to speak. But why make a comparison to images of the new, then? The important point about aesthetic values requires unpacking the *comparison* between old cameras and radios and images allegedly desired by mainstream Finnish critics and the Tourism Bureau. They are the very group allied with Stubb and his national brand project.

The cited passage compares two lists, one of old objects and a shorter one of images not included in Kaurismäki's films, which he says critics wish he would include. In Kaurismäki's view, officials have noticed the films lack the iconography disseminated by the Finnish Tourism Board. Kaurismäki implies that Finnish critics want to see images in his films that would represent Finland in the way the state represents the country to non-Finns. They want Kaurismäki to contribute to the public-diplomacy mission of the Tourism Board and the Foreign Ministry.

Making this remark in an interview with a Swiss journalist, Kaurismäki makes two suggestions about the national status of his films. He implies that his image of Finland is at least influential enough to compete with the advertising campaigns familiar to the Finnish critics. Hence his films are a threat because they may crowd out the official representation of the country to non-Finns, undermining the work of the Tourism Board. Kaurismäki also implies that film critics and officials in the Tourism Board, intellectuals and officials, share an agenda which views cinema as an advertising tool for promoting the nation-state. So while at first glance this remark about aesthetic values seems to be an expression of subjective nostalgia for beautiful old things, on closer inspection it reveals itself also to be a statement that contrasts Kaurismäki's films with the image-making agenda Finnish elites have for national visual culture. What is more, it calls to mind the point made by Donner in the epigraph to this chapter. It attacks the premise that art, thought, and ideas are the expression of the nation-state, suggesting that the particular qualities of the image matter far more than their representation of an entity such as the nation.

We see a premise underlying Kaurismäki's films, which relates to what he means by aesthetic values: people, people's experiences, and the objects that fill their lives have value that cannot be effaced by the new, the desirable, and the commercially available. Here we again see an echo of the argument about everyday nostalgia explored in the previous chapter. These objects insinuate a disruptive socio-political ethics into the instrumental rationality of the late-modern welfare state. It is no mistake that his list of the old in the passage above is not a list of images, but a list of objects. By representing the objects in ways that ascribe value to them, Kaurismäki contests images of the new, whose value in his films tends to be cast in negative terms.

A target of Kaurismäki's critique is the project of building a cohesive image around a specific agenda. The stakes of that agenda are brought out by the comments of one prominent viewer of *The Man Without a Past*. For this viewer, the story of the homeless amnesiac M's search for his identity created the wrong picture of Finland by featuring shipping containers and Salvation-Army soup lines too prominently. Social Democratic MP and former chair of the parliamentary Health and Human Services Committee, Marjatta Vehkaoja, remarked on seeing the film: 'Bread lines are going to be our new export product once this film goes into worldwide circulation' (STT 2002), a remark made several months before the film generated enthusiasm in Finland on account of its *Grand Prix* at Cannes, an Academy Award nomination, and the Nordic Council film prize. 'When we've organised bread lines in the past, we've been able to help these people. But we need to push ourselves further and remember to ask whether food stamps actually provide people relief in a more dignified manner', said Vehkaoja (Finnish Press Agency 2002). The MP considers bread lines undignified and disjunctive with contemporary institutional practice, and the image it has fashioned of itself. The problem for the MP is that Kaurismäki's film is an export product that creates the wrong image of Finland. Paradoxically, another state institution, the Finnish Film Foundation, is promoting Kaurismäki and his films as a model of cultural export. What we see is the multinational dispute to which Kaurismäki's cinema contributes.

Vehkaoja's comment also makes evident the politicisation of vision we have been discussing, implicitly acknowledging the logic driving such projects as the Commission to Develop Finland's National Brand. In speaking of food stamps as more dignified than bread lines, Vehkaoja is also arguing that one loses dignity when one sees oneself on display for others in a breadline or waiting for soup served by the Salvation Army. The nation loses confidence when it sees itself lining up for help. The premise here is that recognising oneself within an image of poverty creates shame. If a person in need of assistance did not need to display himself lining up for food, then he would not lose dignity, and so would escape shame, calling Laine's argument to mind again. The image and visibility of poverty stigmatises as much as poverty itself does, according to Vehkaoja's account.

Vehkaoja's criticism of the film also relates to the image of stasis she attributes to the Salvation Army. This transnational institution has branded itself as a perennial source of relief to the impoverished. In the film, the Salvation Army's uniforms, store, and soup line operation are represented as timeless and unchanging. In their stasis, they create an image that disrupts the narrative of modernisation and progress, which representatives of the state recurrently emphasise. 'We used to do breadlines,' says Vehkaoja, 'now we do electronic payment cards.' We used to be a 'land won by our fathers' combat, passed up by proud strangers', suggests Stubb and his commission; now we need brand synergy to attract those strangers to visit and invest.[9] The discourse of nation here concerns the images by which nation is made visible to its citizens and others. Such representations must compete for visibility in a crowded media environment. Kaurismäki is hence a threat, for he violates the conventions of representation favoured by the national intelligentsia.

These points bring us back again to Laclau and Mouffe's argument about the hegemonic struggle involved in all forms of representation. Within any representation of social identity, parts stand for wholes. While Nokia and its global economic success may be presented as standing for a national history of innovation and engineering skill, the company and the engineers that built it do not represent another symbolic national tradition of excellence in musical composition and performance, represented by Jean Sibelius, Kaija Saariaho, Karita Mattila, Jussi Björling, Esa-Pekka Salonen, and others. And such representatives of a tradition in musical culure can hardly be said to stand for the story of Finland's wars, its suffering, sacrifice, and impoverishment into the 1950s. To be sure, some try to reconcile these. But any representation of the nation, or brand, must also involve exclusions and misrepresentations. The politics involved in such multinational contests concern who will be represented, and who will be excluded. In engaging the politicisation of visual culture, Kaurismäki uses irony to question and contest the primary narratives of Finnish visual culture. In so doing, his films do not build a cohesive national visual culture, but dissipate and distinguish, contributing in some ways to the formation of a more plural visual culture. In other ways, Kaurismäki's films continue exclusions of gender that have figured prominently in national identity discourse. Categorising Kaurismäki's cinema in national terms, then, must avoid oversimplifying notions of identity and cohesion, which the director has questioned and attacked over the course of his career. Such a view does not entail that his films have nothing to do with national cinema, however.

Kaurismäki as Small-Nation Auteur

We have analysed a set of tensions and contradictions that run through Kaurismäki's cinema understood as a national cinema, noting the way that self-presentation of the director and commentators' agendas weave together strands of national and transnational discourses to address different audiences and to generate various effects. The premise of the argument has been that national cinema is not a homogeneous or unified discourse, but a heterogeneous and conflicted one, which intersects with transnational debates, institutions, and networks. What then is the relationship between the national and transnational dimensions of Kaurismäki's cinema? The best point of departure in examining this interconnection is to analyse Kaurismäki as a small-nation filmmaker in a way that builds on and expands the arguments about this term put forth by Mette Hjort (2005; 2007). While Hjort places emphasis on small-nation factors related to production, Kaurismäki's cinema makes clear that a crucial dimension of small-nation cinema is also distribution and exhibition. Adding these factors to the discussion of small nation helps further enrich this useful category, and provides an account of how Kaurismäki's cinema works as a small-nation cinema.

The small-nation filmmaker makes his films within a context of asymmetric forces. The institutional, economic, and cultural dimensions of these forces have been ingeniously analysed by Hjort in *Small Nations, Global Cinema* (2005) and her edited volume, *Cinema of Small Nations* (with Duncan Petrie, 2007). Hjort argues that the way filmmakers from small nations negotiate the asymmetries of small nationhood figure prominently in the way they make films, the kinds of films they make, and the way these films circulate in and outside their home territories. Small nationhood entails population size, geographical scale, gross domestic product (GDP), but also any nation state's embedding in differentiated relationships of power (see Hjort and Petrie 2007: 3–6). Hjort's argument stresses the extent to which small-nation cinema needs to be conceptualised with attention to a different set of imperatives and opportunities than those of cinemas with larger domestic markets, more widely-spoken languages, and more influence on the nations and markets around them. Asymmetries distinguish the globalisation of Anglo-American popular culture from, say, the global prominence of Malian music, Finnish architecture, or Tibetan Buddhism. Analysing the renaissance in Danish cinema that has occurred since the 1990s, Hjort shows how institutional redesign at the Danish Film Institute, increases in parliamentary appropriations for film, investment in specialised and general film education, 'gift culture'-based collaboration, and creative leadership have together fostered a New Danish Cinema (2005; 2007). This cinema has attracted up to nearly fifty percent of total Danish theatrical admissions since the 1990s, while racking up thousands of screenings and scores of prizes at film festivals around the world. Denmark devotes significantly more money to cinema than the other Nordic countries do, producing almost twice as many films as Norway and Finland respectively, although all are similar in population size and GDP. The other Nordic cinemas have also enjoyed rising cinematic fortunes, but not to the extent of Danish cinema. As Hjort shows, Danish cinema has successfully fostered prolific and high-quality production, creating a reputation that attracts audiences at home and abroad. When it comes to small-nation cinema, then, a key question is how it attracts an audience, and this is a question for an auteur like Kaurismäki as well.

One way that Kaurismäki has attracted an audience has been to maintain and build upon a consistent production practice established early in his career, which generates a distinctive style at a low price. This distinctive style heightens audience recognition of the films, at the same time as it furnishes relative commercial flexibility, as low production costs minimise financial risk. Low-cost production can provide competitive advantage. The underground filmmaking techniques we noted in the discussion of Filmtotal in chapter two have remained significant in Kaurismäki's career since the 1980s. Location shooting, relatively minimal shot planning, economical use of film stock with one-take shooting, sound synchronisation during shooting, and working with the same crew of actors and technicians has kept Kaurismäki's production budgets to a ceiling of €1.2 million, of which the lion's share is covered through grants and pre-sold arrangements with European television channels (see Nestingen 2007). The recurrent, cost-efficient production choices in Kaurismäki's cinema require little financial outlay. For example, the bold, saturated colours that create the films' distinctive palette can be inexpensively achieved. Another example is visible in films such as *Crime and Punishment, Calamari Union, Hamlet, Drifting Clouds, Man Without a Past,* and *Lights in the Dusk,* which include numerous night-time sequences: such a production choice allows shooting in urban locations free of pedestrian and vehicle traffic, and does not require using any of the production budget to close streets or hire police assistance (see Kuosmanen 2007). Kaurismäki has long refused to spend money on expensive musical royalties: one reason no Finnish tango features in *Lights in the Dusk* or *Le Havre* is that F-Music, formerly Fazer Music, which owns most of the Finnish repertoire, has raised the cost of usage rights significantly, causing Kaurismäki to decide to omit such music. Even Kaurismäki's screenwriting has remained 'underground': he still speaks of writing his screenplays in a weekend, or a week in recent years, and many of his films have no script, including *Calamari Union, Hamlet, The Match Factory Girl,* the *Leningrad Cowboys* films, and *Take Care of your Scarf, Tatiana* (see Frodon 2006: 32). Rather than relying on ever larger budgets, then, Kaurismäki has maintained a disciplined production strategy, permitting maximal control and flexibility in how he and his films seek and reach their audience. Because Kaurismäki does not depend on big budgets, he can maintain control of production and have significant input concerning distribution.

While such a production strategy may not be unusual, even for a figure as established as Kaurismäki, it is the basis for an alternative mode of globalisation. In the first place, Kaurismäki is simply maximising the advantages he has: he exploits a distinctive 'brand identity' with an established audience, which has, since 1987, provided access to the premiere international film festivals. We can duly see this as an alternative form of globalisation, to recall Katzenstein's argument and to pick up Hjort's point about the value of analysis that comprehends how small-nation cinema works. Such analysis can help

> pinpoint the causes and dynamics of alternative imaginings that to some extent challenge the dominance of the neoliberal model and especially its tendency to reinforce pre-existing patterns of exploitation or domination, be they political, economic, or cultural ... The challenge is to pinpoint the ways in which the neoliberal conception – one favourable to global capital, to corporations governed by narrow strategic rationalities, and to the priorities and putative entitlements of the United States – itself can become the engine for alternative conceptions while agents in specific contexts mobilise the institutional resources of a local situation and effectively yoke them to the salient features of a globalised world. (2005: 26–7)

What is at issue is not making films that differ from the likes of *Star Wars* (George Lucas, 1977), *Titanic* (James Cameron, 1997), or *Saw VI* (Kevin Greutert, 2009) but rather contribute to a system that sustains alternative modes of filmmaking, distribution, and exhibition. The analysis of small-nation cinema as a part of this system has emphasised the significance and novelty of institutional and production practice and strategy. Yet Kaurismäki has maintained the same model of production, and the Finnish Film Foundation has made few and relatively small changes, compared to Denmark and Norway, for example. What is distinctive about his transnationalism is the role of the film festival, from the establishment of the Midnight Sun Festival to the key role of Berlin and Cannes. Kaurismäki's cinema suggests that small-nation cinema as a category also requires theoretical examination of distribution and exhibition pattern and practice. What we see is a patterns of festival premiere, sale of distribution rights in multiple territories, and subsequent release by an art-house distributor to art-house exhibitors, with more established figures and companies exploiting consistency in distribution and exhibition through pre-production financing arrangements, and the like.

The vitality of this system is hardly evident if we place it within the conventional and much-criticised Hollywood–Europe dichotomy. For example, if we follow Toby Miller and his co-authors' argument in *Global Hollywood* about the New International Division of Cultural Labour, by which they mean multinational entertainment corporations' distribution of labour around the world in pursuit of inexpensive production, it would seem that there is little analytical space for the festival system (see Miller *et al.* 2001: 52–3). The simultaneous theatrical release of the Hollywood majors' blockbuster films, their DVD releases, their availability online as streaming files, and their ancillary products would seem to crowd out other visual culture entirely. Since the 1990s, foreign releases have made up some sixty to seventy percent of Hollywood's worldwide theatrical gross (see Aft 2004: 59). Yet to situate Kaurismäki and small-nation cinema in such a context would be an apples and oranges comparison.

A more telling frame of analysis both for Kaurismäki's cinema and auteur cinema in general is available when we ask the question, What kind of product is the film distributor who purchases the rights to distribute Kaurismäki's cinema buying? What does Sony Film Classics seek to do with *The Man Without a Past,* when it releases it in the US market? One reason for the heavy emphasis on production in analysis of the globalisation of cinema is the fetishisation of the massive media corporations that have been involved in cinema production since the mergers of the 1990s and 2000s. Correspondingly, film scholars have sought to unmask the function of these corporations with critical analysis. Yet as the authors of the media studies and business contribution *The Curse of the Mogul: What's Wrong with the World's Leading Media Companies* (2009) Knee, Greenwald, and Seave argue, any media business (including art-house and small-nation distributors) must face the key issue of competitive advantage. What are the barriers to entry to a market that provide a given enterprise an advantage?

There are only a few true advantages: economies of scale, customer captivity, costs of doing business, and government protection, point out Knee, Greenwald, and Seave. Relative economy of scale provides an advantage in a large market with high costs of doing business: a big established business can spread its costs across more sales, while doing more marketing, making it difficult for smaller companies to compete with it. (This is the key advantage that the Hollywood studios have.) Customer captivity designates the habits and investments of customers, which prevent them from switching their consumer behaviour. Costs of doing business refers to the costs of acquiring technology or locations necessary to successful business, for example patented technology or a strategic production location. Finally, government advantage recognises state support that favours one competitor over another.

The most important competitive advantage for Kaurismäki is the relative low cost of doing business, which involves low production costs and established relationships with distribution companies around Europe, Asia, and the Americas. This arrangement allows Kaurismäki maximum flexibility, for the films' production budgets are covered by grants and pre-production financing arrangements with a variety of co-producers. As a result, Kaurismäki's cinema can count on finding distribution in many niche markets, at a relatively low risk. The distinction I have in mind here is made by Knee, Greenwald, and Seave between mass-media entities and niche speciality entities. The line between general and special interest media is not self-evident. 'What distinguishes true "niche media" is that the product itself is designed around a shared interest or activity. The Food Channel vs. USA Network; *Fly Fisherman* vs. *Newsweek*; dailycandy. com vs. MSN.com' (Knee *et al.* 2009: 21). To speak about more relevant examples for this study, we can distinguish between production companies in the Nordic countries' and their audience address. In the Finnish case, for example, such companies as Solar Film-Nordisk, Matila-Röhr, and Timo Koivusalo's Artista Filmi Ltd. make general interest films for the domestic audience. Their films are released in sixty to eighty prints and have reached audiences in the hundreds of thousands domestically, but do not play at festivals and get limited, if any, foreign distribution. In contrast, a company like Kaurismäki's Sputnik Ltd. releases films in a dozen or fewer prints domestically, but relies on a festival release to generate visibility which propels the film into multiple niche markets that are geographically widely spread. Niche media companies in the Nordic context include auteur and art-house cinema distributors, exhibitors, and producers, such as Lars von Trier and Peter Aalbek-Jensen's Zentropa. These companies market themselves to specific audiences, at the same time as they seek to cultivate a network that enhances their status within a specific market segment, to increase their capacity to conduct business effectively and to enhance interest in their brands, who are their auteurs.

What is striking in examining these niche companies in the domestic context, however, is the extent to which they are construed in terms of general interest. It is often but not always the niche films that generate discussion and debate, gain visibility at festivals, and attract coverage including stories about their long lists of awards and controversies over production, and ultimately when such niche films acheive broad international distribution, they can have much greater economic success than even the most successful general interest domestic releases. Niche films also tend to represent the national culture in critics' comments about national cinema, because of their perceived artistic quality. So when one speaks of Finnish cinema as a small-nation cinema, one tends to think of the Kaurismäki brothers or the documentarist Pirjo Honkasalo, not a Solar Films' release like *Pahat pojat* (*Bad Boys*, Aleksi Mäkelä, 2003), viewed by some twelve percent of the Finnish population according to the Lumiere Database.

In Kaurismäki's case we see disjunctions between the identity of the supposed audience for his cinema, the identities of the institutions which have financed the films, and the film personnel with whom Kaurismäki has collaborated to make the films. Critics both in Finland and abroad tend to assume the films are addressed to a Finnish audience, writing often about their Finnishness, a topic which has proved to be of limited interest to audiences outside the nation's borders. Film scholar and Kaurismäki expert Pietari Kääpä points out that distribution of Kaurismäki's films only confirms the insignificance of the Finnish market for him, releasing his films of the 1980s and 1990s in only four to seven prints. *The Match Factory Girl* was released in Finland on four prints in 1990 (2008: 88–94). These are tiny numbers – although they do predate the saturation release approach, which since the 1990s has seen Finnish blockbusters released in fifty to eighty prints. Further, it must be pointed out that Kaurismäki's films have attracted TV viewership in the hundreds of thousands in Finland. Still, Kaurismäki's films have a niche identity in their domestic market. They are also a niche product in France, Germany, and Italy, but the size of these markets adds up to sixty to seventy percent of the total theatrical admissions of Kaurismaki's films. In the big picture, Kaurismäki's primary audience is outside Finland – hence his handlers' consternation at the provincial Finnish reporter in Hamburg. Kääpä observes that 'while the implied or desired audience of Kaurismäki's films may be constructed on the basis of cultural homogeneity, the reality of the audience constitution differs significantly from this' (2008: 44). Similar contradictions are evident in Kaurismäki's production schemes. While they appear to be national – Kaurismäki having been the single largest recipient of production subsidy from the Finnish Film Foundation since the 1980s (see Arolainen 1999) – the co-financing and co-production arrangements underpinning his cinema have consistently been transnational. Finally, while Kaurismäki is often associated with his troupe of Finnish actors, including Kati Outinen, Matti Pellonpää, Esko Nikkari, Elina Salo, and Kari Väänänen, among others, his use of cameos and guest roles by such directors and actors as Samuel Fuller, Jean-Pierre Léaud, Serge Reggiani, Andre Wilms, Nicky Tesco, and others makes the films diverse. What we have is a small-nation filmmaker who has developed a filmmaking practice that straddles the national and the transnational.

Kaurismäki and many other small-nation auteurs aspire to be a global niche interest and a general interest one at home. Kaurismäki's niche status has become evident in the previous chapters. The bohemian narrative that circulates about Kaurismäki positions him not as mainstream figure, but as idiosyncratic, an outsider, and a social critic. His films' aesthetics, moreover, embrace a niche status, telling stories of outsiders and aliens in an anachronistic and unfashionable, if also appealing cinematic idiom. The release of his films in Finland has also consistently followed niche exhibition practice, released as they have been in small numbers of prints at art-house theatres, attracting audiences over a long period with the help of favourable reviews and word-of-mouth. As the critic Markku Koski (2002) sums it up, Kaurismäki is fiercely opposed to the mainstream. Yet at the same time, the previous chapters have also shown the extent to which Kaurismäki's cinema and the director aspire to the mainstream, to a mass market. When he remarks, 'Tarja Halonen is a good president' to Ville Hammarberg, or talks about political corruption on a national and global scale, he implies he is a commentator whose opinion matters. When commentators present Kaurismäki as the most vital figure in Finnish film history, someone whose stature compares to Jean Sibelius, Alvar Aalto, and other prominent Finns, they are seeking to define the director as a national figure (see von Bagh 2007). As we saw in chapter three, many arguments have insisted that Kaurismäki's niche status is a misrecognition of the director's importance, which *should be* mainstream in the national culture. Yet one of the main arguments for this mainstream status is the director's international niche success. For Kaurismäki, and other small-nation filmmakers, one of the most effective means of enhancing their notoriety, impact, or brand is to shine in the international spotlight. While the actual globalisation of a figure is sure to secure increases in funding, influence, and stature, the appearance of global prominence does the same. The sociologist Dan Steinbock made precisely this point about Kaurismäki in 1989, when the director and his brother Mika's films were featured in a retrospective series at the Museum of Modern Art (MoMA) in New York. While articles in the Finnish press touted Kaurismäki's success, Steinbock observes that the retrospective was barely visible in the New York media. Steinbock attacks the argument that the small-nation auteur is a general interest story outside the national borders by recontextualising the MoMA event in a broader context. Yet Steinbock makes a parochial mistake in his comment as well, for he presumes that the MoMA event is a general interest story, rather than a niche one. MoMA, too, is a niche entity. What we see, though, is the extent to which the appearance of global prominence, even as a niche figure, gives Kaurismäki a means of intervening in national discussion as though he were a globally mainstream figure. At the same time, his filmmaking practice remains aimed at a niche audience, both at home and abroad. And since that niche audience is largest in France, Germany, and Italy, the mode of globalisation that is relevant has to do with effective address of these audiences.

What is clear is that a niche is a nice place to be: that is, it provides the savvy auteur with a way of speaking to multiple audiences, without taking on a risk that would undermine his capacity to address those multiple audiences. The established niche auteur can access his domestic culture as both a niche figure and as a general interest newsmaker, with significant cultural and political clout. At the same time, the established auteur can access the media, debates, and discussions of a number of other territories: Hamburg, Berlin, Cannes, Paris, Venice, London, New York. Kaurismäki deftly exploited this access by stirring up controversy in 2002, when he cancelled his attendance at the New York Film Festival to protest the denial of a visa to Abbas Kiarostami to attend the festival, puckishly inviting Donald Rumsfeld to Finland to go mushroom picking. He employed a similar tactic in spring 2003, when he declined to attend the Academy Awards. The New York Film Festival is of course a niche event, but Kaurismäki recognised that Kiarostami's bit part in George W. Bush's War on Terror was a general interest story globally, which furnished him with a general interest moment to do politics. The Academy Awards are a general interest story globally as well, which Kaurismäki exploited skilfully. Festivals and awards events provide a special context, insofar as they multiply the reputation of a filmmaker, but also inasmuch as the events are general interest and address broad television, print, and online audiences.

The Film Festival and the Small-Nation Auteur

The film festival network, estimated at between 1200 and 1900 festivals in 2007, constitutes a distribution system of its own, positioned in a liminal space between the Hollywood majors, their boutique distribution labels, national cinemas, and third cinemas (see Valck 2007). All of these entities come together at festivals such as Cannes, Venice, Berlin, Toronto, Karlovy Vary, Sundance, and others. The majors give sneak previews at out-of-competition screenings and press conferences. Feature series bring emergent names in the avant-garde and third cinema to global attention. Established auteurs and stars such as Wong Kar Wai, Michael Haneke, Lars von Trier, Gus van Sant, and others figure in the competition series. The system comprises an alternative distribution network built around high profiles, a moving transnational bazaar, which gives niche films visibility, adds cultural and political value through debate and discussion about them, and diversifies film culture by producing surprising and unexpected events (see Valck 2007). Kaurismäki's cinema, and small-nation auteur cinema, works through this festival system, and its global distribution and impact could not be achieved without it. The festival system may sand down national differences, raising questions about the relevance of national and small-nation cinema to the festival system, yet at the same time it provides a showcase for national-cinema institutions to market themselves as vital. The festival system shows the extent to which a notion of small-nation cinema must come to terms with distribution and exhibition practice through which it can be defined as vital.

Kaurismäki's films have risen on the growth in the festival system since the 1980s. Kääpä points out that the Kaurismäki brothers' breakout film *The Liar* won the jury prize at the Henri Langlois Festival at Tours in 1981, as well as other prizes, generating significant Finnish press coverage, although the film was released in one print theatrically in Finland, attracting an audience of some 1,200 (Kääpä 2008: 88). With *Shadows in Paradise* in 1987, Kaurismäki made it into Cannes in the Directors' Fortnight series. *I Hired a Contract Killer* was featured in the competition series at Venice in 1990, winning wide critical favour (see Ylänen 1990). The *Leningrad Cowboys* films and *The Bohemian Life* featured in competition at Berlin. Since then, with the exception of *Juha*, Kaurismäki's films have been in the competition at Cannes.

Kaurismäki has proved a deft hand at generating interest in his films at these festivals with eccentric performances in press conferences, including constant smoking, frequent drinking, and cryptic and laconic statements. The primary time that he makes the headlines in the Finnish media, and is a figure of debate in cultural and cinema discussions in the global media, is in the context of festivals featuring his films. This creates a profound ambivalence, for the festival circuit is largely a business enterprise, as Hammarberg pointed out in the interview with which we began, yet it is also a rich discursive space. The Midnight Sun Festival has involved an eclectic 'affinitive transnationalism', to take a term from Hjort (2007: 17–18), gathering together diverse professionals and audiences around a shared object of pleasure and study: cinema. As we saw in the Introduction and chapter two, Kaurismäki's performances at the mainstream festivals have worked in concert with media coverage to amplify attention to his films and to steer debate towards issues on his agenda, be they geopolitics or his assertions of corruption in Finnish politics. Without the event-based forum created by the film festival system, such interventions would be impossible, and they would not receive the general interest status they enjoy when they occur at festivals. The festival system is crucial to the general interest impact of a niche filmmaker from a small nation, who nevertheless has come to count among the significant cinematic figures of his generation.

In Kaurismäki, then, we have a concrete example of a successful model of niche-market globalisation, but it would seem that the model is largely that of most niche products: exploit one's competitive advantages to define one's relevance to a widely spread, multi-local audience. Kaurismäki's films play best in the art-house theatres of European cities, and for collectors of speciality cinema DVDs. That niche audience is sufficiently large, and sufficiently influential to make Kaurismäki into a figure of cultural importance. That is, returning to Laclau and Mouffe (1985) one more time, Kaurismäki's festival and critical success signifies cultural importance, visibility, and notoriety. That status also provides cultural capital, which is paradoxically most valuable in the Finnish context, where he appears as a distant and powerful representative of world cinema. But it also provides moments of general interest relevance in the global media, which permits interventions of the kind that occurred around the

New York Film Festival and the Academy Awards. Niche importance thus becomes a signifier associated with mainstream importance. Yet we might miss the significance of Kaurismäki's negotiation of these dynamics if we focus analysis on production. By adding analysis of distribution and exhibition, we get a richer picture of Kaurismäki and of small-nation cinema.

Coda

Kaurismäki has always responded ambivalently to his oscillating status as transnational niche figure, and national niche and mainstream figure. He cultivates this ambivalence in his films, I have argued, in ways that foster both cohesion and dissipation of the national cinema, foregrounding issues of multination. In this way, Kaurismäki's greatest contribution to Finnish cinema, and the cinema of small-nations, lies in his unrelenting challenge to question these categories, and the premises that subtend them. We come back around to the national stories told about Kaurismäki and figures like him. As we saw in Ville Hammarberg's interview, the national story furnishes a simple and powerful framework for making sense of the filmmaker and his films. Yet at the same time, as we see in Jörn Donner's ridicule of the Commission to Develop National Brand, the logic by which we make a figure like Kaurismäki a signifier of the nation is arguably premised on worn-out notions of national expression. Kaurismäki's cinema situates us at a rich global crossroads, which leads us towards the nation, at the same time as it reminds us that home today is always dislocated and transnational, part of other cultures, other lives, and other imaginings.

Notes

1 Other markings also appear in the margin. One is the name and phone number of the editor in chief of the newspaper *Satakunnan kansa*, Jouko Jokinen. The title of the newspaper and the article's publication date are also handwritten on the document, apparently in a different hand.
2 Here I am echoing Michael Patrick Gillespie's observation that in analysis of national cinema 'long-established analytic habits have impeded any reconfigurations of traditional conceptions' (2008: xiii).
3 Anderson continues to figure prominently in many studies of national cinema, such as Gillespie (2008: 13).
4 This figure comes from the Lumiere Database, which compiles theatrical admissiosn figures in the territories of the European Union. http://lumiere.obs.coe.int/web/film_info/?id=18716.
5 Pellonpää had long played Kaurismäki's leading man, and his death at age forty-three before *Drifting Clouds* shook the director and his troupe.
6 www.sallypotter.com/cv.
7 Also see Richard Porton (1993).
8 The title tellingly alludes to another famous contribution by Donner, his 1971 book *Finnish Film, Year Zero* (*Suomalainen elokuva vuonna nolla*), which made the

case for the development and funding of a Finnish Film Foundation to support production of domestic cinema.
9   The cited verse is from J. L. Runeberg's poem 'Vårt land'/'Our Land' (1848), which is also the source of the lyrics of Finland's national anthem.

APPENDIX

A Conversation with Aki Kaurismäki

The following interview took place on 17 August 2007 at the Helsinki office of Kaurismäki's production company Sputnik Ltd. The interview was in Finnish, and has been translated and edited for concision by the author.

Audience

Andrew Nestingen (AN): As a foreign viewer of your films, it's interesting to note that although many of your films are regarded as instances of national cinema, they have found an audience throughout Europe and around the world. Who is your audience?

Aki Kaurismäki (AK): Of course you have to take your audience into consideration. The premise is that you have to hoodwink the viewer, get them go along with a story that they assume is true. But I couldn't give a shit about a target audience, in terms of numbers or ages. I don't think about that. For me it's mainly about the viewer; you have to make her laugh and make her cry. So you could say that in that way there is an abstract sense of audience at work in the development of my films. You've got to lead them around by the nose. In Finland my audience tends to be young people and cultured older women. Outside Finland it's more diverse.

AN: Are there differences by country? For example in France and Germany do you think there's a different breakdown than the one in Finland?

AK: I don't really know about statistical differences between countries. When the films play well there tends to be a diverse audience. I think that the consistent audience for my films is younger in Europe than in Finland. But I don't know. About the Finnish audience, I can only say that I have heard many times that there's a remarkable number of cultured older women. And that's a wonderful thing, if that's the case.

Production

AN: What is the cost of making a film in Finland? You have to pay salaries, of course, but what kinds of costs are involved in location shooting? What are the most expensive items in your budget?

AK: You don't really have to pay for location shots in Finland. Well, you do have to pay for interior location shots, but it's not much. But they don't charge for location shots on public streets. In the capital city, you can get a general photography permit. And then you go where you want – as long as you don't block traffic on major thoroughfares without permission for very long.

Things are pretty clear budget wise: half goes for salaries and the other half gets divided into various production costs. About a third of that is for sets, a third for laboratory costs, and a third for everything else: lighting, costumes, coffee, rolls, posters, and whatever else is in there. Of course it's not quite so straightforward, but about half goes to salaries. I don't use much on material or supplies, so that cost is significantly less for me than for others. I don't spend much on sets. We pretty much use recycled and used stuff on our sets – whatever happens to be lying on the side of the street when we're shooting and whatever leftover paint is sitting in the corner. If you want to sum it all up, we're talking about 1.5 million US dollars.

AN: A glance at the credits for your films shows that the films are made with funding from many different sources in many different countries, production companies, television channels, as well as film institutes. How has this system developed for you?

AK: The productions have really been Finnish-German-French cooperation for years. The Germans and French have their funding sources, which they want included in the credits. In practice, they don't have a relationship with me in my role as producer. I maintain one hundred percent control of the films' rights, despite the number of parties involved. They only receive distribution rights.

AN: Does that mean that when production commences, the money is in place, but no one but you is responsible for final production decisions?

AK: I am the producer. If there's a script, I let people read it, but usually there's no script. Sure, I give them a scenario of the film. But these are relationships based on trust. This is the way we've done it since the 1970s and 1980s; we've worked with the same people. I definitely know exactly what budget I need, as well as the amount or revenue a picture will produce, and how much it's wise to use on production. I make films so cheap that no one takes on a large risk. The budgets are really insignificant, since we have to cover all our costs.

Music

AN: You've spoken in previous interviews about musical decisions you've made on the basis of budget concerns. You included some recordings of Shostakovich, if I remember, in order to avoid rights costs. Have you made decisions in order to maintain your low budget, while trying to preserve some freedom of choice?

AK: I did use Shostakovich years ago and had to pay like hell for it, but I switched to Tchaikovsky who had the sense to die earlier. Musical rights ownership is concentrated in the hands of a couple of big firms. Almost all Finnish music is controlled by Warner, which bought up Fazer and the smaller firms, which Fazer had rolled into itself. I don't even have the money to use Finnish tango, because the Yanks control the rights, and they're brutal. Their bids are just brutal.

AN: Wasn't there a tango-sequence in *Lights in the Dusk*?

AK: Yes, it's Carlos Gardel.

AN: So you had to pay for that nonetheless? Are the prices in the same class as the Finnish tangos?

AK: I didn't actually have to pay for that one, since Gardel died in 1935, and copyright had expired on 1 January 2006. But that wasn't the reason I used Gardel. It was just a coincidence.

AN: But expensive rights could be an obstacle?

AK: Sure, but in the Gardel case, the recordings are so old they are in the public domain. Of course I don't try to find music that's free. But the bids on some of the music are such that one song would use up as much as I have budgeted for all the music in the film. It doesn't really work. So now I scrape things together from here and there.

AN: Here's an interesting musical question for me as a foreign viewer: What do The Renegades mean to you? What were they as a phenomenon? They have featured frequently in your films.

AK: They're the toughest rock-n-roll (*rautalanka*) band of all time.[1] In comparison to The Renegades, The Shadows belong in a sandbox at the local daycare. When I was a kid and there was only one coin to put in the jukebox, it was always went to The Renegades. They were an English band who became famous in Finland and Italy, but nowhere else.

AN: Do you know why it was only Finland and Italy?

AK: What I do know is that they came to Finland and got an explosive reception here. They even recorded their albums here. They had two LPs released by a Finnish record company during the 1960s.

Finnish Cinema

AN: In your view, where is contemporary Finnish cinema in historical terms?

AK: Throughout the 1950s, it was the idyllic countryside and the sinful city. Then there was a sort of new wave in the 1960s, which flew off every which way, as new waves tend to do. Then things got stuck: it was portraits of great men and grandiose national themes during the 1970s. We kicked up a little more speed in the early 1980s, but we were pretty lonely in our kicking. In the 1990s film started to win popularity with audiences again. But nothing substantive is going on there. Finnish cinema is a bitter pill. Or rather, if there's passion for it, then it's Finnish passion, so it's not easily visible.

AN: You spoke about the idyllic countryside and the sinful city. In your films, a man often arrives from the countryside to the city. Does the source of that narrative lie in the history of Finnish cinema?

AK: Of course it comes from there, too. I myself moved from the country to the city, to Helsinki. I know what it's like to be a newcomer. The films I was thinking of involve a different kind of story. Usually it was something like a farm daughter falling in love with a hired hand, which created a scandal, until the hired hand was revealed to be an agronomist or the son of a wealthy family in the city. And then it wasn't such a big deal. There were about thirty excellent films made in Finland before 1960 and perhaps about the same number since then. That totals about sixty.

AN: You have spoken in the past about Valentin Vaala, Teuvo Tulio, and other figures from Finland's studio period. What do you find in their work?

AK: Nyrki Tapiovaara, too – if he had lived.[2] He could have done whatever he wanted. But Tulio is special, a real master of melodrama. Amazing stuff. It approaches costume drama social-democratically, although they do it skillfully. Vaala's *People in the Summer Night* [*Ihmiset suviyössä*, 1948] is an excellent film, I have to say. Tulio's melodramas are amazing films even when you compare them with an international standard. It's a shame that their technical level was quite a bit more developed than their screenplays. The writing could be pretty elementary. On the other hand, staging, cinematography, costumes, and the other technical elements were pretty good on a European level.

AN: What do you mean that the scripts were flawed?

AK: Well they were a little bit like Finnish summer theatre. I don't know who actually did the screenwriting for those films. The dialogue is sort of fluffed discussion, and it can also be exaggeratedly rigid. When the characters are in the city, the dialogue is just so fluffy there's nothing left, and when they're in the countryside you don't hear anything but grunts.

Melodrama and Film History

AN: You mentioned melodrama, which is something you yourself dip into. What does melodrama mean to you?

AK: In American cinema, it means Douglas Sirk at his purest, but these days you can still find more than a few melodramas. Melodrama is life's actions and events taken to the second power. Quotidian occurrences are taken to their extreme, and the music too. When it storms, it's a booming thunderstorm. When the sky darkens, the clouds are black and there's a lot of them. Melodrama doesn't differ from naturalism, except for in its exaggerated quality.

AN: Towards what end?

AK: So that the spectator can feel that the massive expression of feeling represents herself. It's an exaggerated reality. In a sense it's the opposite of naturalism, or naturalism to the third power.

AN: In *Juha* there's the wonderful moment in which Shemeikka's Corvette arrives, and we see that the hood ornament alludes to Sirk, a central figure in melodrama, as you noted.

AK: His original German surname was Sierck. It's of course an allusion for the couple of people who know the German surname. If you want to amuse yourself, find it there.

AN: But Douglas Sirk is also known for his excessive irony, which on the one hand creates emotional intensity, but on the other criticised the contemporary notion of the American dream in the United States in the 1950s. Is Sirk's tradition of irony also a part of your films?

AK: Yes, the reference is certainly a hint in that direction, that, look out, Sirk's repertoire is in use here. In both the irony and the exaggeration. The entire figure of Shemeikka is based on playing that card. You can't really take the character seriously.

AN: In your essay on Robert Bresson, 'The Wolf', you describe Bresson as the opposite of Douglas Sirk. What do you mean by that?

AK: Bresson is nothing more than Douglas Sirk. I wrote something like that, it's true.

AN: You see Bresson as a melodramatist, then?

AK: What I'm driving at is largely a formal distinction between Bresson and Sirk. The only difference separating them is form. They tell the same story, but with completely divergent forms. One is a minimalist, the other blows things up to their maximum.

AN: Bresson was known for his inexpressive and silent actors, too. Could you talk a little about what Bresson signifies for you?

AK: I'm a lot nicer than Bresson. He was mean. The actress who appeared in *L'Argent*, in the final sequence, in which everyone is murdered. She washes clothes in one scene. Bresson made her wash clothes all day, made her practise for hours, until he was satisfied with the way she was washing clothes.

AN: What do you think of that kind of method-acting technique?

AK: I don't believe in aerobics. Take hold of it and go. Ten minutes to practise dialogue, then we take a look at it. I shoot the first practice run, and that's it. If there's a mistake, then I'll shoot a second take. But in general it's one take.

AN: It reminds me of old John Ford, for whom one take was enough. He built the films in the cutting room.

AK: I sincerely believe that the actors already act in the first take. Of course as a producer, I also see it as the least expensive way to make a film. But I've never noticed that the scene gets better with more takes. If there's some technical mistake, then of course we'll do it again. Otherwise, once is enough. It's unusual to do a scene twice. Then again, if the scene involves a number of people and it would be expensive to set it up a second time, we'll do a second take just in case, but we'll nevertheless use the first take.

AN: Many commentators argue that your films have an important relationship to the history of cinema. It's obvious that the films are built on a knowledge of film history, and that they often allude to other films. In *Leningrad Cowboys Meet Moses*, for example, there's the scene in the factory in which you yourself imitate Charles Chaplin in *Modern Times*, working on the assembly line.

AK: Actually, I'm Chaplin and Buster Keaton at the same time. That scene came about when we were shooting in a tractor factory. We were shooting images of the machines, and so they let the workers take an early lunch break. There was nobody to man the machines, so I had to do it myself as the lone worker.

AN: Are there specific figures in films, or directors, to which you return frequently as a viewer or in your thoughts, for example when you think about how you might resolve a sequence in one of your films?

AK: I don't think of anything when I make films. Directing is automatic writing. So many thoughts scuttle through your head, compress in your head; you can't really know what you're thinking. Otherwise I've noticed that I keep going back to the comics, Chaplin and Buster Keaton and others. They really had it all together.

AN: What about Harold Lloyd?

AK: A little bit, but I'm not enamoured with him.

AN: Why not? What makes him different?

AK: He's so upper class. He had his own car and everything.

AN: And a very large house.

AK: He really managed to cash in, and he didn't lose it, not even in the stock market crash. He was one of the few true businessmen. Most everyone else lost everything. Or were wager-workers at heart.

National Nostalgia

AN: Many media accounts of your career mention that you have been politically active all along the way, from peace marches to the Kirsti Paakkanen matter. In such instances, ethical and moral issues are at stake. Is there a relationship between such issues and your films?

AK: I don't know, since film is a lousy vehicle for saying anything. Or you have to be so subtle. I guess it should tell you something that my films haven't paid any attention to people in power, or to the upper class. They're completely irrelevant; at most they're caricatures who play the fool for a maximum of thirty seconds. There's no political reason for that, they're just such dull characters, all of them.

AN: Not far from your offices here is the memorial to president Urho Kekkonen, and I noticed his picture hanging there on your wall, as well.[3] A lot of people have talked about your films' nostalgia. How would you characterise Kekkonen's time?

AK: What can you conclude from my office? Whose picture hangs highest? Kekkonen was not without his flaws, not even in that neighbourhood. But nowadays it's easy to miss a real politician when you take a look at the herd of cattle and children romping around up there in parliament. Even that business, that groping around, requires sufficient professional skill to spare the nation unceasing humiliation. They're so lousy at corruption that it's obvious to everyone.

AN: What corruption?

AK: It's a *quid pro quo* principle. If someone leaves politics, well then a position needs to be arranged for him. It's not even called corruption, but I have no idea why Esko Aho is head of SITRA, collecting a handsome salary and spreading around capital to his friends at Nokia.[4] What happened to Sinikka Mönkäre, after she drove through Finland's fifth nuclear plant?[5] I wondered, how many weeks will this take? Sure enough, three weeks later she was the newly appointed head of Finland's Slot-Machine Association (*RAHA-automaattiyhdistys*). Ministers lose their posts; and what happens? Let them run the postal service or the lottery. That's the way it is, laundered corruption. None of these people has any professional competency for these jobs. But when someone has been a minister of government, well then he can run the railroads or the postal service. These people can't do anything but collect a big paycheck. As if Finland is the least corrupt country in the world.

AN: I read an amusing remark by a Czech writer who settled as a political refugee in Norway following the Prague spring. He remarked that in Norway there's no corruption, everyone just went to the same secondary school. Are you saying that Finland works on the same principle?

AK: Well, Norway is an even smaller country than Finland. The Finns didn't go to the same secondary school, but the same school, yes. It's clearly a *quid pro quo* system. One party gives tacit approval to some questionable decision, but that just means that next time it'll be their guy or girl. This has been going on as long as I've been following things, which is some forty years.

AN: So in Kekkonen's time, too?

AK: Yes, of course, more openly, but also more honestly.

AN: So now there's more effort spent on concealment?

AK: Right, like I just happened to end up in this job.

AN: A perfectly natural arrangement.

The Political Economy of Food

AK: Kekkonen's contemporaries fought in restaurants. They knew how to drink and have a good time. But nobody wants to pay attention to today's anaemic broilers. And besides that, they make such poor decisions. At least the old-fashioned politicians made bad decisions with some flair. The lying has increased. Lies are told to the nation every day. Any statement you can imagine begins with a lie. Now they're talking about genetically-modified animal feed. They're beginning to import genetically-modified soy products to feed swine in Finland. Of course there was a big outcry. But Farmer John says this is the only way that Finnish meat production can remain profitable. And then they just trot out the lies, plain as can be. There's supposedly a five percent price difference per kilo between animals fed with regular feed and those fed with cheaper, genetically-modified feed. I don't really think it matters whether the price per kilo is 10.70 or 10.80 euros. But then they get all upset that people raise food-safety questions. Of course the farmers raising the livestock wouldn't want to eat dangerous food. And a third of Americans have eaten meat produced with this kind of feed in the last ten years, they say.

AN: Look at us Americans.

AK: I want to ask them – since the argument raises certain suspicions – when four in five Americans are overweight, shouldn't some alarm bells go off? There should be fuller analysis of the safety issues.

AN: The American journalist Michael Pollan has written on this topic, especially in a book called *The Omnivore's Dilemma* – super book. He takes four meals and explores their political economy, from the soil to the plate. The first is a McDonald's meal, which he eats in a car with his family. That's a meal subsidised by cheap oil, which contributes to the fertilisers necessary for farming high yields of cheap corn, which is one of the main sources of calories in American food and especially meat production. Yet corn famers can barely survive, because the price of corn has been driven so low.

AK: What were the other meals?

AN: One is an organic meal, what he calls industrial organic. It's a big trend these days. There's a national grocery chain, Whole Foods, which produces organic food by a similar industrial system to mainstream food production. It's just as dependent on oil. Then there's a meal of what he calls deep organic, farmers who've opted out of the system for local farming, no chemicals of any kind, etc. Finally, there's a hunted and foraged meal, wild boar and mushrooms, which the author acquires himself in the forests of California. Interesting book.

AK: I just saw some study that stated that organic farming could feed the world population. Organic methods are actually more efficient in the developing world than industrial methods. Particularly in the developing world.

AN: The food industry tries to break up the circle of life and insert their products, since it's more profitable.

AK: Apocalyptic companies like Monsanto. It's right out of a horror movie, right out of Hitler's vault.

AN: When you study little things like food packages you can discover quite a bit about how the system works.

AK: That's about it. I've been thinking, should it be obligatory to label pork products produced with pigs that have been fed genetically-modified feed? The EU doesn't currently require it. They argue that the genetically-modified feed is not actually a part of the consumer product. Of course a pig is what it eats. Hopefully the agricultural producers themselves will demand that kind of labelling. I've done my thinking about this, and I said to myself, I can get out of this dilemma right away. I don't have to eat pork, and I don't have to eat meat. So they get their five percent savings through feed, but they lost one customer for all of their products. The companies that initiated the change in feed all ended up being boycotted. So a couple of percent savings ended up being quite a twisted ankle for them.

AN: Hog farming seems to be the worst offender, since pigs can be fed just about anything.

AK: There was a farm in France that got shut down because they fed the pigs human waste.

AN: There's that scene in Veijo Meri's novel *The Manilla Rope* [*Mannillköysi*], which describes an escaped herd of swine during the Continuation War, which started eating human remains, Russian soldiers.

AK: They ate some Finns, too.

Finland and Its Others

AN: About the relationship between Russia and Finland, it's noticeable that in the opening sequence of *Lights in the Dusk*, there are some Russians walking down the street talking about Pushkin and Gogol in Russian. (The sequence is not subtitled in the Finnish release.) It seems that they are presented as stereotyped outsiders, meriting suspicion, even though they are talking about literature in a humanistic way. You yourself live in Portugal part of the year. What does otherness and being a foreigner in a foreign land mean to you?

AK: Living in Portugal is easy, since I'm not dark skinned, even though there's not much racism there. It hasn't been that difficult, it's a small community. They finally figured out my job, and that, OK, the guy has some job. Then they were happy that I had a job and that I wasn't just loafing around, a good-for-nothing. He's got a job, seems like a nice guy. Fine. The commonplace advice there, which I pass on to others, is that if a big BMW with tinted windows drives in and out of your place, someone's going to keep track, and maybe break in. Not the neighbour's office. Or they'll burglarise some little café. That's normal. Great. People don't expect that in Finland. So when someone gets flown in from some devastated place, and he thinks he's acting normal out in some Finnish town, Finns can have a tough time relating. And the language only makes it worse. But racism will disappear from Finland. It's not a part of people's worldview here, it is an expression of fear of the new and unknown. And it's just as quickly directed at Norwegians and Swedes, as at people of colour. The real disgrace here is Finland's refugee policy, which is shameful. We refuse refugee status on the flimsiest of grounds and send people back to secure places like Darfur, Iraq, and Somalia. 'It's perfectly safe, go ahead.' Our policy is a stain among the Nordic nations. Shameful.

AN: You've said a lot about the Finnish state and nation. Your films are often held up as an example of Finnish national cinema. But on the other hand, you relate very critically to any number of aspects of Finnish politics and society. Is there a contradiction there?

AK: One can't equate my films with my person, but when the films received awards outside Finland, Finns thought it was just grand. This nation is so insecure that it's just the greatest thing ever if some foreigner says something nice about Finland, or some Finn jumps or hops or bounces further than anybody else. In that sense, when you have some success internationally, then that success is accepted here, too. Before that, my films were part of the freak show. And of course the films are more exotic to foreigners than to Finns, since for Finns about half of what the films show is everyday life, which is exotic to everybody else.

AN: In looking at the reception of your films outside Finland, it often seems that critics categorise them as expressions of Finnishness because they can't think of another way to categorise them. They don't really know what Finnish film is, but don't what else to say about them.

AK: There is no national cinema in Finland. It's spread out across a couple of groups of people, who do whatever they do. I don't see a national cinema in the US, either, unless you count that disgrace in Hollywood. There's hardly anyone who'd want to declare that *Transformers* represents the national culture. I suppose there's something to be found there, if you put some time into studying it, perhaps there are some deep seams of meaning. But you'd have to look for them in independent productions. There's no sense in mixing up Hollywood and cinema. They're two different things. Hollywood is business, the entertainment business. There's no point in demanding anything else from Hollywood. If you ask for anything more complicated, you just get frustrated.

Notes

1. Kaurismäki does not use the term rock-n-roll, but *rautalanka,* which is a musical genre similar to the instrumental rock and surf rock popularised in the early 1960s by such bands as The Shadows and The Ventures. It was the first form of rock-blues music associated with youth culture in Finland, gaining a foothold through off-shore radio broadcasts around 1960, and agitating against the cultural edification programming promulgated by state-controlled broadcasting. *Rautalanka* literally means 'iron string'.
2. Tapiovaara was killed in action in 1940, during Finland's Winter War.
3. Centre Party politician Urho Kekkonen dominated Finnish public life during his tenure as President (1956–1982). He is remembered for his pragmatically acquiescent relationship with the Soviet Union, which preserved Finland's independence, but also for his strong and paternalistic leadership in domestic affairs.
4. SITRA is a venture capital fund established by the Finnish parliament in 1967 with the purpose of cultivating Finland's economic growth. Esko Aho of the Finnish Centre Party served as Finnish Prime Minister from 1991 to 1995.
5. Mönkäre served as a Social-Democratic MP, as well as Minister of Commerce and Minster of Health and Social Services in several governments since the 1990s. While expansion of nuclear power has been popular on the right, the left and the greens have opposed it. Mönkäre's ministerial-level support of permitting construction of a fifth Finnish nuclear plant proved decisive in 2002 when the matter came up for a parliamentary vote. Yet her position was unpopular in her party and on the left.

FILMOGRAPHY

Feature films directed or co-directed by Aki Kaurismäki

Saimaa-ilmiö (*The Saimaa Gesture*)
Finnish Theatrical Premiere: 11 September 1981
International Premiere: Figuera da Foz Festival (Portugal), 1982
Production Company: Villealfa Filmproductions Ltd.
Directors: Aki Kaurismäki, Mika Kaurismäki
Producer: Mika Kaurismäki
Planning: Aki Kaurismäki, Mika Kaurismäki
Cinematography: Lasse Naukkarinen, Timo Salminen, Toni Sulzbeck, Olli Varja
Sound: Mikael Sievers, Jouko Lumme
Concert Recording: Mika Sundqvist
Film Editing: Antti Kari
Principal Cast: Juice Leskinen Slam, Eppu Normaali, Hassisen kone

Rikos ja rangaistus (*Crime and Punishment*)
Finnish Theatrical Premiere: 2 December 1983
International Premiere: 23 August 1990 (Museum of Modern Art, New York)
Production Company: Villealfa Filmproductions Ltd.
Director: Aki Kaurismäki
Producer: Mika Kaurismäki
Production Manager: Jaakko Talaskivi
Screenplay: Aki Kaurismäki, Pauli Pentti
Based on the novel by Fyodor Dostoevsky
Original Music: Pedro Hietanen
Cinematography: Timo Salminen
Sound: Mikael Sievers
Film Editing: Veikko Aaltonen
Production Design: Matti Jaaranen
Principal Cast: Markku Toikka (Antti Rahikainen), Aino Seppo (Eeva Laakso), Esko Nikkari (Inspector Pennanen), Hannu Lauri (Store Owner), Matti Pellonpää (Nikander), Pentti Auer (Pennanen), Asmo Hurula (Bartender)

Calamari Union
Finnish Theatrical Premiere: 8 February 1985
International Premiere: 23 August 1990 (Museum of Modern Art, New York)
Production Company: Villealfa Filmproductions Ltd.
Director: Aki Kaurismäki
Producer: Aki Kaurismäki
Production Manager: Jaakko Talaskivi
Original Music: Mikko Mattila, Jone Takamäki, Casablanca Vox
Cinematography: Harri Laakso, Mikko Mattila, Heikki Ortamo, Timo Salminen
Sound: Jouko Lumme
Film Editing: Aki Kaurismäki, Raija Talvio
Principal Cast: Timo Eränkö (Frank), Kari Heiskanen (Frank), Asmo Hurula (Frank), Sakke Järvenpää (Frank),

Sakari Kuosmenen (Frank Armoton), Mikko Mattila (Frank), Pate Mustajärvi (Frank), Pirkka-Pekka Petelius (Frank), Matti Pellonpää (Frank), Pertti Sveholm (Frank), Matti Syrjä (Frank), Pantse Syrjä (Frank), Markku Toikka (Pekka)

Varjoja paratiisissa (*Shadows in Paradise*)
Finnish Theatrical Premiere: 17 October 1986
International Premiere: 7–19 May 1987 (Directors' Fortnight, Cannes International Film Festival)*
Director: Aki Kaurismäki
Producer: Mika Kaurismäki
Production Manager: Jaakko Talaskivi
Screenplay: Aki Kaurismäki
Cinematography: Timo Salminen
Sound: Jouko Lumme
Film Editing: Raija Talvio
Art Direction: Pertti Hilkamo, Heikki Ukkonen
Production Company: Villealfa Filmproductions Ltd.
Principal Cast: Matti Pellonpää (Nikander), Kati Outinen (Ilona), Sakari Kuosmanen (Melartin), Esko Nikkari (Nikander's co-worker)

Hamlet liikemaailmassa (*Hamlet Goes Business*)
Finnish Theatrical Premiere: 21 August 1987
International Premiere: 17 February 1988 (Berlin International Film Festival)
Production Company: Villealfa Filmproductions Ltd.
Director: Aki Kaurismäki
Producer: Aki Kaurismäki
Production Manager: Jaakko Talaskivi
Screenplay: Aki Kaurismäki
Based on the play by William Shakespeare
Cinematography: Timo Salminen
Sound: Veikko Aaltonen, Jouko Lumme
Film Editing: Raija Talvio
Art Direction: Pertti Hilkamo
Principal Cast: Pirkka-Pekka Petelius (Hamlet), Esko Salminen (Klaus), Kati Outinen (Ofelia), Elina Salo (Gertrud), Esko Nikkari (Polonius), Kari Väänänen (Lauri Polonius), Puntti Valtonen (Simo), Mari Rantasila (Helena), Turo Pajala (Rosencranz), Åke Kalliala (Gildenstern), Pentti Auer (Father/Ghost), Matti Pellonpää (Sentinel)

Ariel
Finnish Theatrical Premiere: 21 October 1988
International Premiere: 16 February 1989 (Berlin International Film Festival)
Production Company: Villealfa Filmproductions Ltd.
Director: Aki Kaurismäki
Producer: Aki Kaurismäki
Production Manager: Jaakko Talaskivi
Screenplay: Aki Kaurismäki
Cinematography: Timo Salminen
Sound: Jouko Lumme
Film Editing: Raija Talvio
Production Design: Risto Karhula
Principal Cast: Turo Pajala (Taisto Olavi Kasurinen), Susanna Haavisto (Irmeli Katariina Pihlaja), Matti Pellonpää (Mikkonen), Eetu Hilkamo (Riku), Erkki Pajala (Taisto's father)

Leningrad Cowboys Go America
Finnish Theatrical Premiere: 24 March 1989
International Premiere: 4 August 1989 (Swedish Theatrical Release)
Production Company: Swedish Film Institute, Villealfa Filmproductions Ltd.
Director: Aki Kaurismäki
Producers: Aki Kaurismäki, Klaus Heydemann, Katinka Faragó
Production Manager (Finland): Jaakko Talaskivi
Production Manager (US): Lisa Blok-Linson
Production Manager (US): Phil Linson
Screenplay: Aki Kaurismäki
Original Story: Sakke Järvenpää, Aki

Kaurismäki, Mato Valtonen
Cinematography: Timo Salminen
Sound: Jouko Lumme
Film Editing: Raija Talvio
Musical Score: Mauri Sumén
Art Directors: Heikki Ukkonen, Kari Laine
Principal Cast: Matti Pellonpää (Vladimir Kuzmin), Kari Väänänen (The Mute), Leningrad Cowboys, as themselves, Nicky Tesco (Lost Cousin), Richard Boes (Music Promoter), Jim Jarmusch (Car Salesman)

Likaiset kädet (*Dirty Hands*)
Finnish Television Premiere: 5 October 1989 (YLE TV1)
Production Company: Sputnik Ltd., YLE TV 1 (Finnish National Broadcasting Service)
Director: Aki Kaurismäki
Screenplay: Aki Kaurismäki
Based on the play by Jean-Paul Sartre
Producer: Hannu Kahakorpi
Production Manager: Leena Franssila
Cinematography: Matti Kurkikangas
Sound: Lasse Litovaara
Film Editing: Paavo Eskelinen
Principal Cast: Matti Pellonpää (Hugo), Kati Outinen (Jessica), Sulevi Peltola (Hoederer), Kaija Pakarinen (Olga), Pertti Sveholm (Louis), Kari Väänänen (Ivan), Pirkka-Pekka Petelius (Slick)

Tulitikkutehtaan tyttö (*The Match Factory Girl*)
Finnish Theatrical Premiere: 12 January 1990
International Premiere: 14 February 1990 (Berlin International Film Festival)
Production Company: Swedish Film Institute, Villealfa Filmproductions Ltd.
Director: Aki Kaurismäki
Producers: Aki Kaurismäki, Klas Olofsson, Katinka Faragó
Production Manager: Klaus Hedyemann
Production Supervision: Jaakko Talaskivi
Screenplay: Aki Kaurismäki
Cinematography: Timo Salminen
Sound: Jouko Lumme
Film Editing: Aki Kaurismäki
Production Design: Risto Karhula
Principal Cast: Kati Outinen (Iris Rukka), Elina Salo (Mother), Esko Nikkari (Stepfather), Vesa Vierikko (Aarne), Reijo Taipale (Singer)

I Hired a Contract Killer
International Premiere: 13 September 1990 (Venice International Film Festival)
Finnish Theatrical Premiere: 12 October 1990
Production Company: Swedish Film Institute, Villealfa Filmproductions Ltd.
Director: Aki Kaurismäki
Producer: Aki Kaurismäki
Production Manager: Klaus Heydemann
Assistant Production Managers: Jaakko Talaskivi, Pauli Pentti
Screenplay: Aki Kaurismäki
Cinematography: Timo Salminen
Sound: Timo Linnasalo
Film Editing: Aki Kaurismäki
Production Design: John Ebden
Art Direction: Mark Lavis
Principal Cast: Jean-Pierre Léaud (Henri Boulanger), Margi Clarke (Margaret), Kenneth Colley (Harry, Killer), Serge Reggiani (Vic), Nicky Tesco (Pete), Charles Cork (Al)

La vie de Bohème (*The Bohemian Life*)
International Premiere: 18 February 1992 (Berlin International Film Festival)
Finnish Theatrical Premiere: 28 February 1992
Production Company: Sputnik Ltd.
Director: Aki Kaurismäki
Producers: Klaus Heydemann, Aki Kaurismäki
Executive Producers: Francis Boespflug, Paula Oinonen
Production Managers: Gilles Sacuto, Raili Salmi

Screenplay: Aki Kaurismäki
Based on the novel by Henri Murger
Cinematography: Timo Salminen
Sound: Timo Linnasalo, Jouko Lumme
Film Editing: Veikko Aaltonen
Production Design: John Ebden
Principal Cast: Matti Pellonpää (Rodolfo), Evelyne Didi (Mimi), André Wilms (Marcel), Kari Väänänen (Schaunard), Christine Murillo (Musette), Jean-Pierre Léaud (Blancheron)

Total Balalaika Show
Finnish Television Premiere: 29 December 1993 (YLE TV 1)
Finnish Theatrical Premiere: 2 July 1994
International Premiere: 8 September 1994 (Toronto International Film Festival)
Production Company: Sputnik Ltd.
Director: Aki Kaurismäki
Original Music: B. Alexandrov
Original Music: Tipe Johnson
Cinematography: Heikki Ortamo
Film Editing: Timo Linnasalo
Principal Cast: Alexandrov Red Army Ensemble, Atte Blom (himself), Leningrad Cowboys

Pidä huivista kiinni, Tatjana (*Take Care of Your Scarf, Tatiana*)
Finnish Theatrical Premiere: 14 January 1994
International Premiere: 12-23 May 1994 (Directors' Fortnight, Cannes International Film Festival)*
Production Company: Sputnik Ltd.
Director: Aki Kaurismäki
Producer: Aki Kaurismäki
Screenplay: Sakke Järvenpää, Aki Kaurismäki
Cinematography: Timo Salminen
Sound: Jouko Lumme
Film Editing: Aki Kaurismäki
Art Direction: Kari Laine, Markku Pätilä, Jukka Salmi
Principal Cast: Kati Outinen (Tatiana), Matti Pellonpää (Reino), Kirsi Tykkyläinen (Klavdia), Mato Valtonen (Valto)

Leningrad Cowboys Meet Moses
International Premiere: 25 February 1994 (Berlin International Film Festival)
Finnish Theatrical Premiere: 16 Feburary 1994
Production Company: Sputnik Ltd.
Director: Aki Kaurismäki
Executive Producers: Reinhard Brundig, Paula Oinonen, Fabienne Vonier
Producer: Aki Kaurismäki
Production Manager: Jaakko Talaskivi
Story: Sakke Järvenpää, Aki Kaurismäki, Mato Valtonen
Original Music and Musical Supervision: Mauri Sumén
Cinematography: Timo Salminen
Sound: Jouko Lumme, Timo Linnasalo
Film Editing: Aki Kaurismäki
Production Design: John Ebden
Art Direction: Mark Lavis
Principal Cast: Matti Pellonpää (Vladimir Kuzmin, alias Moses), Kari Väänänen (The Mute), André Wilms (Johnson, alias Raymond Lazar, alias Elijah), Leningrad Cowboys, as themselves

Kauas pilvet karkaavat (*Drifting Clouds*)
Finnish Theatrical Premiere: 26 January 1996
International Premiere: 15 May 1996 (Cannes International Film Festival)
Production Company: Sputnik Ltd.
Director: Aki Kaurismäki
Producer: Aki Kaurismäki
Executive Producer: Erkki Astala
Co-Producers: Reinhard Brundig, Fabienne Vonier, Eila Werning
Assistant Producer: Klaus Heydemann
Screenplay: Aki Kaurismäki
Cinematography: Timo Salminen
Sound: Jouko Lumme
Film Editing: Aki Kaurismäki
Production Design: Markku Pätilä, Jukka

Salmi
Principal Cast: Kati Outinen (Ilona), Kari Väänänen (Lauri), Elina Salo (Mrs. Sjöholm), Sakari Kuosmanen (Melartin), Markku Peltola (Lajunen), Matti Onnismaa (Forsström), Matti Pellonpää (child in the photograph)

Juha
International Premiere: 13 February 1999 (Berlin International Film Festival)
Finnish Theatrical Premiere: 25 February 1999
Production Company: Sputnik Ltd.
Director: Aki Kaurismäki
Producer: Aki Kaurismäki
Screenplay: Aki Kaurismäki
Based on the novel *Juha* by Juhani Aho
Original Music: Anssi Tikanmäki
Cinematography: Timo Salminen
Sound: Jouko Lumme
Film Editing: Aki Kaurismäki
Art Design: Markku Pätilä
Principal Cast: Sakari Kuosmanen (Juha), Kati Outinen (Marja), André Wilms (Shemeikka), Markku Peltola (Chauffeur), Elina Salo (Shemeikka's sister)

Mies vailla menneisyyttä (*The Man Without a Past*)
Finnish Theatrical Premiere: 1 March 2002
International Premiere: 22 May 2002 (Cannes International Film Festival)
Production Company: Sputnik Ltd.
Director: Aki Kaurismäki
Producer: Aki Kaurismäki
Executive Producer: Ilkka Mertsola
Screenplay: Aki Kaurismäki
Cinematography: Timo Salminen
Editing: Timo Linnasalo
Sound: Jouko Lumme, Tero Malmberg
Art Design: Markku Pätilä, Jukka Salmi
Principal Cast: Markku Peltola (M, Jaakko Lujanen), Kati Outinen (Irma), Juhani Niemelä (Nieminen), Kaija Pakarinen (Kaisa Nieminen), Sakari Kuosmanen (Anttila), Annikki Tähti (Salvation Army Leader)

Laitakaupungin valot (*Lights in the Dusk*)
Finnish Theatrical Premiere: 3 Feburary 2006
International Premiere: 22 May 2006 (Cannes International Film Festival)
Production Company: Sputnik Ltd.
Director: Aki Kaurismäki
Producer: Aki Kaurismäki
Executive Producer: Ilkka Mertsola
Screenplay: Aki Kaurismäki
Cinematography: Timo Salminen
Sound: Jouko Lumme, Tero Malmberg
Film Editing: Aki Kaurismäki
Art Direction: Markku Pätilä
Principal Cast: Janne Hyytiäinen (Koistinen), Maria Järvenhelmi (Mirja), Maria Heiskanen (Aila), Ilkka Koivula (Lindholm)

Le Havre
Finnish Theatrical Premiere: 9 September 2011
International Premiere: 17 May 2011 (Cannes International Film Festival)
Production Company: Sputnik Ltd.
Director: Aki Kaurismäki
Producer: Aki Kaurismäki
Co-producers: Karl Baumgartner, Reinhard Brundig, Fabienne Vonier
Executive Producer: Hanna Hemilä
Screenplay: Aki Kaurismäki
Cinematography: Timo Salminen
Sound: Tero Malmberg
Film Editing: Timo Linnasalo
Production Design: Wouter Zoon
Principal Cast: André Wilms (Marcel Marx), Kati Outinen (Arletty), Jean-Pierre Darroussin (Monet), Blondin Miguel (Idrissa), Elina Salo (Claire), Evelyne Didi (Yvette), Quoc Dung Nguyen (Chang)

Short and feature films to which Aki Kaurismäki has contributed artistically:

Valehtlija (*The Liar*)
Finnish Premiere: 6 February 1981 (Tampere International Short Film Festival)
International Premiere: Henri Langlois Memorial Film Festival, Tours (France), March 1982
Production Company: Hochchule für Fernsehen und Film München, Mika Kaurismäki
Director: Mika Kaurismäki
Producer: Mika Kaurismäki
Production Manager: Lars Lindberg
Screenplay: Aki Kaurismäki, Pauli Pentti, Veikko Aaltonen
Cinematography: Tony Sulzbeck
Sound: Mikael Sievers
Film Editing: Antti Kari
Principal Cast: Aki Kaurismäki (Ville Alfa), Pirkko Hämäläinen (Tuula), Juuso Hirvikangas (Juuso), Lars Lindberg (Harri, Ville's brother), Matti Pellonpää (Raymond Chandler Fan)

Arvottomat (*The Worthless*)
Finnish Theatrical Premiere: 15 October 1982
International Premiere: Gothenburg Film Festival, 1983
Production Company: Villealfa Filmproductions Ltd.
Director: Mika Kaurismäki
Assistant Director: Aki Kaurismäki
Screenplay: Aki Kaurismäki, Mika Kaurismäki
Cinematography: Timo Salminen
Sound: Mikael Sievers
Film Editing: Antti Kari
Production Design: Aki Kaurismäki, Heikki Ukkonen, Timo Eränkö
Principal Cast: Matti Pellonpää (Manne), Pirkko Hämäläinen (Veera), Juuso Hirvikangas (Harri), Esko Nikkari (Hägström), Jorma Markkula (Mitja), Asmo Hurula (Väyry), Aki Kaurismäki (Ville Alfa)

Jackpot 2
Finnish Theatrical Premiere: 5 March 1982
Production Company: Production Group "Jackpot", Villealfa Filmproductions Ltd.
Director: Mika Kaurismäki
Screenplay: Aki Kaurismäki, Mika Kaurismäki
Cinematography: Raimo Paananen, Kaj Troberg, Olli Varja, Heikki Ortamo
Sound: Mikael Sievers, Veikko Aaltonen
Film Editing: Mika Kaurismäki
Assistant film editing, production design, costuming, organisation, and smoke: Aki Kaurismäki, Pauli Pentti
Principal Cast: Martti Syrjä, Tina Bergström, Jukka Mikkola, Eero Tuomikoski, Eero Manner, Matti Pellonpää, Anna-Maija Kaurismäki, Aki Kaurismäki

'Dogs Have No Hell' (*The Trumpet: Ten Minutes Older*)
International Premiere: 18 May 2002 (Cannes International Film Festival)
Director: Aki Kaurismäki
Production Manager: Ilkka Mertsola
Screenplay: Aki Kaurismäki
Cinematography: Aki Kaurismäki, Olli Varja
Sound: Tero Malmberg
Production Design: Markku Pätilä
Principal Cast: Kati Outinen (Woman), Markku Peltola (Man), Sulevi Peltola (Man in the Tire Store), Kirsi Tykkyläinen (Ticket Salesperson), Aare Karén (Goldsmith), Janne Hyytiäinen (Waiter), Pirkko Hämäläinen (Woman in the Restaurant)

'Bico' (*Visions of Europe*)
International Theatrical Premiere: 1 May 2004
Finnish Television Premiere: 30 April 2006
Multiple Production Companies
Director ("Bico"): Aki Kaurismäki
Cinematography: Timo Salminen
Sound: Jouko Lumme
Film Editing: Aki Kaurismäki
Music: Abel Alves

Short films by Aki Kaurismäki

Rocky VI (1986)
Production Company: Villealfa Filmproductions Ltd., Megamania Musiikki Ltd.
Director: Aki Kaurismäki
Producers: Aki Kaurismäki, Atte Blom
Screenplay: Aki Kaurismäki, Sleepy Sleepers
Assistant Cinematographers: Timo Markko, Tuomas Salminen
Sound: Jouko Lumme, Tom Forsström
Film Editing: Aki Kaurismäki, Raija Talvio
Music: Sleepy Sleepers
Cast: Silu Seppälä (Rocky), Sakari Kuosmanen (Igor), Heinäsirkka (Doris), Mato Valtonen (Manager), Juuso Hirvikangas (Sparring partner), Matti Pellonpää (Alyosha, Igor's coach), Jaakko Talaskivi (Dmitri), Press Photographer (Aki Kaurismäki)

Thru the Wire (1987)
Production Company: Megamania Musiikki Ky, Villealfa Filmproductions Ltd.
Producers: Aki Kaurismäki, Atte Blom
Director: Aki Kaurismäki
Screenplay: Leningrad Cowboys
Cinematography: Timo Salminen
Sound: Jouko Lumme
Film Editing: Aki Kaurismäki, Raija Talvio
Music: Silu Seppälä, Nicky Tesco. Leningrad Cowboys
Cast: Nicky Tesco, Marja-Leena Helin, Mato Valtonen, Sakke Järvenpää

Melrose: Rich Little Bitch (1987)
Production Company: Villealfa Filmproductions Ltd.
Director: Aki Kaurismäki
Producer: Aki Kaurismäki
Cinematography: Timo Salminen
Sound: Jyrki Hytti
Film Editing: Aki Kaurismäki, Raija Talvio
Music: Tokela
Performers: Melrose

L.A. Woman (1987)
Production Company: Megamania Musiikki Ky, Villealfa Filmproductions Ltd.
Director: Aki Kaurismäki
Cinematography: Timo Salminen
Sound: Jouko Lumme
Film Editing: Raija Talvio
Performers: Leningrad Cowboys
Music: The Doors: 'L.A. Woman'

Those Were the Days (1991)
Production Company: Sputnik Ltd.
Director: Aki Kaurismäki
Screenplay: Aki Kaurismäki
Cinematography: Timo Salminen
Sound: Jouko Lumme
Film Editing: Aki Kaurismäki
Cast: Silu Seppälä (Lonely Cowboy), Kirsi Tykkyläinen (Bartender's wife), Leningrad Cowboys

These Boots (1992)
Production Company: Sputnik Ltd.
Director: Aki Kaurismäki
Cinematography: Timo Salminen
Sound: Jouko Lumme
Film Editing: Aki Kaurismäki
Cast: Kirsi Tykkyläinen, Leningrad Cowboys

Oo aina ihminen (*Always be Humane*, 1996)
Production Company: Sputnik Ltd.
Director: Aki Kaurismäki
Screenplay: Aki Kaurismäki
Cinematography: Timo Salminen
Sound: Jouko Lumme
Music: Taisto Wesslin
Performers: Markus Allan, Pauli Granfelt, Kari Lindqvist, Pentti Mutikainen, Tomi Parkkonen, Taisto Wesslin

Välittäjä (*The Employment Agent*, 1996)
Production Company: Sputnik Ltd.
Director: Aki Kaurismäki
Producer: Aki Kaurismäki
Screenplay: Aki Kaurismäki
Cinematography: Timo Salminen
Sound: Jouko Lumme
Film Editing: Aki Kaurismäki
Cast: Sulevi Peltola (Employment Agent), Kati Outinen (Unemployed Woman)

Valimo (*The Foundry*, 2006)
Production Company: Sputnik Ltd.
Director: Aki Kaurismäki
Producer Aki Kaurismäki
Screenplay: Aki Kaurismäki
Cinematography: Olli Varja
Sound: Jouko Lumme, Tero Malmberg
Production Design: Jukka Salmi, Jukka Rautiainen
Costumes: Marja-Leena Hukkanen
Film Editing: Aki Kaurismäki
Cast: Matti Hyvönen, Arto Malmberg, Tarmo Nyholm, Jukka Rautiainen, Jukka Salmi, Marie-Chrstine Möller, Carl-Erik Calamnius

This filmography has been compiled from information published in volumes of The Finnish National Filmography, the online database of the Finnish National Audiovisual Archives (www.elonet.fi), and the Internet Movie Database (www.imdb.com).

*When impossible to ascertain a feature film's exact date of premiere, I have provided approximate dates, or dates of the festival at which a premiere occurred.

BIBLIOGRAPHY

Aft, Rob (2004) 'The Global Markets', in J. E. Squire (ed.) *The Movie Business Book*. New York: Simon and Schuster, 458–82.
Agamben, Giorgio (1998) *Homo Sacer: Sovereign Power and Bare Life*, Daniel Heller-Roazen (trans.). Stanford: Stanford University Press.
Alanen, Antti (2005) 'Levottomat', in Sakari Toiviainen (ed.) *Suomen kansallisfilmografia, Vol. 12*. Helsinki: Edita, 618–24.
Alapuro, Kristiina (1983) 'Aki ja Alfa', *Suomen Kuvalehti*, 33, 42–3.
Alasuutari, Pertti (1996) *Toinen tasavalta: Suomi 1946–1996*. Tampere: Vastapaino.
Alasuutari, Pertti and Petri Ruuska (1999) *Post-patria: Globalisaation kulttuuri Suomessa*. Tampere: Vastapaino.
Anderson, Benedict (1991) *Imagined Communities: Reflections on the Origin and Spread of Nationalism*. New York: Verso.
Andrew, Dudley (1995) *Mists of Regret: Culture and Sensibility in Classic French Film*. Princeton, NJ: Princeton University Press.
Andrew, Geoff (1997) 'Original Finn', *Time Out London*, no. 1398, 4 June.
____ (2003) 'The Mighty Finn', *Time Out*, 15–22 January.
Anon. (1990) 'En tee elokuvaia enää Suomessa', *Iltalehti*, 5 September.
____ (2002a) 'Vihdoin menestystäkin', *Helsingin Sanomat*, 29 May.
____ (2002b) 'Omaperäisyys kannattaa', *Iltalehti*, 28 May.
____ (2002c) 'Aki Kaurismäki mursi myytin', *Ilta-Sanomat*, 28 May.
____ (2007) 'Oiva hotellista tuli hoivakoti', *Metro-Helsinki*, 9 March.
Apo, Satu (2001) *Viinan voima: Näkökulmia suomalaisten kansanomaiseen alkoholiajatteluun ja-kulttuuriin*. Helsinki: Finnish Literature Society.
Arolainen, Teuvo (1999) 'Kaurismäet ovat elokuvatuen suosikkeja', *Helsingin Sanomat*, 24 April.
Asikainen, Merja (2003) 'Näkisipä tämän Oscar-gaalassa', *Ilta-Sanomat*, 13 February.

Bacon, Henry (2003) 'Aki Kaurismäen sijoiltaan olon poetiikka', in Kimmo Ahonen, Janne Rosenqvist, Juha Rosenqvist, Päivi Valotie (eds) *Taju kankaalle: Uutta suomalaista elokuvaa paikantamassa*. Turku: Kirja-Aurora, 88–97.

____ (2004) *Audiovisuaalisen kerronnan teoria*. Helsinki: Finnish Literature Society.

Baudelaire, Charles (2006 [1861]) 'LXXXIII: Héautontimoroumenos', Francis Scarfe. (ed. and trans.) *Baudelaire: The Complete Verse, Vol. 1*. London: Anvil Press Poetry, 163–4.

____ (2008 [1845]) 'The Painter of Modern Life', Jonathan Mayne (ed. and trans.), *The Painter of Modern Life and Other Essays*. London: Phaidon, 1–41.

Bazin, André (1967) *What is Cinema, Vol. 1*, Hugh Gray (trans.). Berkeley, CA: University of California Press.

Bergdahl, Gunnar (1989) 'Akis filmer säger allt – och ingenting', *Göteborgs-Posten*, 3 March.

Bhabha, Homi (ed.) (1990) *Nation and Narration*. New York: Routledge.

Blåfeld, Ville (2003) 'Kulttuuriministeri ei tavoittanut Kaurismäkeä', *Ilta-Sanomat*, 13 February.

Bloch, Judy (1989) 'The Brothers Kaurismäki', *Pacific Film Archive Calendar*, February, 3–4.

Bordwell, David (1985) *Narrative in the Fiction Film*. Madison: University of Wisconsin Press.

Bordwell, David, Janet Staiger, and Kristin Thompson (1985) *The Classical Hollywood Cinema: Film Style and Mode of Practice to 1960*. New York: Columbia University Press.

Bourdieu, Pierre (1996) *The Rules of Art: Genesis and Structure of the Literary Field*, Susan Emanuel (trans.). Stanford, CA: Stanford University Press.

Boym, Svetlana (2001) *The Future of Nostalgia*. New York: Basic Books.

British Film Institute (2000) *Directors' Top Ten Poll*, British Film Institute, http://www.bfi.org.uk/sightandsound/topten/poll/voter.php?forename=Aki&surname=Kaurism%C3%A4ki.

Brooks, Peter (1976) *The Melodramatic Imagination: The Mode of Excess in Balzac, James, and Dickens*. New Haven, CT: Yale University Press.

Bruun, Seppo, Jukka Lindfors, Santtu Luoto, and Markku Salo (1998) *Jee, jee, jee: Suomalaisen rockin historia*. Porvoo: WSOY.

Cardullo, Bert (2006) 'Finnish Character: An Interview with Aki Kaurismäki', *Film Quarterly*, 59, 4, 4–10.

Caruth, Cathy (1996) *Unclaimed Experience: Trauma, Narrative, and History*. Baltimore, MD: Johns Hopkins University Press.

Certeau, Michel de (1984) *The Practice of Everyday Life*, Steven Rendall (trans.). Berkeley, CA: University of California Press.

Connah, Roger (1991) *K/K: A Couple of Finns and Some Donald Ducks*. Helsinki: VAPK.

Cook, Pam (2005) *Screening the Past: Memory and Nostalgia in Cinema*. London: Routledge.

Coslovich, Gabriella (2003) 'The Finnish Touch', *The Age*, 14 March.

Darsey, David (1989) 'Morning Edition', *National Public Radio*, 2 February.
Davis, Natalie Zemon (2008) 'The Quest of Michel de Certeau', *New York Review of Books*, 15 May, 57–60.
Dika, Vera (2003) *Recycled Culture in Contemporary Art and Film: The Uses of Nostalgia*. Cambridge: Cambridge University Press.
Donner, Jörn (2003) 'Kännissä Cannessa', *Ilta-Sanomat*, 22 May.
____ (2008) 'Onko Jörn Donner oikeassa Suomi-brändistä?' *SuomenKuvalehti.fi*, 17 October, <http://suomenkuvalehti.fi/blogit/viikon-puheenaihe/onko-jorn-donner-oikeassa-suomi-brandista> (accessed 7 June 2012).
Donner, Jörn and Martti Häikiö (1990) *Suomi-kuva vuonna nolla*. Porvoo: WSOY.
Dostoevsky, Fyodor (1997 [1866]) *Crime and Punishment*. London: Penguin.
Drouzy, Martin (1982) *Carl Th. Dreyer født Nilsson, Vol. 1*. Copenhagen: Gyldendal.
Ďurovičová, Nataša and Kathleen Newman (eds) (2010) *World Cinemas, Transnational Perspectives*. New York: Routledge.
Dyer, Richard (1979) *Stars*. London: British Film Institute.
Elsaesser, Thomas (2005) *European Cinema: Face to Face with Hollywood*. Amsterdam: University of Amsterdam Press.
____ (2010) 'Pohjalla: Aki Kaurismäki ja abjekti subjekti', *Lähikuva*, 2, 7–27.
____ (2011) 'Hitting Bottom: Aki Kaurismäki and the Abject Subject', *Journal of Scandinavian Cinema*, 1, 1, 105–22.
Eskilson, Stephen J. (2007) *A New History of Graphic Design*. New Haven, CT: Yale University Press.
Esping-Andersen, Gøsta (1990) *Three Worlds of Welfare Capitalism*. Princeton, NJ: Princeton University Press.
Finnish Foreign Ministry (2009) *Jorma Ollila luomaan Suomelle maabrändiä*. On-line. Available at: http://formin.finland.fi/public/default.aspx?contentid=136484&no deid=15145&contentlan=1&culture=fi-FI (accessed 14 October 2009).
Fitzgerald, F. Scott (1999 [1925]) *The Great Gatsby*. New York: Scribner.
Floyd, Nigel (1991) 'Do the right Finn', *Time Out*, 1068, 6 February.
Foster, Hal (2006 [2004]) 'An Archival Impulse', Charles Merewether (ed.), *The Archive*. Cambridge, MA: MIT Press, 143–148.
Franzen, Jonathan (2010) *Freedom*. New York: Farrar, Strauss, Giroux.
Frodon, Jean-Michel (2006) 'Aki Kaurismäki', *Cahiers du cinéma*, May, 32–4.
Galt, Rosalind and Karl Schoonover (eds) (2010) *Global Art Cinema: New Theories and Histories*. New York: Oxford University Press.
Genette, Gerard (1980) *Narrative Discourse: An Essay in Method*, Jane E. Lewin (trans). Ithaca, NY: Cornell University Press.
Gerstner, David A. and Janet Staiger (eds) (2003). *Authorship and Film*. New York: Routledge.
Gillespie, Michael Patrick (2008) *The Myth of an Irish Cinema: Approaching Irish Themed Films*. Syracuse, NY: Syracuse University Press.
Gledhill, Chrstine (ed.) (1991) *Stardom: Industry of Desire*. New York: Routledge.
Gluck, Mary (2000) 'Theorizing the Cultural Roots of the Bohemian Artist', *Modernism/Modernity*, 7, 3, 351–78.

____ (2005) *Popular Bohemia: Modernism and Urban Culture in Nineteenth-Century Paris*. Cambridge, MA: Harvard University Press.
Gordon, Tuula, Katri Komulainen, and Kirsti Lempiäinen (eds) (2002) *Suomineitonen, hei! Kansallisuuden sukupuoli*. Tampere: Vastapaino.
Gregory, James (2005) *The Southern Diaspora: How the Great Migrations of Black and White Southerners Transformed America*. Chapel Hill, NC: University of North Carolina Press.
Hammarberg, Ville (2002) 'Mies vailla...', *Satakunnan kansa*, 6 October.
Hämäläinen, Anna-Liisa (1981) 'Elokuvaveljekset Mika ja Aki Kaurismäki', *Seura*, 9. (No page numbers; on file at Finnish National Audiovisual Archive, Helsinki).
____ (1984) 'Elämän perusarvoille pitää nauraa', *Seura*, 1, 52–3.
Harvey, David (1991) *The Condition of Postmodernity: An Enquiry into the Origins of Cultural Change*. Oxford: Blackwell.
Helén, Ilpo (1991) 'Ajan läpi?', *Filmihullu*, 5, 12–18.
Highmore, Ben (2006) *Michel de Certeau: Analysing Culture*. New York: Continuum.
Higson, Andrew (1995) *Waving the Flag: Constructing a National Cinema in Britain*. Oxford: Clarendon.
Hillier, Jim (ed.) (1986) *Cahiers du Cinéma: 1960–1968: New Wave, New Cinema, Reevaluating Hollywood*. Cambridge, MA: Harvard University Press.
Hirvikorpi, Helinä (1999) 'Samurai Karkkilan paratiisissa', *Talouselämä*, 24, 18–21.
Hjort, Mette (2005) *Small Nation, Global Cinema: The New Danish Cinema*. Minneapolis: University of Minnesota Press.
____ (2010) 'On The Plurality of Cinematic Transnationalism', Nataša Ďurovičová and Kathleen Newman (eds.) *World Cinemas, Transnational Perspectives*. New York: Routledge, 12–33.
Hjort, Mette and Duncan Petrie (eds.) (2007) *The Cinema of Small Nations*. Edinburgh: Edinburgh University Press.
Hohtokari, Marit (1981) 'Valehtelija: Mika Kaurismäki puhuu totta', *Filmaaja* 3, 14–15.
Huyssen, Andreas (2000) 'Present Pasts: Media, Politics, Amnesia', *Public Culture* 12, 1, 21–38.
Hyvärinen, Aimo (1985) 'Uudistuva suomalainen elokuva', *Suomi-lehti*, 11 January.
Hyvönen, Eero (1990) 'Aki Suuri', *City-lehti*, 19, 21–5.
Jäckel, Anne (2003) *European Film Industries*. London: British Film Institute.
Jameson, Fredric (1991) *Postmodernism, or, The Cultural Logic of Late Capitalism*. Durham, NC: Duke University Press.
____ (1998) 'Notes on Globalization as a Philosophical Issues', in Fredric Jameson and Masao Miyoshi (eds) *The Cultures of Globalization*. Durham, NC: Duke University Press, 54–80.
Jensen, Jorn Rossing (1994) 'Sealed with a K', *Moving Pictures*, 10 Feburary, 30.
Jutila, Ville (1999) 'Idiootit ohjaavat Suomea', *Ilta-Sanomat*, 2 September.
Kääpä, Pietari (2008) 'The National and Beyond: The Globalisation of Finnish Cinema in the Films of Aki and Mika Kaurismäki, 1981–1995', unpublished PhD dissertation, School of Film and Television Studies, University of East Anglia.

Kaurismäki, Aki (1979) 'Luis Buñuel ja Jumalan kuolema', *Monroe*, 2, 4–10.
____ (1980) 'Baudelaire, kuumehoureita', *Filmihullu*, 8, 5–6.
____ (1990a) Manuscript of press release for *I Hired a Contract Killer*. Held at the Finnish National Audiovisual Archives, Helsinki.
____ (1990b) 'Aki Kaurismäki – Interview 1990', from Television Program *Cinema Cinemas*, http://www.youtube.com/watch?v=d9tp8rAaTsE (accessed 21 September 2010).
____ (1990c) Manuscript of press release for *The Match Factory Girl*. Held at the Finnish National Audiovisual Archives, Helsinki.
____ (1999) Press release for *Juha*. Held at the Finnish National Audiovisual Archives, Helsinki.
____ (2001) 'Kunniantohtoruus ja tapausten kulku', *Helsingin Sanomat*, 1 February.
Keskimäki, Ilmo (1982) 'Aki Kaurismäki – suomalainen sankari', 12–13, *Contactor*. (No page numbers; on file at Finnish National Audiovisual Archive, Helsinki).
Kierkegaard, Søren (1989 [1841]) *The Concept of Irony, with Continual Reference to Socrates: Together with Notes of Schelling's Berlin Lectures*, Howard V. Hong and Edna H. Hong (trans.). Princeton, NJ: Princeton University Press.
Kivimäki, Sanna (2010) 'Nainen vailla kaikkea – sukupuoli, luokka ja rikos Aki Kaurismäen elokuvassa *Tulitikkutehtaan tyttö (1990)*', *Lähikuva*, 2, 28–45.
____ (2012) 'Working-Class Girls in a Welfare State: Finnishness, Social Class and Gender in Aki Kaurismäki's Workers' Trilogy' (1986—1990)', *Journal of Scandinavian Cinema* 2, 1, 73–88.
Knee, Jonathan A., Bruce Greenwald and Ava Seave (2009) *The Curse of the Mogul: What's Wrong with the World's Leading Media Companies*. New York: Portfolio.
Koivunen, Anu (2003) *Performative Histories, Foundational Fictions: Gender and Sexuality in Niskavuori Films*. Helsinki: Finnish Literature Society.
____ (2006) 'Do You Remember Monrepos? Melancholia, Modernity and Working-Class Masculinity in *The Man Without a Past*', in C. Claire Thomson (ed.) *Northern Constellations: New Readings in Nordic Cinema*. Norwich: Norvik Press. 133–48.
Korhonen, Antti (1999) 'Kaurismäen kaatopaikkarealismi ei jaksa kiinnostaa katsojaa', *Aamulehti*, 10 April.
Koski, Markku (2006) 'Aki Kaurismäen nostalgian politiikkaa', *Aki Kaurismäki*, presented by the Orimattila Municipal Library <http://www.orimattila.fi/kirjasto/index.php?option=com_content&task=viewid=133&itemid=94> (accessed 10 November 2010).
Koskinen, Maaret (2002) *I begynnelsen var ordet: Ingmar Bergman och hads tidiga författarskap*. Värnamo: Wahlström och Widstrand.
____ (2009) 'From Erotic Icon to Clan Chief: The Auteur as Star', in Tytti Soila (ed.) *Stellar Encounters: Stardom in European Cinema*. New Barnett: John Libbey, 73–82.
Kosonen, Pekka (1987) *Hyvinvointivaltion haasteet ja pohjoismaiset mallit*. Tampere: Vastapaino.
Kuosmanen, Jukka (2007) 'Kaurismäen kääntöpiiri', YLE Radio, Channel 1, 10 March.

Kuusi, Pekka (1956) *Alkoholijuomien käyttö maaseudulla: Kokeellinen tutkimus alkoholijuomien käytöstä eräissä maalaiskunnissa ja kauppaloissa*. Helsinki: Väkijuomakysymyksen tutkimussäätiö.

Kyösola, Satu (2000) 'Työlaisista ja torakasta, eli rikos ja rangaistus Aki Kaurismäen elokuvatuotannossa', in Sakari Toiviainen (ed.) *Suomen kansallisfilmografia: 1981– 1985, Vol. 9*. Helsinki: Edita, 291–6.

____ (2004a) 'Kadotettu par(at)iisi eli boheemielämää Aki Kaurismäen tuotannossa', in Sakari Toiviainen (ed.) *Suomen kansallisfilmografia: 1991–1995, Vol. 11*. Helsinki: Edita, 145–50.

____ (2004b) 'The Archivist's Nostalgia', *Journal of Finnish Studies* 7, 2, 46–62.

____ (2007) 'Viattomuuden kadotettu aika: Särkynyt unelma katjaisesta kansasta Aki Kaurismäen elokuvissa', in H. Bacon, A. Lehtisalo and P. Nyssönen (eds.), *Suomalaisuus valkokankaalla: Kotimainen elokuva toisin katsoen*. Helsinki: Like, 167–188.

Laclau, Ernesto and Chantal Mouffe (1985) *Hegemony and Socialist Strategy: Towards a Radical Democratic Politics*. London: Verso.

Laine, Kimmo (2000) *'Pääosassa Suomen kansa': Suomi-filmi ja Suomen Filmiteollisuus kansallisen elokuvan rakentajina 1933–1939*. Helsinki: Finnish Literature Society.

Laine, Tarja (2004) 'Shame and Desire: Intersubjectivity in Finnish Visual Culture', unpublished PhD dissertation', Cinema and Media Studies, University of Amsterdam.

Latomaa, Sirkku (2010) Personal communication, 19 October.

Lea, John (2002) *Crime and Modernity: Continuities in Left Realist Criminology*. London: Sage.

Leppä, Asta (1996) 'Vaitelias pienuuden puhemies', *Anna*, 11, 8–11.

Levinson, Marc (2006) *The Box: How the Shipping Container Made the World Smaller and the World Economy Bigger*. Princeton, NJ: Princeton University Press.

Lewis, Sinclair (1995 [1920]) *Main Street*. New York: Penguin.

Lim, Dennis (2009) 'At Uneven Berlin Film Festival, Notions of Globalism Abound', *International Herald Tribune*, 12 February.

Lindqvist, Antti (1982) 'Uuden aallon vanavedessä', *Kansan Uutiset*, 10 June.

____ (1985) 'Miesten tie' *Katso!*, 8, 51.

Lindstedt, Leo (2002) 'Onnen hetkiä', *Turun Sanomat*, 31 May.

Löppönen, Paavo (2008) 'Myyttien ja kertomusten valta', in Ilkka Niiniluoto and Juha Sihvola (eds.) *Tarkemmin ajatellen: Kansakunnan henkinen tila*. Helsinki: Gaudeamus Helsinki University Press, 89–135.

Luomi, Merja-Terttu (2007) 'Onnea, Aki', *Seura*, 14–15, 94.

Luukka, Teemu (2008) 'Aki Kaurismäki sai akateemikon arvon suurtangon tahdissa', *Helsingin Sanomat*, 23 May.

Lyotard, Jean-Francois (1984) *The Postmodern Condition: A Report On Knowledge*, Geoff Bennington and Brian Massumi (trans.). Minneapolis: University of Minnesota Press.

Lyytikäinen, Pirjo (2004) 'Kullervo's Curse: The Transgression Tradition in Finnish Literature', Lecture delivered at University of Washington, Seattle, 13 April.

Mäkinen, Esa (2008) 'Akateemikko Kaurismäen julkikuva on tarkasti luotu', *Helsingin Sanomat*, 22 May.
Makkonen, Veli-Pekka (1988) 'Tasi Kasurinen ja ilman henki', *Tiedonantaja*, 25 October.
Mann, Andrew (2003) 'Kaurismatic', Review of *The Man Without a Past*, *LA Weekly*, 11–17 April.
Mattila, Ilkka (2009) 'Kansallisen musiikkimaun vangit', *Helsingin Sanomat*, 9 May, <http://www.hs.fi/kulttuuri/artikkeli/Kansallisen+musiikkimaun+vangit/1135249809018> (accessed 15 September 2010).
Mazierska, Eva and Laura Rascaroli (2006) *Crossing New Europe: Postmodern Travel and the European Road Movie*. London and New York: Wallflower Press.
Miller, Toby, Nitvin Govill, John McMurria, and Richard Maxwell (2001) *Global Hollywood*. London: British Film Institute.
Montonen, Mikko (1983) 'Menneisyyttä nykypäivässä: Rikos ja rangaistus Helsingissä', *Ilta-Sanomat*, 3 August.
Murger, Henri (2004 [1852]) *The Bohemians of the Latin Quarter*, Ellen Marriage and John Selwyn (trans.). Philadelphia: University of Pennsylvania Press.
Mykkänen, Jouni (2002) 'Valtion tuki elokuvalle on nostettava kaksinkertaiseksi', *Savon Sanomat*, 12 June.
____ (2004) 'Kulttuurista seuraava menstystarina', *Savon Sanomat*, 28 June.
Myllyoja, Essi (2007) 'Tiedotuspäälliköllä oli kosteat eväät kassissaan', *Aamulehti*, 8 March.
Naski, Kaarina (1985) 'Vasta toisella katselulla huomasin, että se on surullinen', *Kaleva*, 4 March.
Näveri, Tuomas (2002a) 'Cannes-hitistä tuli Kaurismäen uran suurin kassamagneetti', *Ilta-Sanomat*, 2 July.
____ (2002b) 'Hiljaa hyvä tulee', *Ilta-Sanomat*, 29 May.
____ (2002c) 'Kaurismäen leffalle historiallinen sopimus Yhdysvaltoihin', *Ilta-Sanomat*, 29 May.
____ (2003) 'Kaurismäki-hitin lipputulot 10 miljoonaa euroa', *Ilta-Sanomat*, 18 October.
Nestingen, Andrew (2007) 'A Conversation with Aki Kaurismäki', at Sputnik Ltd., Helsinki, Finland, 17 August. Printed here as Appendix.
____ (2008) *Crime and Fantasy in Scandinavia: Fiction, Film, and Social Change*. Seattle & Copenhagen: University of Washington Press & Museum Tusculanum.
Niemelä, Ilkka (Tähystäjä) (1978) 'Silmälappuja ja saippuakupla', *Kino Lehti*, 4, 15.
Nieminen, Tommi (2007) 'Katsokaa meitä', *Helsingin Sanomat*, 4 March.
Nikkilä-Kiiski, Raija (1999) 'Parantolan puutarha oli Kaurismäen veljesten mummola', *Hyvinkään Sanomat*, 17 October.
Noukka, Reijo (1981) 'Rokkarit Saimaalla', *Aamulehti*, 13 September.
____ (2002) 'Kaurismäki uskalsi puuttua Suomen häpeäpilkkuun', *Aamulehti*, 31 May.
Numminen, M. A. (1986) *Baarien mies: Faktapohjainen romaani suomalaisista keskiolutbaareista*. Helsinki: Kirjayhtymä.

Paavolainen, Pentti, and Aino Kukkonen (2005) *Näyttämöllä: Teatterihistoria Suomesta*. Helsinki: WSOY.

Pantti, Mervi (2005) 'Art or Industry: Battles Over Finnish Cinema Since the 1960s', Andrew Nestingen and Trevor G. Elkington (eds.) *Transnational Cinema in a Global North: Nordic Cinema in Transition*. Detroit: Wayne State University Press, 165–90.

Pasanen, Inkeri (1984) 'Aki Kaurismäki Viitasaarella: Kaurismäki-ilmiötä ei ole', *Keskisuomalainen*, 31 March.

Peltonen, Matti (1988) *Viinapäästä kolerakauhuun: Kirjoituksia soisaalihistoriasta*. Helsinki: Hanki ja Jää.

Porton, Richard (1993) 'La vie de Bohème', review of *The Bohemian Life*, *Cineaste* XX, 2, 47–8.

Pouta, Helena (2003) 'Mies ja hänen menneisyytensä', *Apu*, 13, 38–41.

Puukko, Martti (2000) 'Keskustelu Aki Kaurismäen kanssa', *Parnasso*, 4, 468–473.

Raeste, Juha-Pekka (1990) 'Kaurismäen reilu meininki myy Euroopassa', *Helsingin Sanomat*, 28 July.

Räihä, Merja (1991) 'Juhlimme työn merkeissä: Kaurismäkien tuotantoyhtiö Villealfa täytti 10 vuotta', *Ilta-Sanomat*, 12 April.

Riihiranta, Lilli (ed.) (1982) *Hyvinvointikakarat*. Helsinki: Weilin+Goös.

Romney, Jonathan (1997) 'The Kaurismaki effect', *Sight & Sound*, 7, 6, 10–14.

____ (2003) 'Last Exit to Helsinki', *Film Comment*, XXXIX, 2, 43–45, 47.

Roos, Eerika (2003) 'Kati Outinen ja Markku Peltola peruivat lähtönsä Oscar-gaalaan: En voisi elää itseni kanssa"', *Iltalehti*, 20 March.

Rosen, Philip (2006) 'History, Textuality, Nation: Kracauer, Burch and Some Problems in the Study of Naitonal Cinemas', V. Vitali and P. Willemen (eds.) *Theorising National Cinema*. London: British Film Institute, 17–28.

Rossi, Riikka, and Katja Seutu (2007) 'Nostalgian lukijalle', in Riikka Rossi and Katja Seutu (eds) *Nostalgia*. Helsinki: Finnish Literature Society, 1–8.

Runeberg, Johan Ludvig (1938 [1848]) 'Our Land', in Charles Wharton Stork (ed. and trans.) *The Tales of Ensign Stål*. Princeton, NJ: Princeton University Press/ New York: American Scandinavian Foundation, 2–7.

Ryan, Marie Laure (2007) 'Toward a Definition of Narrative', in David Howard (ed.) *The Cambridge Companion to Narrative*. Cambridge: Cambridge University Press, 22–38.

Sallinen, Otto (1998) 'Aki Kaurismäki: Suomi-elokuvan suuri hiljainen puhuu', *Like Uutiset*, 6, 5–7.

Sarris, Andrew (2003 [1962]) 'Notes on Auteur Theory in 1962', in Leo Braudy and Marshall Cohen (eds) *Introduction to Film Theory and Criticism*. Oxford: Oxford University Press, 515–18.

Seigel, Jerrold (1986) *Bohemian Paris: Culture, Politics, and Boundaries of Bourgeois Life, 1830–1930*. New York: Viking.

Sekula, Allan (2006) 'The Body and the Archive', in Charles Mereweather (ed.) *The Archive*. Cambridge, MA: MIT Press, 70–5.

Sihvola, Juha (2008) 'Ramones ja mä', on-line source, <http://www.ramopunk.com/R/77/1977komm4.htm>, (accessed 12 November 2010).

Siikala, Kirsikka (1978) 'Pete Q. räjäyttää vanhat auktoriteetit', *Helsingin Sanomat*, 10 July.
Siistonen, Miia (2006) 'Aki muiden silmin', *Anna*, 4, 26–30.
Social Issues Research Council (1998) *Social And Cultural Aspects of Drinking: A Report to the European Council*. Oxford: The Social Issues Research Centre.
Soila, Tytti (2003) 'The Landscape of Memories in the Films of the Kaurismäki Bros.', *Film International*, 3, 4–15.
Spangenberg, Mia (2009) 'It's Reigning Men! Masculinities in Contemporary Finnish Fiction and Film', unpublished PhD dissertation, Scandinavian Studies, University of Washington, Seattle.
Sputnik Ltd. (1994) *'Pidä huivista kiinni, Tatjana'* (publicity brochure).
Ståhlhammer, Leo (1985) 'Aki Kaurismäen mustan komedian Helsinki on maailma pienoiskoossa', *Suomenmaa*, 13 February.
Stecher, Thorsten (2002) *'Das Weltwoche-Gespräch*: "Ich glaube an Bäume, nicht an Gott"', *Die Weltwoche*, 37, 2, 12 September, <http://www.weltwoche.ch/ausgaben/2002-37/artikel/2002/37/ich-glaube-an-baeume-nicht-an-gott.html> (accessed 10 November 2010).
Steinbock, Dan (1989) 'Miten Aki Kaurismäelle todella kävi New Yorkissa', *Uusi Suomi*, 7 October.
STT (Finnish Press Agency) (2002) 'Kaurismäen elokuva vie Suomen ruokajonot taas maailmalle', *Kymen Sanomat*, 2 March.
Sundström, Hans (2002) 'I melankolins finska ruinlandskap', review of *The Man Without a Past*, *Hufvudstadsbladet*, 1 March.
____ (2002) 'Unik triumf', *Hufvudstadsbladet*, 27 May.
Suominen, Raili (2002) 'Kaurismäen saavutus mannaa kansalle', *Turun Sanomat*, 28 May.
Suvanto, Pertti (1981) 'Valehtelija välittää ajan tuntoja', *Ylioppilaslehti*, 26, February, 16–17.
Tainola, Rita (2002) 'Ministeri Lindén vaivautui Kaurismäestä', *Ilta-Sanomat*, 25 May.
Taubin, Amy (1992) 'Berlin Stories', *Village Voice*, 11, 58.
Thompson, Kristin and David Bordwell (2003) *Film History: An Introduction*. New York: McGraw Hill.
Timonen, Lauri (2005) 'Päämme päällä ja sisällämme moraalilaki', in Sakari Toiviainen (ed.) *Suomen kansallisfilmografia, 1996–2000, Vol. 12*. Helsinki: Edita, 54–62.
____ (2006) *Aki Kaurismäen elokuvat*. Helsinki: Otava.
Toiviainen, Sakari (1981) *'Valehtelija & Matkalla'*, *Ilta-Sanomat*, 27 February.
____ (1985) 'Jengin unelma Eirasta,' *Ilta-Sanomat*, 8 February.
____ (2002) *Levottomat sukupolvet: Uusin suomalainen elokuva*. Helsinki: Finnish Literature Society.
____ (2004) 'The Kaurismäki Phenomenon' in Lola Rogers (trans.), *Journal of Finnish Studies* 7, 2, 8–34.
Tuukko, Usko (1985) 'Filmtotal: elokuvatehdas Helsingissä', *Helsinki-lehti*, 14 March.

Valck, Marijke de (2007) *Film Festivals: From European Geopolitics to Global Cinephilia*. Amsterdam: University of Amsterdam Press.
Valkola, Jarmo (2002) 'Kaurismäki vangitsee elegaansillaan', *Keskisuomalainen*, 28 May.
Van Gelder, Lawrence (2000) 'Humanizing Those Other Pilots With the Right Stuff', review of *The Red Stuff* and *The Total Balalaika Show*, in *The New York Times*, 11 October.
Vermeulen, Tim (2007) 'The Loneliest Man of the Crowd: A Loser's Guide to Helsinki', *Aki Kaurismäki*, Presented by the Orimattila Municipal Library, <http://www.orimattila.fi/kirjasto/index.php?option=com_content&task=view&id=200&itemid=94> (accessed 10 November 2010).
Viertola, Ritva (1990) 'Aki Kaurismäki valloitti italialaiset', *Turun Sanomat*, 18 September.
Vihavainen, Timo (1991) *Kansakunta rähmällään: Suomettumisen lyhyt historia*. Helsinki: Otava.
Villealfa Filmproductions Ltd. (1983) 'F.M. Dostoevsky's *Crime and Punishment*: A film about love, revenge and guilt' (publicity brochure).
von Bagh, Peter (1984) 'Kellarin filosofia', *Filmihullu*, 7, 4–10.
_____ (1991) 'Työmiehen muotokuva', *Filmihullu*, 5, 4–11.
_____ (1997) 'The Comedy of Losers', in Marjaleena Hukkanen (ed.) *Shadows in Paradise: Photographs from the Films of Aki Kaurismäki*. Helsinki: Otava, 5–21.
_____ (2002a) 'Aki Kaurismäen elokuvat kertovat ankarasta arjesta ja ihmisarvosta', *Lapin Kansa*, 4 March.
_____ (2002b) 'Suurten tunteiden voitto', *Kaleva*, 1 June.
_____ (2002c) 'Aki Kaurismäki ja suomalainen todellisuus', in S. Toiviainen (ed.), *Suomen kansallisfilmografia, 1986–1990, Vol. 10*. Helsinki: Edita, 138–45.
_____ (2006) *Aki Kaurismäki*. Helsinki: WSOY.
_____ (2007) *Sininen laulu: Itsenäisen Suomen taiteiden tarina*. Helsinki: WSOY.
Warhol, Andy (2006 [1975]) 'The Philosophy of Andy Warhol (From A to B and Back Again)', in Charles Mereweather (ed.) *The Archive*. Cambridge, MA: MIT Press, 31.
Wexman, Virginia (ed.) (2003). *Film and Authorship*. New Brunswick, NJ: Rutgers University Press.
Wilson, Eric (2009) 'Smile and say "No Photoshop"', *New York Times*, 27 May, http://www.nytimes.com/2009/05/28/fashion/28RETOUCH.html (accessed 10 November 2010).
Wollen, Peter (1998) *Signs and Meaning in the Cinema*. London: British Film Institute.
Wood, Robin (2008 [1977]) 'Ideology, Genre, Auteur', in Barry Keith Grant (ed.) *Authors and Authorship: A Film Reader*. Oxford: Blackwell, 84–92.
Ylänen, Helena (1985) '18 miestä, mutta vain yksi tarina', *Helsingin Sanomat*, 9 February.
_____ (1987) 'Kaurismäki ;en elokuvateatteri on valmis', *Helsingin Sanomat*, 19 August.

_____ (1990) 'Aki Kaurismäki ensi kerran isoissa kisoissa', *Helsingin Sanomat*, 3 September.

_____ (1991) 'Suomalaiset katsovat vain amerikkalaisia tai suomalaisia elokuvia', *Helsingin Sanomat*, 11 February.

_____ (2000) 'Suomalaisen elokuvan vaikea vuosikymmenen', *Helsingin Sanomat*, 30 April.

Yritys, Olli (1981) Review of *Saimaa-ilmiö*, in *Turun Ylioppilaslehti*, 25 September.

INDEX

Aalto, Alvar 119, 136
Aaltonen, Veikko 63–4, 68, 70
Akerman, Chantal 116
Akin, Fatih 116
Alanen, Antti 118–19
Anderson, Benedict 3, 118, 139
Ariel 5, 19, 27, 39, 42, 62, 79, 100, 105–10, 123

Ballard, Carrol 116
Bazin, André 4, 18, 99
Benjamin, Walter 24
Björling, Jussi 130
Blixen, Karen 93
Bogart, Humphrey 103
Bordwell, David 3, 93–4
Boulanger, Henri 45, 47, 102
Broken Blossoms 34
Buñuel, Luis 24, 54, 56, 86

Calamari Union 5, 24, 28, 30, 36, 68–9, 126–7, 132
Capra, Frank 82, 90–1

de Sica, Vittorio 82
Dika, Vera 93
Dinesen, Isak 93
Dostoevsky, Fyodor 15, 19, 30, 91

Drifting Clouds 19, 29, 37–8, 42, 45–6, 75–9, 92, 100–1, 108, 123, 132, 139

Earle, Roy 103

Fassbinder, Rainer Werner 15
Ford, John 146
Freedom 11–12
Fuller, Samuel 33, 58, 72, 116, 136

Gardel, Carlos 143
Gitai, Amos 116
Godard, Jean-Luc 4, 13, 23–4, 39, 64, 69, 86, 103, 111
Griffith, D. W. 24

Häikkiö, Martti 128
Hamlet liikemaailmassa (*Hamlet Goes Business*) 20, 28, 32, 67
Harvey, David 93, 102
Haynes, Todd 112
Hess, Jared 45
Hyvönen, Eero 71

I Hired a Contract Killer 19–20, 26, 28, 37, 42, 45–7, 54, 106, 127, 138

Jameson, Fredric 93
Jarmusch, Jim 23, 38, 45, 71–2, 90
Juha 14, 20, 23, 29, 32–6, 63, 79, 92, 119–20, 138, 145

Käkriäinen, Juutas 119
Kauas pilvet karkaavat (Drifting Clouds) 19, 29, 37–8, 42, 45–6, 54, 70, 75–9, 89, 92, 100–1, 108, 110, 123, 132, 139
Keaton, Buster 15, 44–5, 90, 146–7
Koivunen, Anu 89, 92–4, 100, 109, 125

La vie de Bohème (The Bohemian Life) 5, 20, 32–3, 58, 77, 90, 122, 138
Laclau, Ernesto 118, 126, 130
Laitakaupungin valot (Lights in the Dusk) 20–1, 23, 35, 42, 46, 62, 79, 89, 106, 122–6, 132, 143, 150
Lang, Fritz 4, 7
Lantier, Jacques 103
Le Havre 20, 60, 132
Léaud, Jean-Pierre 27, 33, 45, 47
Lee, Ang 71, 112
Lehtonen, Joel 114, 119
Leigh, Mike 90, 112
Leningrad Cowboys Meet Moses 5, 29, 36, 40, 51, 90, 146
Liitovaara, Lasse 33
Likaiset kädet (Dirty Hands) 33–4, 91
Lloyd, Harold 147
Lumme, Jouko 33
Lyotard, Jean-Francois 17

Manda, Georges 47, 122
Mattila, Karita 130
Mies vailla menneisyyttä (The Man Without a Past) 1–2, 5, 13–14, 17, 20–1, 23, 29, 35, 48, 51, 62, 71, 77, 79, 88–92, 94, 100–2, 106, 119, 122–5, 129
Mönkäre, Sinikka 148, 152
Mouffe, Chantal 118, 126

Mykkänen, Jouni 81, 83

Orwell, George 63

Pakkasvirta, Jaakko 66
Pentti, Pauli 63–4
Pidä huivista kiinni, Tatjana (Take Care of Your Scarf, Tatiana) 19, 29, 36, 39–40, 75, 77, 92, 97, 100, 132
Pollack, Sydney 93

Queen Kelly 34

Reggiani, Serge 136
Renoir, Jean 4, 60, 91, 122
Rikos ja rangaistus (Crime and Punishment) 12, 19, 30, 32, 48, 54, 71, 74, 86, 97, 100, 132
Rosen, Philip 118–19, 121
Rossellini, Roberto 4
Rossi, Rikka 88, 102

Saariaho, Kaija 130
Saimaa-ilmiö (The Saimaa Gesture) 28, 30, 48–52, 55, 69, 71, 75
Salminen, Timo 33
Salonen, Esa-Pekka 130
Sartre, Jean-Paul 33–4, 91
Schoonmaker, Thelma 116
Sedergren, Jari 86
Seutu, Katja 88, 102
Sibelius, Jean 15, 119, 127–8, 130
Steinbock, Dan 136

Taubin, Amy 125
Thompson, Kristin 93–4
Tikanmäki, Anssi 34
Total Balalaika Show 28–30, 48, 52–3
Truffaut, François 4, 23, 30, 103
Tulitikkutehtaan tyttö (The Match Factory Girl) 15, 19, 27–8, 42–4, 51, 68, 86, 100, 102, 122–5, 132, 135

Valo, Ville 119

Varjoja paratiisissa (*Shadows in Paradise*)
   13, 19, 27, 42, 46, 75–6, 103, 125, 138
Vinterberg, Thomas 71
Virén, Lasse 119

Zhangke, Jia 90

GPSR Authorized Representative: Easy Access System Europe, Mustamäe tee 50, 10621 Tallinn, Estonia, gpsr.requests@easproject.com